I0010596

FORWARD/COMMENTARY

The National Institute of Standards and Technology (NIST) is a measurement standards laboratory, and a non-regulatory agency of the **United States Department of Commerce**. Its mission is to promote innovation and industrial competitiveness. Founded in 1901, as the National Bureau of Standards, NIST was formed with the mandate to provide standard weights and measures, and to serve as the national physical laboratory for the United States. With a world-class measurement and testing laboratory encompassing a wide range of areas of computer science, mathematics, statistics, and systems engineering, NIST's cybersecurity program supports its overall mission to promote U.S. innovation and industrial competitiveness by advancing measurement science, standards, and related technology through research and development in ways that enhance economic security and improve our quality of life.

The need for cybersecurity standards and best practices that address interoperability, usability and privacy has been shown to be critical for the nation. NIST's cybersecurity programs seek to enable greater development and application of practical, innovative security technologies and methodologies that enhance the country's ability to address current and future computer and information security challenges.

The cybersecurity publications produced by NIST cover a wide range of cybersecurity concepts that are carefully designed to work together to produce a holistic approach to cybersecurity primarily for government agencies and constitute the best practices used by industry. This holistic strategy to cybersecurity covers the gamut of security subjects from development of secure encryption standards for communication and storage of information while at rest to how best to recover from a cyber-attack.

Why buy a book you can download for free?   **We print this so you don't have to.**

Some are available only in electronic media. Some online docs are missing pages or barely legible.

We at 4th Watch Publishing are former government employees, so we know how government employees actually use the standards. When a new standard is released, an engineer prints it out, punches holes and puts it in a 3-ring binder. While this is not a big deal for a 5 or 10-page document, many NIST documents are over 100 pages and printing a large document is a time-consuming effort. So, an engineer that's paid $75 an hour is spending hours simply printing out the tools needed to do the job. That's time that could be better spent doing engineering. We publish these documents so engineers can focus on what they were hired to do – engineering. It's much more cost-effective to just order the latest version from Amazon.com

If there is a standard you would like published, let us know. Our web site is https://usgovpub.com/

NIST Special Publication 1108r3

NIST Framework and Roadmap for Smart Grid Interoperability Standards, Release 3.0

Smart Grid and Cyber-Physical Systems Program Office
and Energy and Environment Division,
Engineering Laboratory

in collaboration with
Quantum Measurement Division,
Semiconductor and Dimensional Metrology Division,
and Electromagnetics Division,
Physical Measurement Laboratory
and
Advanced Network Technologies Division
and Computer Security Division,
Information Technology Laboratory

http://dx.doi.org/10.6028/NIST.SP.1108r3

National Institute of
Standards and Technology
U.S. Department of Commerce

NIST Special Publication 1108r3

NIST Framework and Roadmap for Smart Grid Interoperability Standards, Release 3.0

Smart Grid and Cyber-Physical Systems Program Office
and Energy and Environment Division,
Engineering Laboratory

in collaboration with
Quantum Measurement Division,
Semiconductor and Dimensional Metrology Division,
and Electromagnetics Division,
Physical Measurement Laboratory
and
Advanced Network Technologies Division
and Computer Security Division
Information Technology Laboratory

This publication is available free of charge from:
http://dx.doi.org/10.6028/NIST.SP.1108r3

September 2014

U.S. Department of Commerce
Penny Pritzker, Secretary

National Institute of Standards and Technology
Willie May, Acting Under Secretary of Commerce for Standards and Technology and Acting Director

Certain commercial entities, equipment, or materials may be identified in this document in order to describe an experimental procedure or concept adequately. Such identification is not intended to imply recommendation or endorsement by the National Institute of Standards and Technology, nor is it intended to imply that the entities, materials, or equipment are necessarily the best available for the purpose.

National Institute of Standards and Technology Special Publication 1108r3
Natl. Inst. Stand. Technol. Spec. Publ. 1108r3, 239 pages (September 2014)
CODEN: NSPUE2

This publication is available free of charge from:
http://dx.doi.org/10.6028/NIST.SP.1108r3

Table of Contents

Executive Summary 1

Accomplishments since NIST Framework Release 2.0 8

What's Included in Release 3.0 9

What's New in Release 3.0 11

1. Purpose and Scope 14
   1.1. Overview and Background 14
   1.2. Use of this Framework 18
   1.3. Key Concepts 19
      1.3.1. Definitions 20
      1.3.2. Applications and Requirements: Nine Priority Areas 22
   1.4. Framework Content Overview 24

2. Smart Grid Visions 25
   2.1. Overview of Smart Grid: Definitions, Costs, Benefits, and Standards 25
   2.2. Importance to National Energy Policy Goals 30
   2.3. International Smart Grid Standards 33
   2.4. International Efforts to Align Smart Grid Architectures 35
   2.5. Smart Grid Key Attributes--Standards and Conformance 36

3. Smart Grid Interoperability Panel (SGIP 40
   3.1. Overview 40
   3.2. Pre-SGIP: 2008 and 2009 40
   3.3. SGIP, the Public-Private Partnership: 2010 - 2012 42
   3.4. SGIP, the Industry-Led Non-Profit Organization: 2013 - Ongoing 46
   3.5. SGIP Catalog of Standards 48

4. Standards Identified for Implementation 51
   4.1. Guiding Principles and Process Used for Identifying Interoperability Standards 51
   4.2. Overview of the Standards Identification Process 56
   4.3. Current List of Standards Identified by NIST 58
   4.4. Process for Future Smart Grid Standards Identification 122

5. Architectural Framework 123
   5.1. Introduction 123
   5.2. Architectural Goals for the Smart Grid 124
   5.3. Smart Grid Architecture Model 125

5.3.1. Overview – Conceptual Domain Model 125

5.3.2. Description of Smart Grid Architecture Model (SGAM) 128

5.3.3. Architecture Process - Evolution of the Conceptual Architecture to SGAM 129

5.3.4. Description of Legacy Logical Application Types within the Context of the Conceptual Domains 138

5.4. Use Cases 140

5.5. Ongoing Work of the Smart Grid Architecture Committee (SGAC) 142

5.5.1. Conceptual Business Services 142

5.5.2. Architecture Development Working Party 143

5.5.3. The SGAC Smart Grid Semantic Framework 144

5.5.4. Standards Review by the SGAC 145

6. Cybersecurity Strategy 147

6.1. Cybersecurity in the Smart Grid 147

6.2. NIST's Role in Smart Grid Cybersecurity 149

6.3. Progress to Date 151

6.3.1. Release of National Institute of Standards and Technology Interagency Report (NISTIR) 7628 and Companion Documents 151

6.3.2. Standards Reviews 153

6.3.3. Risk Management Framework 154

6.3.4. Cyber-Physical System Research 154

6.3.5. Advanced Meter Upgradeability Test Guidance 155

6.4. Future Activities 156

7. Smart Grid Testing and Certification Framework 157

7.1. NIST Role in Smart Grid Testing and Certification 157

7.2. NIST-Initiated Efforts Supporting the Framework Development 157

7.2.1. Testing and Certification Framework Development Guide 158

7.2.2. Assessment of Existing Smart Grid Standards Testing Programs 159

7.3. SGTCC Framework Development Activities 160

7.3.1. Interoperability Process Reference Manual (IPRM) 161

7.4. SGTCC Progress since Framework 2.0 164

7.4.1. IPRM Version 2 164

7.4.2. Engagement with ITCAs, Labs, Certifiers, and Accreditors 165

7.4.3. SGTCC Input for SGIP CoS Review 166

7.5. Current Smart Grid Testing Initiatives 167

7.5.1. Prioritization of Test Programs – Gaps/Opportunities 167

7.5.2. Outreach 168

7.6.   Future Directions 169

7.6.1. Incubation of New Testing Initiatives via Priority Action Plans 170

7.6.2. Catalog of Test Programs 170

7.6.3. IPRM Version 3 170

7.6.4. International Engagement 171

8.   Cross-Cutting and Future Issues 172

8.1.   Introduction 172

8.2.   Electromagnetic Disturbances and Interference 174

8.3.   Implementability, Safety, Reliability and Resiliency 179

8.3.1. Implementability and Safety 179

8.3.2. Reliability and Resiliency 180

8.3.3. SGIP action 182

8.4.   The Smart Grid Community Effort to Further Define R&D Needs 183

8.5.   Framework Updates 184

Appendix A: List of Acronyms and Abbreviations 185

Appendix B: Specific Domain Diagrams 189

Appendix C: Smart Grid Service Orientation and Ontology 206

Appendix D: SGIP Committees, DEWGs, and PAPs 218

DISCLAIMER

This document has been prepared by the National Institute of Standards and Technology (NIST) and describes standards research coordination activities in support of its mandate under the Energy Independence and Security Act of 2007 (EISA) and its smart grid standards and technology research program.

Certain commercial entities, equipment, or materials may be identified in this document in order to describe a concept adequately. Such identification is not intended to imply recommendation or endorsement by the National Institute of Standards and Technology, nor is it intended to imply that these entities, materials, or equipment are necessarily the best available for the purpose.

Executive Summary

Framework Release 3.0 Background

Since the release of the last edition of the *NIST Smart Grid Framework and Roadmap for Interoperability Standards (Release 2.0)*,[1] in February 2012, significant technological advances in smart grid infrastructure have been implemented, supported by standards development across the entire smart grid arena. Examples include widespread deployment of wireless-communication power meters, availability of customer energy usage data through the Green Button initiative, remote sensing for determining real-time transmission and distribution status, and protocols for electric vehicle charging. The first release of the *NIST Framework and Roadmap for Smart Grid Interoperability Standards (Release 1.0)*[2] was published in January 2010. Release 3.0 updates NIST's ongoing efforts to facilitate and coordinate smart grid interoperability standards development and smart grid-related measurement science and technology, including the evolving and continuing NIST relationship with the Smart Grid Interoperability Panel (SGIP) public-private partnership.

Over the last decade, Congress and the Administration have outlined a vision for the smart grid and have laid the policy foundation upon which it is being built. The Energy Independence and Security Act of 2007 (EISA) codified the policy of the United States to modernize the nation's electricity transmission and distribution system to create a smart electric grid.[3] The American Recovery and Reinvestment Act of 2009 (ARRA) accelerated the development of smart grid technologies, investing $4.5 billion for electricity delivery and energy reliability activities to modernize the electric grid and implement demonstration and deployment programs (as authorized under Title XIII of EISA).[4][5] The president, in his 2011 and 2012 State of the Union Addresses, reiterated his vision for a clean energy economy,[6] and he underscored the Administration's commitment in the "Blueprint for a Secure Energy Future."[7] In June 2011 and February 2013, the White House released reports by the Cabinet-level National Science and

---

[1] See http://www.nist.gov/smartgrid/upload/NIST_Framework_Release_2-0_corr.pdf

[2] See http://www.nist.gov/public_affairs/releases/upload/smartgrid_interoperability_final.pdf

[3] Energy Independence and Security Act of 2007 [Public Law No: 110-140]. http://www.gpo.gov/fdsys/pkg/PLAW-110publ140/pdf/PLAW-110publ140.pdf

[4] The White House, "American Recovery and Reinvestment Act: Moving America Toward a Clean Energy Future." Feb. 17, 2009. See http://www.whitehouse.gov/assets/documents/Recovery_Act_Energy_2-17.pdf

[5] "Economic Impact of Recovery Act Investments in the Smart Grid", April 2013. See http://www.smartgrid.gov/sites/default/files/doc/files/Smart%20Grid%20Economic%20Impact%20Report.pdf

[6] The White House, Office of the Press Secretary, "Remarks by the President in State of the Union Address." January 25, 2011 and January 24, 2012. See http://www.whitehouse.gov/the-press-office/2011/01/25/remarks-president-state-union-address and http://www.whitehouse.gov/the-press-office/2012/01/24/remarks-president-state-union-address

[7] The White House, "Blueprint for a Secure Energy Future." March 30, 2011. See http://www.whitehouse.gov/sites/default/files/blueprint_secure_energy_future.pdf

Technology Council (NSTC) entitled "A Policy Framework for the 21st Century Grid: Enabling Our Secure Energy Future" and "A Policy Framework for the 21st Century Grid: A Progress Report."[8]

Several reports from the Department of Energy (DOE) and the Federal Energy Regulatory Commission (FERC) further document the progress, with specific mention of the positive role played by the National Institute of Standards and Technology and the Smart Grid Interoperability Panel. DOE released reports in May 2013 ("Economic Impact of Recovery Act Investments in Smart Grid"[9]) and October 2013 ("Smart Grid Investment Grant, Progress Report II"[10]). A report from FERC, "Assessment of Demand Response & Advanced Metering, Staff Report," was also released in October 2013.[11]

The advanced power grid relates to a number of key scientific and technological areas. These include power quality, reliability, and resilience; widespread integration of grid-tied renewables along with attendant large-scale storage; widespread deployment of grid sensors; and secure cyber-based communication within the grid. The smart grid also has the potential to ameliorate climate change through the reduction of energy waste in homes, businesses, and factories, and the accommodation of millions of electric vehicles (EVs) through innovative approaches to battery charging.[12] [13]

The federal government promotes development and deployment of a secure cyber-physical electric power grid.[14] In his 2013 State of the Union address, the president noted the critical issue of cybersecurity as it pertains to the present and future national power grid.[15] Two documents relating to critical infrastructure protection, Executive Order 13636 (*Improving Critical Infrastructure Cybersecurity*) and Presidential Policy Directive (PPD)-21(*Critical Infrastructure Security and Resilience*), articulate the federal government's commitment toward improving

---

[8] See NSTC reports at http://www.whitehouse.gov/sites/default/files/microsites/ostp/nstc-smart-grid-june2011.pdf . and http://www.whitehouse.gov/sites/default/files/microsites/ostp/2013_nstc_grid.pdf

[9] See report at http://www.smartgrid.gov/document/economic_impact_recovery_act_investments_smart_grid

[10] See report at http://www.smartgrid.gov/sites/default/files/doc/files/SGIG_progress_report_2013.pdf

[11] See report at http://www.ferc.gov/legal/staff-reports/2013/oct-demand-response.pdf

[12] "The President's Climate Action Plan", June 2013. See http://www.whitehouse.gov/sites/default/files/image/president27sclimateactionplan.pdf

[13] http://energy.gov/sites/prod/files/Presentation%20to%20the%20EAC%20-%20Impact%20of%20Smart%20Grid%20Projects%20Funded%20by%20ARRA%20-%20Joe%20Paladino.pdf

[14] See http://energy.gov/sites/prod/files/Presentation%20to%20the%20EAC%20-%20Impact%20of%20Smart%20Grid%20Projects%20Funded%20by%20ARRA%20-%20Joe%20Paladino.pdf

[15] See full text at http://www.nytimes.com/2013/02/13/us/politics/obamas-2013-state-of-the-union-address.html?pagewanted=all

cyber-based infrastructure security and the ability to recover from all potential disasters and damage to grid infrastructure. [16] [17]

As noted, EISA articulates the critical role of standards for the smart grid. The June 2011 and February 2013 NSTC reports also advocate the development and adoption of standards to ensure that today's investments in the smart grid remain valuable in the future; to catalyze innovations; to support consumer choice; to create economies of scale to reduce costs; to highlight best practices; and to open global markets for smart grid devices and systems.

Ongoing Response of the National Institute of Standards and Technology (NIST)

EISA assigns to the National Institute of Standards and Technology (NIST) the "primary responsibility to coordinate development of a framework that includes protocols and model standards for information management to achieve interoperability[18] of smart grid devices and systems…."[19]

In response to the urgent need to establish interoperability standards and protocols for the smart grid, NIST developed an initial (now completed) three-phase plan:

1) To accelerate the identification and consensus on smart grid standards
2) To establish a robust Smart Grid Interoperability Panel (SGIP) that sustains the development of the many additional standards that will be needed
3) To create a conformity testing and certification infrastructure

Beginning in 2008 and continuing throughout 2009, NIST convened workshops and meetings that brought together experts and a diverse group of stakeholders to begin the implementation of the three-phase plan (a detailed timeline is provided in Figure 1-1). By the end of 2009, significant progress and consensus had been achieved in developing a roadmap and identifying an initial set of standards (Phase I of the NIST plan). The publication in January 2010 of the *NIST Framework and Roadmap for Smart Grid Interoperability Standards, Release 1.0*[20] represented an important milestone and documented the progress made up to that time. This publication was updated in February 2012 by the *NIST Framework and Roadmap for Smart Grid Interoperability Standards, Release 2.0.*[21]

---

[16] See full text at   http://www.gpo.gov/fdsys/pkg/FR-2013-02-19/pdf/2013-03915.pdf

[17] For extended press release, see http://www.whitehouse.gov/the-press-office/2013/02/12/presidential-policy-directive-critical-infrastructure-security-and-resil

[18] "Interoperability" refers to the capability of two or more networks, systems, devices, applications, or components to exchange and readily use information—securely, effectively, and with little or no inconvenience to the user.

[19] Energy Independence and Security Act of 2007 [Public Law No: 110-140], Sec. 1305

[20] http://www.nist.gov/public_affairs/releases/upload/smartgrid_interoperability_final.pdf

[21] See http://www.nist.gov/smartgrid/upload/NIST_Framework_Release_2-0_corr.pdf

Release 1.0 of the NIST Framework described a high-level conceptual reference model for the Smart Grid, identified 75 existing standards that are applicable (or likely to be applicable) to the ongoing development of the Smart Grid, specified 15 high-priority gaps and harmonization issues for which new or revised standards and requirements are needed, documented action plans with aggressive timelines by which designated standards development organizations (SDOs) and standards-setting organizations (SSOs) will address these gaps, and described the strategy to establish requirements and standards to help ensure Smart Grid cybersecurity.

Release 2.0 of the NIST Framework updated and expanded the lists of standards and described advanced-stage progress made since the establishment of the SGIP in November 2009, in Phases 2 and 3 of NIST's three-phase plan.

The SGIP was established to further the development of consensus-based smart grid interoperability standards. NIST staff hold key technical positions in the SGIP. These include Chair or NIST Lead of two committees, Smart Grid Cybersecurity Committee (SGCC), and the Testing and Certification Committee (TCC), and several domain expert working groups (DEWGs), including the Building-to-Grid (B2G), Industrial-to-Grid (I2G), Home-to-Grid (H2G), Transmission and Distribution (TnD), Vehicle-to-Grid (V2G), Business and Policy (BnP), and Distributed Renewables, Generation, and Storage (DRGS) groups. NIST personnel also serve on almost all of the 25 Priority Action Plans (PAPs). NIST leadership on these committees and working groups provides strong support for the acceleration of the standards necessary for the safe, secure, and reliable smart grid.

In January 2013, the SGIP transitioned to an industry-led incorporated non-profit organization (sometimes referred to as SGIP 2.0), in which NIST continues to serve in a technical leadership role. NIST also continues to provide financial support for the SGIP through a cooperative agreement. The new SGIP public-private partnership also raises funding through membership dues. As of June 2014, SGIP 2.0 had 194 members. As of August 2014, there have been 59 standards accepted into the SGIP Catalog of Standards (CoS). See Chapter 3 for a detailed discussion of the evolution of the SGIP.

Under EISA, the Federal Energy Regulatory Commission (FERC) is charged with instituting rulemaking proceedings to adopt the standards and protocols as may be necessary to ensure smart grid functionality and interoperability once, in FERC's judgment, the NIST-coordinated process has led to sufficient consensus.[22] FERC obtained public input through two Technical Conferences on Smart Grid Interoperability Standards in November 2010[23] and January 2011,[24] and through a supplemental notice requesting comments in February 2011.[25] As a result, FERC issued an order in July 2011 stating that while there was insufficient consensus for it to institute a rulemaking at that time, FERC "encourages stakeholders to actively participate in the NIST

---

[22] Energy Independence and Security Act of 2007 [Public Law No: 110-140], Sec. 1305.

[23] http://ferc.gov/EventCalendar/EventDetails.aspx?ID=5505&CalType=&CalendarID=116&Date=11/14/2010&View=Listview

[24] http://ferc.gov/EventCalendar/EventDetails.aspx?ID=5571&CalType=%20&CalendarID=116&Date=01/31/2011&View=Listview

[25] http://ferc.gov/EventCalendar/Files/20110228084004-supplemental-notice.pdf

interoperability framework process to work on the development of interoperability standards and to refer to that process for guidance on smart grid standards."[26]

Content of Framework Release 3.0

This document, Release 3.0 of the *NIST Framework and Roadmap for Smart Grid Interoperability Standards,* updates progress made during 2012 and 2013, and reviews the achievements and direction of the SGIP during a period of transition to an industry-led organization. In Release 3.0, smart grids are viewed from the perspective of cyber-physical systems (CPS)—hybridized systems that combine computer-based communication, control, and command with physical equipment to yield improved performance, reliability, resiliency, and user and producer awareness.

Major advancements in smart grid architecture, cybersecurity, and testing and certification are covered in Release 3.0. The list of standards, Table 4-1, has been updated and expanded. Additional smart grid standards from the SGIP Priority Action Plans (PAPs) fill gaps identified in Release 2.0 and have been added to the list of identified smart grid standards. Listed standards have undergone an extensive vetting process to serve over time as useful building blocks for companies producing devices and software for the smart grid, as well as for utilities, regulators, academia, and other smart grid stakeholders. The sections below entitled "What's Included in Release 3.0" and "What's New in Release 3.0" provide additional summary information about the contents of this document.

The reference model, standards, gaps, and action plans described in this document offer a solid foundation for a secure, interoperable smart grid. They are consistent with the president's executive order on improving critical infrastructure cybersecurity.[27] However, the smart grid will continually evolve as new requirements and technologies emerge. Engaging the diverse community of smart grid stakeholders, the SGIP public-private partnership establishes a robust ongoing mechanism to develop requirements to guide the standardization efforts now spanning more than 25 standards-development organizations (SDOs) and standards-setting organizations (SSOs).[28]

The smart grid stakeholder groups who may find this Release 3.0 document most useful include:

- Utilities and suppliers concerned with how best to understand and implement the smart grid (especially Chapters 4, 5, 6, and 7)

- Testing laboratories and certification organizations (especially Chapter 7)

---

[26] http://www.ferc.gov/EventCalendar/Files/20110719143912-RM11-2-000.pdf

[27] Executive Order: "Improving Critical Infrastructure Cybersecurity", February 12, 2013. See http://www.whitehouse.gov/the-press-office/2013/02/12/executive-order-improving-critical-infrastructure-cybersecurity

[28] http://www.sgiclearinghouse.org/standards?page=1

- Academia (especially Section 5.1 and Chapter 8)
- Regulators (especially Chapters 1, 4, and 6, and also Section 3.5)

Cross-Cutting and Future Issues

Execution of current and future Priority Action Plans (PAPs) continue until identified gaps in the standards portfolio have been accomplished. As new gaps and requirements are identified, the SGIP will initiate PAPs to address them. Many of the U.S. Department of Energy (DOE) Smart Grid Investment Grant projects, funded by ARRA, are reaching their conclusions. In their proposals, awardees were required to describe how the projects would support the NIST Framework. As experience with new smart grid technologies is gained from these projects, NIST and the SGIP will use these "lessons learned" to further identify gaps and shortcomings of standards upon which these technologies are based.[29] NIST and the SGIP will continue to work with SDOs, SSOs, and other stakeholders to fill the gaps and improve the standards that form the foundation of the smart grid.

Work on the SGIP Catalog of Standards will continue to fully populate the Catalog and ensure robust architectural and cybersecurity reviews of the standards. New cybersecurity guidelines will address emerging new threats. NIST will continue to explore partnership opportunities with the private sector for the creation of testing and certification programs consistent with the SGIP testing and certification framework. NIST will continue to ensure coordination with related international smart grid standards efforts, maintaining U.S. leadership going forward.

NIST will support the needs of regulators in standardization matters in the regulatory arena. State and local regulators play important roles in establishing the regulatory framework for the electrical industry. Broad engagement of smart grid stakeholders at the state and local levels is essential to ensure the consistent voluntary application of the standards being developed, and both NIST and SGIP leaders have met frequently with this stakeholder group. The National Association of Regulatory Utility Commissioners (NARUC) has indicated its support for the SGIP process, stating that "When evaluating smart grid investments, State commissions should consider how certified smart grid interoperability standards may reduce the cost and improve the performance of smart grid projects and encourage participation in the Smart Grid Interoperability Panel, a public-private partnership that is coordinating and accelerating the development of interoperability standards for the smart grid."[30]

A key objective of NIST's effort is to create a self-sustaining, ongoing standards process that supports continuous innovation as grid modernization continues in the decades to come.[31] Grid modernization should ensure backward compatibility with existing technology to the greatest

---

[29] "Economic Impact of Recovery Act Investments in the Smart Grid", April 2013, p.9. See http://www.smartgrid.gov/sites/default/files/doc/files/Smart%20Grid%20Economic%20Impact%20Report.pdf

[30] http://www.naruc.org/Resolutions/Resolution%20on%20Smart%20Grid%20Principles.pdf

[31] As part of this process, the SGIP will help to prioritize and coordinate smart grid-related standards. See Chapter 5 for further discussion.

extent practical. NIST envisions that the standards development processes put in place by the SGIP will provide the mechanism to evolve the smart grid standards framework as new requirements and technologies emerge. In addition to its leadership role in the SGIP, NIST is increasing its measurement research program in areas related to smart grid interoperability. This research facilitates the development of smart grid interoperability standards including measurement advancements in the areas of cybersecurity, power conditioning, synchrophasors, power metering accuracy, precision timing, communications on the smart grid, sensor interfaces, and energy storage. To this end, NIST is developing an integrated smart grid testbed facility for full measurement, characterization, and validation of smart grid technology and interoperability standards, with particular emphasis on smart microgrids.

Mitigation of diverse natural and man-made events such as electromagnetic interference (EMI), geomagnetic storms, high-altitude nuclear detonations, and severe weather all pose a potential threat to grid reliability and resiliency. Electromagnetic interference can degrade or disable effective two-way communication and control on the grid; geomagnetic storms can damage large transformers and other equipment through induced currents,[32] and a high-altitude nuclear detonation would produce an electromagnetic pulse that can damage unprotected integrated circuits as well as large electrical equipment. Severe storms such as Hurricane Sandy in October 2012 produce long-term outages resulting in billions of dollars in infrastructure damages and lost business revenue. The future incorporation of microgrids offers the possibility of improved resiliency (i.e., the ability to recover from an outage event) to the effect of severe wind storms. After Hurricane Sandy, the Gridwise Alliance issued a report of lessons learned that recommended microgrids be considered for enhancing the resiliency of electric infrastructure serving critical loads.[33] The incorporation of microgrids to boost resiliency to the effects of storms is consistent with the President's Climate Action Plan.[34]

---

[32] See "Comment: Astrophysics: Prepare for the coming space weather storm" at
http://www.nature.com/nature/journal/v484/n7394/index.html

[33] http://www.gridwise.org/documents/ImprovingElectricGridReliabilityandResilience_6_6_13webFINAL.pdf

[34] "The President's Climate Action Plan", June 2013, p. 13, see
http://www.whitehouse.gov/sites/default/files/image/president27sclimateactionplan.pdf.

Accomplishments since NIST Framework Release 2.0

The major accomplishments in the NIST Smart Grid Program since Release 2.0 of the framework in February 2012 include the following:

Smart Grid Interoperability Panel

- The NIST-established SGIP has transitioned to an industry-led non-profit organization.
- SGIP has grown to 194 members as of June 2014, providing > 50% of funding through member dues.
- SGIP CoS has grown to 59 consensus entries.
- The number of PAPs has grown to 25 (including PAP00).
- The total number of completed PAPs is now up to 13

Regulatory Engagement and International Leadership

- FERC and NARUC point to the NIST framework and SGIP process for guidance in the coordination, development, and implementation of interoperability standards.
- Numerous liaison/working relationships have been established with international organizations.

Outcomes with Major Contributions from NIST

- Multiple new or revised standards, including Open ADR 2.0, SEP2, IEEE 1547, NAESB REQ18, and UL 1741 standards
- SGIP EMIIWG report on electromagnetic compatibility issues
- Two documents—"Technology, Measurement, and Standards Challenges for the Smart Grid" and "Strategic R&D Opportunities for the Smart Grid"—resulting from an August 2012 workshop hosted by NIST and the Renewable and Solar Energy Institute (RASEI)
- NISTIR 7823 (AMI Smart Meter Upgradeability Test Framework)
- Precision Time Protocol (IEEE 1588) Testbed, Dashboard, and Conformance Test Plan
- Revision 1 of NISTIR-7628 ("Guidelines for Smart Grid Cybersecurity"), published in September 2014.

What's Included in Release 3.0

Chapter 1

"Purpose and Scope" outlines the role of NIST with respect to the smart grid, including NIST's relationship with the newly independent Smart Grid Interoperability Panel (SGIP), defines key concepts and priorities discussed in the document, identifies potential uses of the document, and describes the basic content of the document. (A list of acronyms and abbreviations appears in Appendix A.)

Chapter 2

"Smart Grid Visions" provides a high-level description of the envisioned smart grid and describes major organizational drivers, opportunities, challenges, and anticipated benefits.

Chapter 3

"Smart Grid Interoperability Panel" presents the mission and structure of the SGIP. Following a transition period in late 2012 and early 2013, the SGIP is now a membership-based dues-supported and incorporated non-profit organization established to support NIST and to identify, prioritize, and address new and emerging requirements for smart grid standards. Working as an incorporated non-profit organization, the SGIP provides a process for stakeholders to interact in the ongoing coordination, acceleration, and harmonization of standards development for the smart grid. NIST maintains a prominent leadership role in the activities of the SGIP, and provides funding through a cooperative agreement program. (Additional details are provided in Appendix D.)

Chapter 4

"Standards Identified for Implementation" presents and describes an updated list of existing standards and emerging specifications applicable to the smart grid. It includes descriptions of selection criteria and methodology, a general overview of the standards identified by stakeholders in the NIST-coordinated process, and a discussion of their relevance to smart grid interoperability requirements.

Chapter 5

"Architectural Framework" presents an architectural process that includes views (diagrams) and descriptions that facilitate the discovery of appropriate characteristics, uses, behavior, interfaces, requirements, and standards of the smart grid. Because the smart grid is an evolving networked system of systems, the high-level model provides guidance for standards-setting organizations (SSOs) developing more detailed views of smart grid architecture. (Additional details are provided in Appendices B and C.)

Chapter 6

"Cybersecurity Strategy" discusses NIST's role in the SGIP Smart Grid Cybersecurity Committee's six current subgroups. These subgroups include cloud computing and the NISTIR 7628 User's Guide for the updated NISTIR 7628 document that deals with cyber protection of utilities and other entities implementing smart grid technology.

Chapter 7
"Testing and Certification Framework" reviews the key components and deliverables from the testing and certification framework development activities. The emerging implementation phase projects and activities are discussed, as well as views on the longer term implementation needs and challenges in maintaining a robust testing and certification ecosystem for interoperable smart grid systems and devices.

Chapter 8

"Cross-Cutting and Future Issues" contains a high-level overview of some of the currently foreseen areas of interest to the smart grid community, including reliability and resiliency of the grid through the implementation of standards.

What's New in Release 3.0

This document, Release 3.0, builds on the work reported in Release 2.0. Throughout the document, facts, figures, and tables have been updated. In addition to the subjects highlighted below, a number of chapters include forward-looking sections that outline current and future activities.

Chapter 1

New subjects in this chapter include:

- The history of NIST and the smart grid has been updated to include activities from 2012 and 2013, and the key events are highlighted in a timeline. (Figure 1-1.)
- New key concepts have been added to the "Definitions" section. (Section 1.3.1.)

Chapter 2

Section 2.2 ("Importance to National Energy Policy Goals") has been updated to include information from the 2013 State of the Union address and the 2013 National Science and Technology Council report. The broadening of the smart grid vision beyond the borders of the United States is reflected in two new sections that have been added to this chapter: "International Smart Grid Standards" and "International Efforts to Harmonize Architectures" (Sections 2.3 and 2.4, respectively).

Chapter 3

Major new topics described in this chapter include:

- SGIP transition from a federally-funded membership organization to a non-profit organization, known as SGIP 2.0, in December 2012, and the associated Memorandum of Understanding (MOU) and Cooperative Agreement with NIST.
- Organization of staff and activity within the new SGIP.
- Explanation of the SGIP Standing Committees and Permanent Working Groups. (See also Appendix D.)
- A discussion of criteria for inclusion of a proposed standard in the SGIP Catalog of Standards (CoS).
- A description of the Domain Expert Working Groups (DEWGs) and Priority Action Plans (PAPs). (See also Appendix D.)

Chapter 4

With the establishment of the Smart Grid Interoperability Panel, the process for identifying standards has evolved, and the standards listed in this chapter reflect that evolving process. (Section 4.2)

A new section, "Process of Future Smart Grid Standards Identification," details the process that will be used in the future (Section 4.4).

The heart of Chapter 4, in both Release 2.0 and Release 3.0, is found in the lists of standards:

- Table 4-1 ("Identified Standards") is discussed in Section 4.3 ("Current List of Standards Identified by NIST"). In Release 3.0, the number of entries in Table 4-1 has increased from 34 to 71, as compared to the list in Release 2.0.

In addition to the new standards added to the list in Release 3.0, the list includes a number of updates to those presented in Release 2.0. Links to relevant SGIP-related Web pages have been added. A list corresponding to Table 4.2 in Release 2.0 is not included in Release 3.0.

Chapter 5

The architectural framework described in this chapter in Release 3.0 provides a significant expansion to the conceptual reference model, which had been the primary architecture-related topic discussed in Release 1.0's Chapter 3. A description of the architectural framework, now under development, includes the following:

- Architectural goals for the smart grid (Section 5.2)

- Architecture methodology, which comprises the original NIST conceptual domain architecture, EU-M490 Reference Architecture, IEC 62357 and the combined reference model (Section 5.3)

- An extensive discussion of smart grid architecture methodology appears in Section 5.3.

- Recent work by the Smart Grid Architecture Committee (SGAC) is discussed in Section 5.5.

- Appendices B and C contain additional architecture-related details.

Chapter 6

New material documents the many developments related to smart grid cybersecurity since the topic was discussed in Chapter 6 of Release 2.0. Major new topics described in this chapter include the following.

- The transformation of the SGIP Cybersecurity Working Group (CSWG) into the Smart Grid Cybersecurity Committee (SGCC), and a description (Table 6.1) of the SGCC's six subgroups and their recent activities.

- Recently released *Guide for Assessing the High-Level Security Requirements in NISTIR 7628, Guidelines for Smart Grid Cyber Security (Assessment Guide)* and the *NISTIR 7628 User's Guide*, which facilitate use of the previously published National Institute of Standards and Technology Interagency Report (NISTIR) 7628, *Guidelines for Smart*

Grid Cyber Security; and the SGCC's work with the U.S. Department of Energy in developing the document, *Electricity Subsector Cybersecurity Risk Management Process.*

- Release of the document *NISTIR 7823, Advanced Metering Infrastructure Smart Meter Upgradeability Test Framework.*

- The NIST cybersecurity team's future plans as it maintains a leadership role within the SGIP SGCC.

Chapter 7

New material reviews the key components and deliverables from the testing and certification framework development activities. The emerging implementation phase projects and activities since Release 2.0 are then discussed, as well as views on the longer term implementation needs and challenges in maintaining a robust testing and certification approach for interoperable smart grid systems and devices. New topics discussed include

- Update of Smart Grid Test Program Landscape

- Discussion of Smart Grid Testing and Certification Committee (SGTCC) progress since Framework 2.0

- Discussion of the Interoperability Process Reference Manual (IPRM) version 2

- SGTCC 2012 working group analysis of standards proposed for inclusion in the SGIP Catalog of Standards (CoS)

- Engagement with interoperability testing and certification authorities (ITCAs), labs, certifiers, and accreditors

- Current and future smart grid testing initiatives

Chapter 8

- Discussion of electromagnetic compatibility

- Discussion of reliability, resiliency, implementability, and safety

- IEC and IEEE standards relating to electromagnetic compatibility that are under consideration for smart grid applications

- Discussion of R&D needs for the smart grid, including results of the August 2013 NIST/RASEI Smart Grid Workshop in Boulder, CO

1. Purpose and Scope

1.1. Overview and Background

Under the Energy Independence and Security Act of 2007 (EISA), the National Institute of Standards and Technology (NIST) was assigned *"primary responsibility to coordinate development of a framework that includes protocols and model standards for information management to achieve interoperability of Smart Grid devices and systems..."* [EISA Section 1305].[35] This responsibility comes at a time when the electric power grid and electric power industry are undergoing the most dramatic transformation in many decades. Very significant investments are being made by industry and the federal government to modernize the power grid. To realize the full benefits of these investments—and the continued investments forecast for the coming decades—there is a continued need to establish effective smart grid[36] standards and protocols for interoperability.

A major impetus behind the increased investments has been the American Recovery and Reinvestment Act of 2009 (ARRA), which provided the U.S. Department of Energy (DOE) with $4.5 billion to modernize the electric power grid and to implement Title XIII of EISA. Two of the programs established by DOE, the Smart Grid Investment Grants (SGIG) and the Smart Grid Demonstration Program (SGDP), have generated a significant impact on the U.S. economy and have resulted in substantial deployment of smart grid technologies.

An April 2013 report from DOE found that, as of March 2012, the total invested value of these two programs—$2.96 billion, including $1.48 billion of ARRA funds and $1.48 billion of private sector matching funds—generated at least $6.8 billion in total economic output.[37] The report estimates that, by the conclusion of these two programs, $9.56 billion will have been spent by the federal government and the private sector.

Recent investments in smart meters and synchrophasors are examples of the increasing investments in technology seen across the smart grid ecosystem as a result of these two programs

---

[35] The Department of Energy (DOE) is the lead federal agency with responsibility for the smart grid. Under the American Recovery and Reinvestment Act (ARRA), DOE has sponsored cost-shared smart grid investment grants, demonstration projects, and other R&D efforts. The Federal Energy Regulatory Commission (FERC) is tasked with initiating rulemakings for adoption of smart grid standards as necessary to ensure functionality and interoperability when it determines that the standards identified in the NIST Framework development efforts have sufficient consensus. See Section 1305 of the Energy Independence and Security Act of 2007. See http://www.gpo.gov/fdsys/pkg/PLAW-110publ140/content-detail.html

[36] While recognizing that the different names used for the future grid have meaningful distinctions to some stakeholders, this report generally uses the term "smart grid." The decision to use "smart grid" is not intended to discount or supersede other terms used to describe a modernized grid that enables bidirectional flows of energy and uses two-way communication and control capabilities that will lead to an array of new functionalities and applications. Both capitalized and lower-case versions of the term are used in the Energy Independence and Security Act of 2007. In this document, the lower-case version is used unless referring to a specific program, office, or title.

[37] "Economic Impact of Recovery Act Investments in Smart Grid," Department of Energy, April 2013. http://www.smartgrid.gov/document/economic_impact_recovery_act_investments_smart_grid

- Smart meters are being widely deployed. In 2011, there were more than 37.3 million smart meters installed by 492 U.S. electric utilities.[38] It is estimated that 61.8 million smart meters will have been deployed in the U.S. by the end of 2013.[39] On a global basis, the International Energy Agency projects that cumulative installations of smart meters will increase to almost one billion before the end of 2018.[40]

- Installation of synchrophasors (or phasor measurement units, PMUs), sensors that provide real-time assessments of power system health to provide system operators with better information for averting disastrous outages, has accelerated rapidly. The Western Interconnection Synchrophasor Program (WISP), which includes participants in ten western states, had installed more than 465 Phasor Measurement Units (PMUs) PMUs throughout the west as of June 2013.[41] DOE anticipates that once all of the ARRA synchrophasor projects have been completed, there will be at least 1,043 networked PMUs in place (compared to 166 in 2010), providing significantly greater coverage of the U.S. bulk power system.[42]

These recent U.S. investments in smart grid technology are just the beginning of a decades-long, global effort to modernize the electric power grid. Internationally, many other countries are also making significant smart grid investments. A recent forecast projects that the global market for smart grid-related products and services will exceed $400 billion cumulatively by 2020.[43]

To ensure that the mounting investments made in smart grid technologies will be cost-effective, the smart grid community needs to establish standards and protocols for interoperability. In the absence of standards, there is a risk that the diverse smart grid technologies will become prematurely obsolete or, worse, be implemented without adequate security measures. Lack of standards may also impede future innovation and the realization of promising applications, such as smart appliances responsive to price and demand response signals. Standards adopted or

---

[38] http://www.eia.gov/tools/faqs/faq.cfm?id=108&t=1 [Most recent annual data available as of January 10, 2013.]

[39] http://smartgridresearch.org/standard/u-s-smart-meter-trends/

[40] "Tracking Clean Energy Progress 2013," International Energy Agency, http://www.iea.org/publications/TCEP_web.pdf (see page 106 and 109).

[41] See
http://www.google.com/url?sa=t&rct=j&q=&esrc=s&frm=1&source=web&cd=1&ved=0CCQQFjAA&url=http%3
A%2F%2Fwww.wecc.biz%2Fcommittees%2FBOD%2F20130625%2FLists%2FPresentations%2F1%2FMark%252
0Maher%2520CEO%2520Update%25206-26-
2013.pdf&ei=D5AgU_jIHuqp2QWu34HYCw&usg=AFQjCNEjXn12qDVToOH4Rc5lLwNx9m-
y6w&bvm=bv.62788935,d.eW0

[42] "Synchrophasor Technologies and their Deployment in the Recovery Act Smart Grid Programs," Department of Energy, August 2013. See
http://www.smartgrid.gov/sites/default/files/doc/files/Synchrophasor%20Report%2008%2009%202013%20DOE%2
0(2)%20version_0.pdf

[43] "Global Smart Grid Technologies and Growth Markets 2013 – 2020," GTM Research, July 2013.
http://www.greentechmedia.com/articles/read/smart-grid-market-to-surpass-400-billion-worldwide-by-
2020?utm_source=Daily&utm_medium=Picture&utm_campaign=GTMDaily

developed in support of this transition must also fully account for backward compatibility with deployed technologies.

Moreover, standards enable economies of scale and scope that help to create competitive markets in which vendors compete on the basis of a combination of price and quality. Market competition promotes faster diffusion of smart grid technologies and realization of customer benefits. As summarized in *"A Policy Framework for the 21st Century Grid: A Progress Report,"* a February 2013 report from the White House's National Science and Technology Council, "interoperability standards make markets more efficient, help open new international markets to U.S. manufacturers, and reduce the costs of providing reliable, safe power to U.S. households and businesses."[44]

The importance of interoperability standards was highlighted in EISA as a key element of U.S. energy policy. This document, Framework 3.0, provides a summary of NIST's efforts to fulfill its EISA role—to coordinate development of a framework that includes protocols and model standards for information management to achieve interoperability of smart grid devices and systems.

Since 2009, NIST has worked cooperatively with industry to develop and refine this framework. The process has resulted in a solid foundation and platform. Key standards have been identified, and critical standards gaps have been filled. Guidance and tools have been provided to advance smart grid architectures, cybersecurity, and testing and certification. A robust consensus-building stakeholder engagement process and organization—the Smart Grid Interoperability Panel—has been established, and it is expected to provide for continued development and implementation of standards to meet the needs of industry and consumers and to keep pace with the rapid advance of technology.

However, NIST's job—as well as the job of the broader national and global smart grid community—is far from complete. Development of a standard is not a one-time project. Initially developed standards are reviewed and revised periodically in a continual process of maturation. Similarly, the NIST Framework has undergone reviews and revisions as technology matures. This document is the third installment in an ongoing standards coordination and harmonization process. Ultimately, this process will deliver the hundreds of communication protocols, standard interfaces, and other widely accepted and adopted technical specifications necessary to build an advanced, secure electric power grid with two-way communication and control capabilities.

The *NIST Framework and Roadmap for Smart Grid Interoperability Standards, Release 3.0,* builds upon the work in Releases 1.0 (January 2010) and 2.0 (February 2012). Releases 1.0 and 2.0 of the NIST Framework document contained information obtained through an open public process that engaged both the broad spectrum of smart grid stakeholder communities and the general public. NIST also consulted with stakeholders through extensive outreach efforts. The timeline for the development of the Release 1.0, Release 2.0, and Release 3.0 Framework documents is displayed in Fig. 1-1, which shows the history of NIST activities in smart grid.

---

[44] http://www.whitehouse.gov/sites/default/files/microsites/ostp/2013_nstc_grid.pdf

A History of NIST and the Smart Grid

⊙ 2007/2008	⊙ 2009	⊙ 2010	⊙ 2011	⊙ 2012	⊙ 2013
December Energy Independence & Security Act (EISA) signed by President Bush	**April** NIST announces Three-Phase Plan for Interoperability Standards	**January** NIST seeks nominations for new Smart Grid Advisory Committee		**January** Green Button Initiative launched to help consumers manage electricity use	**April** NIST publishes R&D Assessment for the Smart Grid
June NIST Smart Grid Coordination Plan drafted, Web site established	**May** NIST holds Smart Grid Interoperability Standards Interim Roadmap Public Workshop	**NIST releases** Framework and Roadmap for Smart Grid Interoperability Release 1.0	**January** Interoperability Process Reference Manual published as Framework for Testing and Certification	**February** NIST releases Framework and Roadmap for Smart Grid Interoperability Release 2.0	**May** With the addition of 15 major utilities, Green Button Initiative reaches 30 million U.S. households
August Smart Grid Stakeholder Domain Expert Working Groups formed	**June** NIST releases Report on Smart Grid Development for public comment	**February** NIST issues expanded draft of Smart Grid Cyber Security Strategy for public comment	**February** SGIP Governing Board agrees on Data-Exchange Standards for Electricity Usage	**July** NIST releases Test Framework for Upgrading Smart Electrical Meters	**June** NIST Presidential Innovation Fellows address Smart Grid issues including improvements in consumer access to energy usage data
November Grid-Interop Smart Grid Interoperability Workshop	**September** NIST issues Framework & Roadmap for Smart Grid Interoperability Standards Release 1.0 for public comment	**September** NIST finalizes initial set of Smart Grid Cyber Security Guidelines	**March** NIST Smart Grid Advisory Committee holds public meeting	**December** NIST & SGIP 2.0 sign Memorandum of Understanding as SGIP transitions to Industry-Led Organization	
	November Smart Grid Interoperability Panel (SGIP) launched		**July** First six entries made to SGIP's Catalog of Standards		

Fig. 1-1. A History of NIST and the Smart Grid

Release 1.0 described a high-level conceptual reference model for the smart grid that identified 75 existing standards that are applicable (or likely to be applicable) to the ongoing development of the smart grid; specified 15 high-priority gaps and harmonization issues (in addition to cybersecurity) for which new or revised standards and requirements are needed; documented action plans with aggressive timelines by which designated standards-setting organizations (SSOs) will address these gaps; and described the strategy to establish requirements and standards to help ensure better smart grid cybersecurity. This document served as guidance for the national and international smart grid community.

Release 2.0 built on the work reported in Release 1.0. Throughout the document, facts and figures were updated. Two new chapters—one on the Smart Grid Interoperability Panel (SGIP) and one on the framework for smart grid interoperability testing and certification—were added. Existing chapters on architecture and cybersecurity were significantly expanded to reflect accomplishments and ongoing work. The number of standards identified as applicable or likely to be applicable to the ongoing development of the smart grid was increased to 96.

The *NIST Framework and Roadmap for Smart Grid Interoperability Standards, Release 3.0*, further builds upon the work in Releases 1.0 and 2.0, and is based on updated information and input from relevant stakeholders. Release 3.0 includes a description of the Smart Grid Interoperability Panel (SGIP) now that it has become an independent entity (Chapter 3); an update to the progress of the Priority Action Plans (PAPs) in closing the previously identified high-priority gaps (Appendix D); a description of the smart grid conceptual reference model and conceptual architectural framework that was developed by the SGIP's Smart Grid Architecture Committee (SGAC) (Chapter 5); an expanded cybersecurity section (Chapter 6); updates to the testing and certification section (Chapter 7); and a summary of cross-cutting and future issues, including discussions of reliability and electromagnetic interference topics (Chapter 8).

While the SGIP is now an incorporated private entity, NIST maintains an active leadership role in many of the SGIP's working groups and committees.

1.2. Use of this Framework

The results of NIST's ongoing technical work reflected in this framework document should assist industry utilities, vendors, academia, regulators, system integrators and developers, and other smart grid stakeholders in future decision making. This document includes a compendium of interoperability standards that, in NIST's engineering judgment, are foundational to the smart grid. Standards identified in Table 4-1, below, have gone through a full vetting process, and are expected to stand the "test of time" as useful building blocks for firms producing devices and software for the smart grid, as well as for utilities, regulators, academia, and other smart grid stakeholders. It is important to note that these standards are not static as they mature. Standards undergo continuing revisions to add new functionalities, integrate with legacy standards, harmonize/align with overlapping standards, and remedy shortcomings that are discovered as their implementations undergo interoperability testing.

The following stakeholder groups will find specific information in this framework document most useful:

- For utilities and suppliers concerned with how best to understand and implement the smart grid, the document provides a compendium of reference standards (Chapter 4), an architectural framework that provides guidance and core services to identify fundamental interactions, applications, requirements and organizational change to establish new or integrate legacy implementations (Chapter 5), an introduction to the extensive body of work available from NIST concerning smart grid privacy and security (Chapter 6), and a taxonomy of the various smart grid domains (Appendix B).

- For testing laboratories and certification organizations, the testing and certification chapter (Chapter 7) provides updates on efforts now under way to enable vendors and other smart grid stakeholders to certify the interoperability of devices being considered for a specific smart grid deployment.

- For those in academia, this document provides a benchmark of considerable progress made in advancing the hundreds of standards required for the smart grid. In addition, Chapter 8 and summaries of various PAP subgroup efforts in Appendix D point to additional research and innovation needed to fill gaps in our collective understanding of the tools, systems, and policies needed to deploy and manage what will be the largest single network yet deployed in the United States.

- For regulators, the framework serves as a general introduction to both the challenge and promise of the Smart Grid (Executive Summary, Chapter 1, and Chapter 2), a guide to workable standards useful to delivering the best value for consumers by ensuring that technical investments by energy providers utilize standards wisely (Chapter 4), and an introduction to extensive work now under way considering smart grid privacy and security matters (Chapter 6).

1.3. Key Concepts

The expedited development and evolution of an interoperability framework and a roadmap for underpinning standards, such as those outlined in this document, is a fundamental aspect of the overall transformation to a smart grid infrastructure. Although electric utilities are ultimately responsible for the safe and reliable operation of the grid, many other participants are involved in the evolution of the existing electric power infrastructure. Technical contributions from numerous stakeholder communities are required to realize an interoperable, secure smart grid. Because of the diversity of technical and industrial perspectives involved, most participants in the roadmapping effort are familiar with only subsets of smart grid-related standards. Few have detailed knowledge of all pertinent standards, even in their own industrial and technical area.

To facilitate broad and balanced input from all smart grid stakeholders, the SGIP[45] was established:

- To create a forum with balanced stakeholder governance that would bring together stakeholders with expertise in the many various areas necessary for the smart grid, including areas such as power engineering, information communication technologies, architecture, systems engineering, and life-cycle management

- To support development of consensus for smart grid interoperability standards

- To provide a source of expert input for the interoperability standards framework and roadmap

This report contributes to an increased understanding of the key elements critical to realization of the smart grid, including standards-related priorities, strengths and weaknesses of individual standards, the level of effective interoperability among different smart grid domains, and cybersecurity requirements.

---

[45] A more detailed description of the SGIP can be found in Chapter 3.

1.3.1. Definitions

Different stakeholders may hold a variety of definitions for the important terms that appear throughout the roadmap. To facilitate clear stakeholder discourse, NIST used the following definitions for the key terms below:

Architecture: The structure and overall organization of the smart grid from the point of view of its use or design. This includes technical and business designs, demonstrations, implementations, and standards that together convey a common understanding of the smart grid. The architecture embodies high-level principles and requirements that designs of smart grid applications and systems must satisfy.[46]

Architecture Process: A process that identifies in a phased fashion the necessary business-through-product requirements to implement a desired functionality with insight into the effects new capability may impose on existing business units' manual and automated processes. It includes a set of views (diagrams) and descriptions that provides the basis for discussing the characteristics, uses, behavior/processes, interfaces, requirements, and standards of the smart grid. This architecture process does not represent the final architecture of the smart grid; rather, it is a tool for describing, discussing, and developing a sustainable architecture.

Energy Services Interface (ESI): The device or application that functions as the gateway between the energy providers and consumers. Located on the consumer side of the exchange, this can have many forms. Its purpose is to facilitate communications between the consumer and the energy provider.

Functional Requirement: A requirement that specifies a function that a system or system component must be able to perform.[47]

Harmonization: The process of achieving technical equivalency and enabling interchangeability between different standards with overlapping functionality. Harmonization requires an architecture that documents key points of interoperability and associated interfaces.

Interchangeability: The ability of two or more devices or components to be interchanged without making changes to the other components or devices and without degradation in system performance.

Interoperability: The capability of two or more networks, systems, devices, applications, or components to work together, and to exchange and readily use information—securely, effectively, and with little or no inconvenience to the user. The smart grid will be a system of interoperable systems; that is, different systems will be able to exchange meaningful, actionable

---

[46] Pacific Northwest National Laboratory, U.S. Department of Energy. *Gridwise™ Architecture Tenets and Illustrations*, PNNL-SA-39480 October 2003.

[47] IEEE 610.12-1990–IEEE Standard Glossary of Software Engineering Terminology. See http://standards.ieee.org/findstds/standard/610.12-1990.html

information in support of the safe, secure, efficient, and reliable operations of electric systems. The systems will share a common meaning of the exchanged information, and this information will elicit agreed-upon types of response. The reliability, fidelity, and security of information exchanges between and among smart grid systems must achieve requisite performance levels.[48]

Mature Standard: A mature standard is a standard that has been in use for a sufficient time that most of its initial faults and inherent problems have been identified and removed or reduced by further development.

Non-Functional Requirement: A non-functional requirement is a statement that specifies a constraint about how a system must behave to meet functional requirements.

Reliability: The ability of a system or component to perform its required functions under stated conditions for a specified period of time. It is often measured as a probability of failure or a measure of availability. However, maintainability is also an important part of reliability engineering. In addition to reliability of information technology, it covers power system equipment and reliability requirements of electric utilities.

Requirement: 1) A condition or capability needed by a user to solve a problem or achieve an objective. 2) A condition or capability that must be met or possessed by a system or system component to satisfy a contract, standard, specification, or other formally imposed document.[49]

Resiliency: The attribute that allows a grid to better sustain and more quickly recover from adverse events such as attacks or natural disasters. Grid resiliency includes hardening, advanced capabilities, and recovery/reconstitution. Although most attention is placed on best practices for hardening, resiliency strategies must also consider options to improve grid flexibility and control. Resiliency also includes reconstitution and general readiness, outage management, use of mobile transformers and substations, and participation in mutual assistance groups.[50]

Standards: Specifications that establish the fitness of a product for a particular use or that define the function and performance of a device or system. Standards are key facilitators of compatibility and interoperability. They define specifications for languages, communication protocols, data formats, linkages within and across systems, interfaces between software applications and between hardware devices, and much more. Standards must be robust so that they can be extended to accommodate future applications and technologies. An assortment of organizations develops voluntary standards and specifications, which are the results of processes that vary on the basis of the type of organization and its purpose. These organizations include, but are not limited to, standards development organizations (SDOs), standards-setting organizations (SSOs), and user groups.

---

[48] GridWise Architecture Council, *Interoperability Path Forward Whitepaper*, November 30, 2005 (v1.0)

[49] IEEE Std 610.12.

[50] "Economic Benefits of Increasing Electric Grid Resilience to Weather Outages," Executive Office of the President, August 2013. See http://energy.gov/downloads/economic-benefits-increasing-electric-grid-resilience-weather-outages

Additional terms pertinent to cybersecurity and to other important security-related considerations relevant to the safety, reliability, and overall performance of the smart grid and its components are defined in the *Guidelines to Smart Grid Cyber Security* (NISTIR 7628[51]).

1.3.2. Applications and Requirements: Nine Priority Areas

The smart grid will ultimately require hundreds of standards. Some are more urgently needed than others. To prioritize its work, NIST chose to focus on seven key functionalities plus cybersecurity and network communications. These functionalities are especially critical to ongoing and near-term deployments of smart grid technologies and services, and they include the priorities recommended by the Federal Energy Regulatory Commission (FERC) in its policy statement:[52]

- **Demand response and consumer energy efficiency:** Provide mechanisms and incentives for utilities, business, industrial, and residential customers to modify energy use during times of peak demand or when power reliability is at risk. Demand response is necessary for optimizing the balance of power supply and demand. With increased access to detailed energy consumption information, consumers can also save energy with efficiency behavior and investments that achieve measurable results. In addition, they can learn where they may benefit with additional energy efficiency investments.

- **Wide-area situational awareness:** Utilizes monitoring and display of power-system components and performance across interconnections and over large geographic areas in near real time. The goals of situational awareness are to understand and ultimately optimize the management of power-network components, behavior, and performance, as well as to anticipate, prevent, or respond to problems before disruptions arise.

- **Distributed Energy Resources (DER):** Covers generation and/or electric storage systems that are interconnected with distribution systems, including devices that reside on a customer premise, "behind the meter." DER systems utilize a wide range of generation and storage technologies such as renewable energy, combined heat and power generators (CHP), fixed battery storage, and electric vehicles with bi-directional chargers. DER systems can be used for local generation/storage, can participate in capacity and ancillary service markets, and/or can be aggregated as virtual power plants. Advanced grid-interactive DER functionalities, enabled by smart inverter interconnection equipment, are becoming increasingly available (and required in some jurisdictions) to ensure power quality and grid stability while simultaneously meeting the safety requirements of the distribution system. Advanced DER functionalities also enable new grid architectures incorporating "microgrids" that can separate from the grid when power is disrupted and can interact in cooperation with grid operations to form a more adaptive resilient power system.

---

[51] http://csrc.nist.gov/publications/PubsNISTIRs.html#NIST-IR-7628

[52] Federal Energy Regulatory Commission, *Smart Grid Policy*, 128 FERC ¶ 61,060 [Docket No. PL09-4-000] July 16, 2009, http://www.ferc.gov/whats-new/comm-meet/2009/071609/E-3.pdf

- **Energy Storage:** Means of storing energy, directly or indirectly. The most common bulk energy storage technology used today is pumped hydroelectric storage technology. New storage capabilities—especially for distributed storage—would benefit the entire grid, from generation to end use.

- **Electric transportation:** Refers primarily to enabling large-scale integration of plug-in electric vehicles (PEVs). Electric transportation could significantly reduce U.S. dependence on foreign oil, increase use of renewable sources of energy, provide electric energy storage to ameliorate peak-load demands, and dramatically reduce the nation's carbon footprint.

- **Network communications:** Refers to a variety of public and private communication networks, both wired and wireless, that will be used for smart grid domains and subdomains. Given this variety of networking environments, the identification of performance metrics and core operational requirements of different applications, actors, and domains—in addition to the development, implementation, and maintenance of appropriate security and access controls—is critical to the smart grid. In addition, as FERC notes, a "… cross-cutting issue is the need for a common semantic framework (i.e., agreement as to meaning) and software models for enabling effective communication and coordination across inter-system interfaces. An interface is a point where two systems need to exchange data with each other. Effective communication and coordination occurs when each of the systems understands and can respond to the data provided by the other system, even if the internal workings of the system are quite different."[53]

- **Advanced metering infrastructure (AMI):** Provides near real-time monitoring of power usage. These advanced metering networks are of many different designs and could also be used to implement residential demand response including dynamic pricing. AMI consists of the communications hardware and software, and the associated system and data management software, that together create a two-way network between advanced meters and utility business systems, enabling collection and distribution of information to customers and other parties, such as the competitive retail supplier or the utility itself.

- **Distribution grid management:** Focuses on maximizing performance of feeders, transformers, and other components of networked distribution systems and integrating them with transmission systems and customer operations. As smart grid capabilities, such as AMI and demand response are developed, and as large numbers of distributed energy resources and PEVs are deployed, the automation of distribution systems becomes increasingly more important to the efficient and reliable operation of the overall power system. The anticipated benefits of distribution grid management include increased reliability, reductions in peak loads, increased efficiency of the distribution system, and improved capabilities for managing distributed sources of renewable energy.

- **Cybersecurity:** Encompasses measures to ensure the confidentiality, integrity, and availability of the electronic information communication systems and the control systems

---

[53] Smart Grid Policy; Final Rule Federal Register / Vol. 74, No. 142 / Monday, July 27, 2009 / Rules and Regulations, FERC. See http://www.gpo.gov/fdsys/pkg/FR-2009-07-27/html/E9-17624.htm

necessary for the management, operation, and protection of the smart grid's energy, information technology, and telecommunications infrastructures.[54]

1.4. Framework Content Overview

Chapter 2, "Smart Grid Visions," provides a high-level description of the envisioned smart grid and describes major organizational drivers, opportunities, challenges, and anticipated benefits.

Chapter 3, "Smart Grid Interoperability Panel," presents the mission and structure of the SGIP. The SGIP is an incorporated private/public non-profit partnership funded by industry stakeholders in cooperation with the federal government. It is a membership-based organization established to support NIST and to identify, prioritize, and address new and emerging requirements for smart grid standards. The SGIP provides a venue for stakeholders to interact with NIST in the ongoing coordination, acceleration, and harmonization of standards development for the smart grid. (Additional details are provided in Appendix D.)

Chapter 4, "Standards Identified for Implementation," presents and describes existing standards and emerging specifications applicable to the smart grid. It includes descriptions of selection criteria and methodology, a general overview of the standards identified by stakeholders in the NIST-coordinated process, and a discussion of their relevance to smart grid interoperability requirements.

Chapter 5, "Architectural Framework," presents an evolution from static reference architectures to a disciplined process identifying requirements and impacts of smart grid requirements. This process includes views (diagrams) and descriptions that are the basis for discussing the characteristics, uses, behavior, processes, interfaces, requirements, and standards of the smart grid. Because the smart grid is an evolving networked system of systems, this methodology provides guidance for SSOs, end-users, and solution providers with detailed views of smart grid architecture. (Additional details are provided in Appendices B and C.)

Chapter 6, "Cybersecurity Strategy," provides an overview of the content of NISTIR 7628 and the go-forward strategy of the Smart Grid Cybersecurity Committee (SGCC). Cybersecurity is now being expanded to address the following: combined power systems; IT and communication systems required to maintain the reliability of the smart grid; physical security of all components; reduced impact of coordinated cyber-physical attacks; and privacy of consumers.

Chapter 7, "Testing and Certification Framework," provides details on an assessment of existing smart grid standards testing programs and high-level guidance for the development of a testing and certification framework. This chapter includes a comprehensive roadmap and operational framework for how testing and certification of smart grid devices will be conducted.

Chapter 8, "Cross-cutting Issues and Future Issues," contains a high-level overview of some of the anticipated areas of interest to the smart grid community, including electromagnetic disturbance and interference, the implementability of standards, and R&D needs.

---

[54] Ibid.

2. Smart Grid Visions

2.1. Overview of Smart Grid: Definitions, Costs, Benefits, and Standards

In the United States and internationally, modernization of the electric power grid is central to national efforts to increase reliability, resiliency, sustainability, and energy efficiency; transition to renewable sources of energy; reduce greenhouse gas emissions; implement secure smart grid technologies and address cybersecurity and privacy issues; support a growing fleet of electric vehicles; and build a sustainable economy that ensures prosperity for future generations.

For the United States, one report from the Electric Power Research Institute[55] estimates that the investment costs,[56] over 20 years, to achieve a fully functioning smart grid may approach $500 billion. Globally, several trillion dollars will be spent in the coming decades to build elements of what ultimately will be "smart" electric power grids. A 2013 report from the International Energy Agency[57] found that 2012 global public and private investment in smart grid technologies and applications was nearly $14 billion, a four-fold increase from 2008. It is expected to increase to more than $25 billion in 2018.

Definitions and terminology vary somewhat, but all notions of an advanced power grid for the 21st century include the addition and integration of many varieties of digital computing and communication technologies and services with the power-delivery infrastructure. Bidirectional flows of energy and two-way communication and control capabilities will enable an array of new functionalities and applications that go well beyond "smart" meters for homes and businesses.

The Energy Independence and Security Act of 2007 (EISA), which directed the National Institute of Standards and Technology (NIST) to coordinate development of this framework and roadmap, states that national policy supports the creation of a smart grid. Distinguishing characteristics of the smart grid cited in EISA include:[58]

- Increased use of digital information and controls technology to improve reliability, security, and efficiency of the electric grid

- Dynamic optimization of grid operations and resources, with full cybersecurity

- Deployment and integration of distributed resources and generation, including renewable resources

---

[55] Estimating the Costs and Benefits of the Smart Grid: A Preliminary Estimate of the Investment Requirements and the Resultant Benefits of a Fully Functioning Smart Grid" EPRI March 2011. See http://www.smartgrid.gov/sites/default/files/doc/files/Estimating_Costs_Benefits_Smart_Grid_Preliminary_Estimate_In_201103.pdf

[56] "estimated *net* investment needed to realize the envisioned power delivery system (PDS) of the future"

[57] "Tracking Clean Energy Progress 2013," International Energy Agency. http://www.iea.org/publications/TCEP_web.pdf (see page 110). Costs include "advanced metering infrastructure, distribution automation, and advanced smart grid applications"

[58] Energy Independence and Security Act of 2007 [Public Law No: 110-140] Title XIII, Sec. 1301.

- Development and incorporation of demand response, demand-side resources, and energy-efficiency resources

- Deployment of ''smart'' technologies for metering, communications concerning grid operations and status, and distribution automation

- Integration of ''smart'' appliances and consumer devices

- Deployment and integration of advanced electricity storage and peak-shaving technologies, including plug-in electric and hybrid electric vehicles, and thermal-storage air conditioning

- Provision to consumers of timely information and control options

- Development of standards for communication and interoperability of appliances and equipment connected to the electric grid, including the infrastructure serving the grid

- Identification and lowering of unreasonable or unnecessary barriers to adoption of smart grid technologies, practices, and services

The smart grid will bring a wide variety of benefits. A list of anticipated benefits is found in Figure 2-1.

Anticipated Smart Grid Benefits
A modernized national electrical grid:

- **Improves power reliability and quality**

- **Optimizes facility utilization and averts construction of backup (peak load) power plants**

- **Enhances capacity and efficiency of existing electric power networks**

- **Improves resilience to disruption by natural disasters and attacks**

- **Enables predictive maintenance and "self-healing" responses to system disturbances**

- **Facilitates expanded deployment of renewable energy sources**

- **Accommodates distributed power sources**

- **Automates maintenance and operation**

- **Reduces greenhouse gas emissions by enabling electric vehicles and new power sources**

- **Reduces fossil fuel consumption by reducing the need for gas turbine generation during peak usage periods**

- **Presents opportunities to improve grid security**

- **Enables transition to plug-in electric vehicles and new energy storage options**

- **Provides consumers with actionable and timely information about their energy usage**

- **Increases consumer choice, and enables new products, services, and markets**

Fig. 2-1. Anticipated Smart Grid Benefits

The U.S. Department of Energy (DOE), which leads the overall federal smart grid effort, has developed a series of metrics to monitor the progress of smart grid deployments in the United

States and assess the benefits achieved to date. In its Report to Congress, DOE tracks activities grouped under six chief benefits/characteristics of the envisioned smart grid:[59]

- Enables informed participation by customers

- Accommodates all generation and storage options

- Enables new products, services, and markets

- Provides power quality for the range of needs

- Optimizes asset utilization and operating efficiency

- Operates resiliently to disturbances, attacks, and natural disasters

In a 2011 report, the Electric Power Research Institute (EPRI) estimated the costs and benefits of a fully functioning smart grid in the United States (see Table 2.1) and found that the benefits outweigh the costs by a ratio of 2.8 to 6.0.[60] (The report is entitled "preliminary," but no further report is available as of August 2014.)

20-Year Total

	($billion)
Net Investment Required	338 – 476
Net Benefit	1,294 – 2,028
Benefit-to-Cost Ratio	2.8 – 6.0

Table 2-1. Summary of Estimated Cost and Benefits of the Smart Grid[61]

An October 2013 report from the Smart Grid Consumer Collaborative provided a review and synthesis of research on smart grid benefits and costs.[62] The report concluded that "smart grid investment is likely to offer economic benefits in excess of costs" and "smart grid investment offers significant reductions in environmental impact." The report's detailed analyses include estimates of direct and indirect economic benefits per customer per year, as well as estimates of "carbon dioxide equivalent reduction" per customer per year. Based on assumptions outlined in

---

[59] U.S. Department of Energy, *2010 Smart Grid System Report*, Biennial Report to Congress, February 2012. See http://energy.gov/sites/prod/files/2010%20Smart%20Grid%20System%20Report.pdf

[60] Estimating the Costs and Benefits of the Smart Grid: A Preliminary Estimate of the Investment Requirements and the Resultant Benefits of a Fully Functioning Smart Grid" EPRI March 2011 http://www.smartgrid.gov/sites/default/files/doc/files/Estimating_Costs_Benefits_Smart_Grid_Preliminary_Estimat e_In_201103.pdf

[61] Estimating the Costs and Benefits of the Smart Grid: A Preliminary Estimate of the Investment Requirements and the Resultant Benefits of a Fully Functioning Smart Grid" EPRI March 2011. See http://www.smartgrid.gov/sites/default/files/doc/files/Estimating_Costs_Benefits_Smart_Grid_Preliminary_Estimat e_In_201103.pdf

[62] http://smartgridcc.org/sgccs-smart-grid-environmental-and-economic-benefits-report

the report, the ratio of benefits to costs for the smart grid ranged from 1.5 ("reference case") to 2.6 ("ideal case").

Role of Standards and Interoperability in Achieving the Smart Grid Vision

Within the context of the significant costs and benefits associated with the smart grid (see Table 2.1), interoperability and cybersecurity standards are key to achieving benefits as well as managing overall costs. Therefore, NIST's EISA-identified role—to coordinate the development of a framework of protocols and model standards—represents a critical element of the overall smart grid vision.

DOE explicitly recognizes that underpinning standards infrastructure will realize benefits:

> The applications of advanced digital technologies (i.e., microprocessor-based measurement and control, communications, computing, and information systems) are expected to greatly improve the reliability, security, interoperability, and efficiency of the electric grid, while reducing environmental impacts and promoting economic growth. Achieving enhanced connectivity and interoperability will require innovation, ingenuity, and different applications, systems, and devices to operate seamlessly with one another, involving the combined use of open system architecture, as an integration platform, and commonly-shared technical standards and protocols for communications and information systems. To realize smart grid capabilities, deployments must integrate a vast number of smart devices and systems.[63]

Similarly, the International Energy Agency, in its 2013 report, highlights the following two key points in the section titled "Technology Developments":[64]

- Integration of the many individual smart grid technologies is the largest challenge in development and deployment of smart grids.

- Interoperability, put into practice through technical standards and grid codes, is a key element of technology development.

In undertaking its important assignment and developing a framework of protocols and model standards, NIST has followed the guidance of EISA, which stipulates that the framework embody the following characteristics:[65]

---

[63] U. S. Department of Energy, Office of Electricity Delivery and Energy Reliability, Recovery Act Financial Assistance Funding Opportunity Announcement, Smart Grid Investment Grant Program, DE-FOA-0000058, June 25, 2009.

[64] "Tracking Clean Energy Progress 2013," International Energy Agency. http://www.iea.org/publications/TCEP_web.pdf (see page 110 and 111)

[65] Quotes in the bulleted list are from the Energy Independence and Security Act of 2007 [Public Law No: 110-140] Title XIII, Sec. 1305.

- That the framework be "flexible, uniform and technology neutral, including but not limited to technologies for managing Smart Grid information"

- That it "be designed to accommodate traditional, centralized generation and transmission resources and consumer distributed resources"

- That it be "designed to be flexible to incorporate regional and organizational differences; and technological innovations"

That it be "designed to consider the use of voluntary uniform standards for certain classes of mass-produced electric appliances and equipment for homes and businesses that enable customers, at their election and consistent with applicable State and Federal laws, and are manufactured with the ability to respond to electric grid emergencies and demand response signals"; and that "such voluntary standards should incorporate appropriate manufacturer lead time."

2.2.   Importance to National Energy Policy Goals

The smart grid is a vital component of the Administration's comprehensive energy plan, which aims to reduce U.S. dependence on foreign oil, to create jobs, and to help U.S. industry compete successfully in global markets for clean energy technology. Throughout the duration of his administration, the president has repeatedly set ambitious long- and short-term goals, necessitating sustained progress in implementing the components, systems, and networks that will make up the smart grid.

In his 2013 "State of the Union" address, the president called once again for infrastructure investment that would include "self-healing power grids," and he set a long-term goal in energy efficiency: to "cut in half the energy wasted by our homes and businesses over the next 20 years."[66] In a major energy policy speech in July 2013, the president also set a shorter-term goal: "Your federal government will consume 20 percent of its electricity from renewable sources within the next seven years."[67]

The smart grid will play an important role in helping the nation achieve these goals. The Pacific Northwest National Laboratory (PNNL) studied nine mechanisms by which the smart grid can reduce energy use and carbon impacts associated with electricity generation and delivery, and has estimated that, by 2030, smart grid-enabled (or facilitated) applications could reduce the nation's carbon-dioxide emissions by 18% annually.[68]

Although national policy to create a smart grid was first stated explicitly in EISA 2007, the policy's implementation received its biggest push two years later, with the enactment of the

---

[66] The White House, Office of the Press Secretary, "Remarks by the President in State of the Union Address." February 12, 2013. See: http://www.whitehouse.gov/the-press-office/2013/02/12/remarks-president-state-union-address

[67] See http://www.whitehouse.gov/the-press-office/2013/06/25/remarks-president-climate-change

[68] The Smart Grid: An Estimation of the Energy and CO2 Benefits, Revision 1 (January 2010) PNNL. See http://energyenvironment.pnnl.gov/news/pdf/PNNL-19112_Revision_1_Final.pdf

American Recovery and Reinvestment Act (ARRA) of 2009. Referred to often as the Recovery Act, this legislation included $11 billion for smart grid technologies, transmission system expansion and upgrades, and other investments to modernize and enhance the electric transmission infrastructure to improve energy efficiency and reliability.[69] The lead role in smart grid was assigned to the Department of Energy (DOE). DOE's Smart Grid Investment Grants (SGIG) and Smart Grid Demonstration Projects (SGDP) have yielded significant results in key areas, such as improving electric distribution system reliability; implementing advanced metering, customer systems, and time-based rates; adding advanced voltage and volt-ampere reactive (VAR) optimization (VVO) technologies; and installing advanced metering infrastructure (AMI).[70] All of the SGIG and SGDP recipients are required to address both interoperability and cybersecurity in their smart grid projects.[71] Figure 2-2 shows the location of the projects funded by Smart Grid Investment Grants (SGIG) program.

Fig. 2-2. The SGIG Program: 99 Projects Involving 228 Electric Utilities and Other Organizations[72] [73]

---

[69] The White House, "American Recovery and Reinvestment Act: Moving America Toward a Clean Energy Future." Feb. 17, 2009. See: http://www.whitehouse.gov/assets/documents/Recovery_Act_Energy_2-17.pdf

[70] See http://energy.gov/oe/downloads/reports-initial-results-smart-grid-investment-grant-projects-december-2012

[71] See http://www.smartgrid.gov/recovery_act/overview/standards_interoperability_and_cyber_security

[72] A breakdown of projects and funding by recipients appears on p. 7 of http://energy.gov/sites/prod/files/Smart%20Grid%20Investment%20Grant%20Program%20-%20Progress%20Report%20July%202012.pdf

[73] Smart Grid Investment Grant Program—Progress Report II, October 2013. See http://www.smartgrid.gov/sites/default/files/doc/files/SGIG_progress_report_2013.pdf

As part of the Recovery Act's overall investment in smart grid, $10 million via DOE was allocated for the interoperability standards effort assigned to NIST, augmented by an additional $2 million from DOE and an additional $5 million from NIST, for a total ARRA-funded investment of $17 million.

Another key policy-related milestone in the smart grid timeline occurred in June 2011, when the White House released a report by the Cabinet-level National Science and Technology Council (NSTC) entitled "A Policy Framework for the 21st Century Grid: Enabling Our Secure Energy Future."[74] This report outlined four overarching goals the Administration would pursue in order to ensure that all Americans benefit from investments in the nation's electric infrastructure:

- Enabling cost-effective smart grid investments
- Unlocking the potential of innovation in the electricity sector
- Empowering consumers and enabling informed decision making
- Securing the grid

The report called for continued federal effort to catalyze the development and adoption of open standards to ensure that the following benefits are realized:

- **Today's investments in the smart grid remain valuable in the future.** Standards can ensure that smart grid investments made today will be compatible with advancing technology. Similarly, standards can ensure that smart grid devices are installed with proper consideration of the necessary security to enable and protect the grid of tomorrow.

- **Innovation is catalyzed.** Shared standards and protocols help reduce investment uncertainty by ensuring that new technologies can be used throughout the grid, lowering transaction costs and increasing compatibility. Standards also encourage entrepreneurs by enabling a significant market for their work.

- **Consumer choice is supported.** In the absence of smart grid interoperability standards, open standards developed in a consensus-based, collaborative, and balanced process can alleviate concerns that companies may attempt to "lock-in" consumers by using proprietary technologies that make their products (and, therefore, their consumers' assets) incompatible with other suppliers' products or services.

- **Costs are reduced.** Standards can reduce market fragmentation and help create economies of scale, providing consumers greater choice and lower costs.

- **Best practices are highlighted as utilities face new and difficult choices.** Standards can provide guidance to utilities as they face novel cybersecurity, interoperability, and privacy concerns.

---

[74] http://www.whitehouse.gov/sites/default/files/microsites/ostp/nstc-smart-grid-june2011.pdf

- **Global markets are opened.** Development of international smart grid interoperability standards can help to open global markets, create export opportunities for U.S. companies, and achieve greater economies of scale and vendor competition that will result in lower costs for utilities and ultimately consumers.

The NSTC has updated its 2011 report with a progress report in February 2013.[75] This report highlights the progress of NIST and the Smart Grid Interoperability Panel in "establishing new interoperability standards to spur private-sector innovation." Reiterating the important role of standards, the report concludes, "Interoperability standards make markets more efficient, help open new international markets to U.S. manufacturers, and reduce the costs of providing reliable, safe power to U.S. households and businesses."

Another important national policy goal for the current administration has been to open up the availability of data to spur innovation, enable consumer choice, and create value. In the energy sector, the success of the Green Button Initiative[76] provides an excellent example of how the work of NIST and the SGIP to coordinate and accelerate interoperable standards is helping to achieve those goals.[77] "Green Button" is the common-sense idea that electricity customers should be able to securely download their own easy-to-understand household energy usage information from their utility or electricity supplier website. As of May 2013, the White House reported that 35 utilities and energy providers had committed to provide 36 million homes and businesses with their own energy usage information in the consensus, industry-standard Green Button format.[78]

2.3. International Smart Grid Standards

The United States is not alone in its initiative to modernize the electric grid. Many other countries—across six continents—have launched significant efforts to encourage the development of the smart grid in their own countries and regions.

As countries move forward with individual initiatives, internationally coordinated and harmonized smart grid efforts will be essential.

International coordination will provide a double benefit:

- As the United States and other nations construct their smart grids, use of international standards ensures the broadest possible market for smart grid suppliers based in the United States. By helping these American companies export their smart grid products, technologies, and services overseas, we will be encouraging innovation and job growth in a high-tech market of growing importance.

---

[75] http://www.whitehouse.gov/sites/default/files/microsites/ostp/2013_nstc_grid.pdf

[76] See http://www.greenbuttondata.org

[77] See http://collaborate.nist.gov/twiki-sggrid/pub/SmartGrid/SGIPMemberNews/SGIPnews_032212.pdf

[78] See http://www.whitehouse.gov/blog/2013/05/02/green-button-enabling-energy-innovation

- The use of international standards results in efficiency for manufacturers and encourages supplier competition. As a result, costs will be lower, and those savings will benefit utilities and consumers.

NIST has devoted considerable resources to and cooperation in bilateral and multilateral engagement with other countries in the development of international standards for the smart grid. The NIST Framework and the Smart Grid Interoperability Panel have received widespread international attention. Examples of recent NIST activities in the international arena include the following:

- In September 2011, NIST and the European Union's Smart Grid Coordination Group (SG-CG) published a white paper outlining the two organizations' plans for collaboration.[79] In December 2011, the SGIP signed a Letter of Intent (LOI) with SG-CG. The cooperative efforts between Americans and Europeans have continued with a number of virtual and face-to-face meetings. The work being undertaken to harmonize architectures has been especially productive. (See Section 2.4 for further details.)

- Under DOE's leadership, NIST and the International Trade Administration (ITA) have helped establish the International Smart Grid Action Network (ISGAN),[80] a multinational collaboration of 24 countries and the European Union. ISGAN complements the Global Smart Grid Federation,[81] a global stakeholder organization which serves as an "association of associations" to bring together leaders from smart grid stakeholder organizations around the world.

- NIST has played a key role in smart grid-related meetings held by the Asia-Pacific Economic Cooperation (APEC). With 21 members—referred to as "member economies"—APEC is the premier Asia-Pacific economic forum, representing approximately 40 percent of the world's population, 54 percent of world GDP, and 44 percent of world trade. APEC's primary goal is to support sustainable economic growth and prosperity in the Asia-Pacific region. The United States, on behalf of the Asia Pacific Economic Cooperation (APEC) Subcommittee on Standards and Conformance, organized a Workshop on Regulatory Approaches to Smart Grid Investment and Deployment, held May 2012 in Quebec City, Canada.

- In July 2011, the SGIP held its first international face-to-face meeting in Montreal, Canada. At that meeting, the SGIP signed an LOI with the Korea Smart Grid Standardization Forum (KSGSF). One outcome from the agreement was a joint workshop held by the two organizations in Irving, Texas in December 2012.

- In 2012, the SGIP also signed LOIs with three other national organizations representing several different countries:
  - The Japan Smart Community Alliance (March 2012)

---

[79] See http://www.nist.gov/smartgrid/grid-091311.cfm

[80] See http://www.iea-isgan.org/

[81] See http://www.globalsmartgridfederation.org/

- o Ecuador's Centro Nacional de Control de Energía (July 2012)

- o Colombia's ICONTEC, the country's national standards organization (December 2012)

- In 2013, the SGIP signed a Memorandum of Understanding with Brazil's Inmetro, the National Institute of Metrology, Quality, and Technology (November 2013).

- On issues related to testing and certification, NIST has held an introductory collaboration meeting including testing with a Korean smart grid delegation, as well as coordination with European Union testing participants within the SG-CG. (See Section 7.5.3 for more details.)

2.4.   International Efforts to Align Smart Grid Architectures

NIST and the SGIP are coordinating with several smart grid stakeholder groups developing different architectures. The coordination with these groups will help align or harmonize evolving architectures existing within the smart grid architectural framework, evaluating how well they support the architectural goals listed in Section 5.2. In the broadest perspective, the architectural framework developed by the Smart Grid Architecture Committee (SGAC) of the SGIP will provide an overarching perspective with respect to other architectural efforts. These architectures will be evaluated against the architecture artifacts, Smart Grid Architecture Model (SGAM), semantic framework, standards and architecture evaluation criteria, and service-oriented principles.

Architecture alignment efforts are under way with (but are not limited to) the following groups:

- The Institute of Electrical and Electronic Engineers (IEEE) P2030 developed a logical-level view of the smart grid organized into three major areas: physical, communications, and information. This logical architecture conforms to the NIST Conceptual Reference Model and provides a set of defined interfaces for the smart grid. A SGAC/P2030 harmonization activity completed in late 2011 provided the IEEE P2030 team with several recommendations that were incorporated into their work.

- The European Commission's Mandate 490 (EU-M490) for Smart Grid with the European Telecommunications Standards Institute (ETSI), European Committee for Standardization (Comité Européen Normalisation - CEN), and the European Committee for Electrotechnical Standardization (CENELEC), completed their first version of the Smart Grid Reference Architecture in November 2012.[82] The document incorporated comments and suggestions from the SGAC. This group is now working on the second release with an aligned architecture approach (SGAM) sharing work developed by both groups. Both groups' goals are to provide the basis for an architectural process leveraging The Open Group Architecture Framework and Service Oriented Ontology. The goal is to provide stakeholders with the tools necessary to quickly identify and define their requirements that include interoperability and application specifications. The work is focused on the requirements of European Union (EU) and NIST/SGIP stakeholders.

---

[82] See http://ec.europa.eu/energy/gas_electricity/smartgrids/doc/xpert_group1_reference_architecture.pdf

ETSI/CEN/CENELEC, NIST, and the SGIP are working on a collaborated architecture.

- The SGAC has also initiated efforts to collaborate on architecture harmonization with:

  - The Chinese Electrical Power Research Institute (CEPRI). (The initial roadmap resembles much of the work done in the EU and the United States, with some very specific changes that support differences in the Chinese market.)

  - The Korea Smart Grid Association (KSGA). (The KSGA has not published an architecture document yet, but pieces of the architecture have been released, including IT, physical field devices, and interfaces.)

  - The EU's SG-CG, the International Electrotechnical Commission (IEC) 62357 (Common Information Model Reference Architecture) and TC8 WG 5 and 6 (Use Cases) teams are working with NIST and the SGAC to define an aligned architectural process consistent with the SGAM including their perspective, recommendations, and artifacts as necessary.

2.5. Smart Grid Key Attributes--Standards and Conformance

The smart grid, unprecedented in its scope and breadth, will demand significant levels of cooperation to fully achieve the ultimate vision described in Section 2.1. Efforts directed toward enabling interoperability among the many diverse components of the evolving smart grid should address the following issues and considerations:

- Standards are critical to enabling interoperable systems and components.
- Mature, robust standards are the foundation of mass markets for the millions of components that will have a role in the future smart grid.
- Standards enable innovation where thousands of companies may construct individual components.

Standards also enable consistency in systems management and maintenance over the life cycles of components. Criteria for smart grid interoperability standards are discussed further in Chapter 4.

Sound interoperability standards will ensure that sizable public and private sector technology investments are not stranded. Such standards enable diverse systems and their components to work together and to securely exchange meaningful, actionable information.

Clearly, there is a need for concerted action and accelerated efforts to speed the development of high-priority standards. But the standards development, prioritization, and harmonization process must be systematic, not ad hoc.

Moreover, while standards are necessary to achieve interoperability, they are not sufficient. A conformance testing and certification framework for smart grid equipment is also essential. The

SGIP has developed an overall framework for conformance testing and certification, and steps have been taken toward implementation. This topic is discussed in greater detail in Chapter 7.

Different Layers of Interoperability

Large, integrated, complex systems require different layers of interoperability, from a plug or wireless connection to compatible processes and procedures for participating in distributed business transactions. In developing the SGAM described in Chapter 5, the high-level categorization approach developed by the GridWise Architecture Council (GWAC) was considered.[83]

Referred to as the "GWAC stack," the eight layers shown in Figure 2-3 comprise a vertical cross-section of the degrees of interoperation necessary to enable various interactions and transactions on the Smart Grid. Very simple functionality, such as the physical equipment layer and software for encoding and transmitting data, is confined to the lowest layers. Communication protocols and applications reside on higher levels, with the top levels reserved for business functionality. As functions and capabilities increase in complexity and sophistication, more layers of the GWAC stack are required to interoperate to achieve the desired results. Each layer typically depends upon—and is enabled by—the layers below it.

---

[83] GridWise Architecture Council, GridWise Interoperability Context-Setting Framework. March 2008.

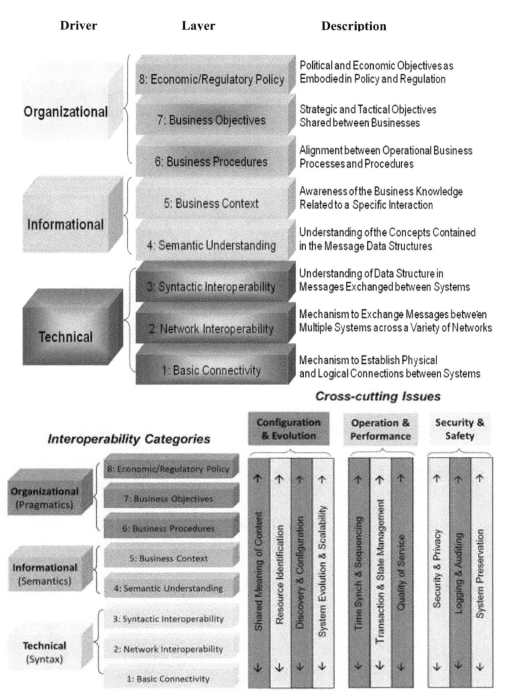

Driver	Layer	Description
Organizational	8: Economic/Regulatory Policy	Political and Economic Objectives as Embodied in Policy and Regulation
	7: Business Objectives	Strategic and Tactical Objectives Shared between Businesses
	6: Business Procedures	Alignment between Operational Business Processes and Procedures
Informational	5: Business Context	Awareness of the Business Knowledge Related to a Specific Interaction
	4: Semantic Understanding	Understanding of the Concepts Contained in the Message Data Structures
Technical	3: Syntactic Interoperability	Understanding of Data Structure in Messages Exchanged between Systems
	2: Network Interoperability	Mechanism to Exchange Messages between Multiple Systems across a Variety of Networks
	1: Basic Connectivity	Mechanism to Establish Physical and Logical Connections between Systems

Fig. 2-3. The GridWise Architecture Council's eight-layer stack provides a context for determining smart grid interoperability requirements and defining exchanges of information.[84]

The most important feature of the GWAC stack is that the layers define well-known interfaces which are loosely-coupled: establishing interoperability at one layer enables flexibility at other

[84] See http://www.gridwiseac.org/about/imm.aspx

38

layers. The most obvious example of this is seen in the Internet: with a common Network Interoperability layer, the Basic Connectivity Layer can vary from Ethernet to WiFi to optical and microwave links, but the different networks can exchange information in the same common way. The GWAC stack is further discussed in the NIST Framework 1.0.[85]

As discussed in Section 2.4, work is being pursued by the SGAC, EU M490, and IEC62357 to align the "GAWC Stack" layers with the SGAM use of The Open Group Architecture Framework (TOGAF).

---

[85] See http://www.nist.gov/public_affairs/releases/upload/smartgrid_interoperability_final.pdf

3.   Smart Grid Interoperability Panel (SGIP)

3.1.   Overview

This chapter summarizes how NIST has worked—and will continue to work—with the smart grid community to coordinate and accelerate the development of standards and protocols that will ensure the interoperability of the smart grid. Section 3.2 reviews the process used during 2008 and 2009, prior to the formal establishment of the Smart Grid Interoperability Panel (SGIP). Section 3.3 reviews the process used during 2010-2012, when SGIP was operating as a public-private partnership under the administration of NIST and the contracted SGIP Administrator. Section 3.4 reviews the process used after January 2013, when SGIP began operating as an industry-led non-profit organization. Section 3.5 discusses the Catalog of Standards, a product of the SGIP.

While the organizational mechanisms and processes that NIST has used to interact with the smart grid community have evolved over the past five years, the underlying purpose and principles guiding this interaction remain the same.

Ideally, NIST's coordination with the smart grid community accelerates the development of interoperable standards and protocols for the smart grid.

The principles that NIST uses to guide its interactions are the following:

1. Openness – NIST-sponsored meetings are open to the public. Documents are posted in a public collaboration environment. Membership is not required to attend meetings or to access the collaborative web site.

2. Balance – NIST seeks input and feedback from across the smart grid community. The SGIP's governance configuration was structured to balance representation across 22 electric industry segments.

3. Consensus – NIST encourages consensus-driven processes. "Consensus" means the general agreement of those involved. For example, chairs of working groups consider all views, proposals, and objections, and endeavor to reconcile them.

4. Harmonization – NIST encourages standards harmonization across multiple Standards-Setting Organizations (SSOs). The SGIP was established to identify and help to coordinate harmonization when overlaps or "identified points of interoperability" require it.

3.2.   Pre-SGIP: 2008 and 2009

This period covers the time between the enactment of "The Energy Independence and Security Act of 2007" (EISA) and the establishment of the Smart Grid Interoperability Panel (SGIP). EISA was signed into law by President George W. Bush on December 19, 2007, and the SGIP was formally launched on November 19, 2009.

Building on initial planning and stakeholder engagement begun in 2008, NIST articulated and began to implement—in early 2009—a three-phase plan to carry out its EISA-assigned responsibilities. The plan was designed to rapidly identify an initial set of standards, while providing a robust process for continued development and implementation of standards as needs and opportunities arise and as technology advances. The three phases were:

- Engage stakeholders in a participatory public process to identify applicable standards and requirements, and gaps in currently available standards, and priorities for additional standardization activities. With the support of outside technical experts working under contract, NIST compiled and incorporated stakeholder inputs from three public workshops into the NIST-coordinated standards-roadmapping effort. Key technical contributions during this time period were provided by a cybersecurity coordination task group and six Domain Expert Working Groups (DEWGs) established by NIST, with the assistance of DOE and GWAC.

- Establish a Smart Grid Interoperability Panel forum to drive longer-term progress. The SGIP was designed to serve as a representative, reliable, and responsive organizational forum which would sustain continued development of interoperability standards.

- Develop and implement a framework for conformity testing and certification. Testing and certification of how standards are implemented in smart grid devices, systems, and processes are essential to ensure interoperability and security under realistic operating conditions. NIST, in consultation with stakeholders, began to develop an overall framework for testing and certification.

NIST was successful in completing the first phase in late 2009, and it laid the foundation for phases two and three.

Release 1.0 of the *NIST Framework and Roadmap for Smart Grid Interoperability Standards*[86] documents the interaction of NIST and the smart grid community during 2008-2009. Section 1.2 of that publication described the steps that NIST undertook to engage diverse stakeholders in the identification of the first set of applicable smart grid standards. It also described the initial priorities for developing new standards that address gaps identified in public workshops and through NIST outreach to stakeholders and formal public reviews of draft versions of the document. The document distilled insights, analyses, and recommendations from members of the general public, proffered during stakeholder-engagement workshops that involved over 1,500 people and four rounds of public review formally announced in *Federal Register* notices. Key deliverables that were developed during the 2008-2009 time period are described in Release 1.0, including the following:

---

[86] The draft of Release 1.0 of the Framework was made available for public review on September 24, 2009 (see http://nist.gov/smartgrid/smartgrid_092409.cfm), and the final version of the document was released on January 19, 2010 (see http://nist.gov/smartgrid/smartgrid_011910.cfm). The full document is available online (see http://www.nist.gov/public_affairs/releases/upload/smartgrid_interoperability_final.pdf).

- A conceptual reference model to facilitate design of an architecture for the smart grid overall and for its networked domains

- An initial set of 75 standards identified as applicable to the smart grid

- Priorities for additional standards—revised or new—to resolve important gaps

- Action plans under which designated standards-setting organizations will address these priorities

- An initial smart grid cybersecurity strategy and associated requirements

3.3. SGIP, the Public-Private Partnership: 2010 - 2012

This period covers the time from the formal establishment of SGIP as a government-funded public-private partnership in November 2009 until SGIP transitioned to an industry-led non-profit organization in December 2012.[87]

A description of how the SGIP was organized, governed, and operated during this period can be found in Chapter 5 ("Smart Grid Interoperability Panel") of Release 2.0 of *NIST Framework and Roadmap for Smart Grid Interoperability Standards*.[88]

The government-funded SGIP, which consisted of organizations spread among 22 categories of smart grid stakeholders, had three primary functions:

- To oversee activities intended to expedite the development of interoperability and cybersecurity specifications by standards-setting organizations (SSOs)

- To provide technical guidance to facilitate the development of standards for a secure, interoperable smart grid

- To specify testing and certification requirements necessary to assess the interoperability of smart grid-related equipment

Overall direction and guidance for the organization was provided by a combination of NIST; EnerNex, which served as the contracted SGIP Administrator; and the Governing Board and its committees.

---

[87] The transition of SGIP from the government-funded to the industry-led organization occurred over a period of several months, with the two organizations operating in parallel for a period in late 2012 and early 2013.

[88] The draft of Release 2.0 of the Framework was made available for public review on October 25, 2011 (see http://nist.gov/smartgrid/grid-102511.cfm), and the final version of the document was released on February 28, 2012. (see http://nist.gov/smartgrid/framework-022812.cfm). The full document is available online (see http://www.nist.gov/customcf/get_pdf.cfm?pub_id=910824).

The SGIP's working groups included the following:

- Priority Action Plans (PAPs) – For more information about the 22 PAPs operating during this time period, see Appendix D.

- Domain Expert Working Groups (DEWGs) – The seven DEWGs operating during this time period were:

  o Building-to-Grid (B2G)

  o Business and Policy (BnP)

  o Distributed Renewables, Generators, and Storage (DRGS)

  o Home-to-Grid (H2G)

  o Industry-to-Grid (I2G)

  o Transmission and Distribution (T&D)

  o Vehicle-to-Grid (V2G)

- Standing Committees and Permanent Working Groups – The four groups operating during this time period were:

  o Cybersecurity Working Group (CSWG)

  o Implementation Methods Committee (IMC)

  o Smart Grid Architecture Committee (SGAC)

  o Smart Grid Testing and Certification Committee (SGTCC)

- Other Working Groups – The two groups operating during this time period were:

  o Electromagnetic Interoperability Issues (EMII)

  o Gas Infrastructure Working Group

The work products and deliverables from these groups were made available to the public (and are currently archived) on the NIST Smart Grid Collaboration Wiki.[89] The Smart Grid Wiki was an open collaboration site for the entire smart grid community to work with NIST on a technical level to develop a framework for smart grid interoperability standards. In addition, the Smart Grid Wiki was a public portal to emerging technical documents written by working groups and committees helping to develop the framework. This site was used by the SGIP during the 2009-2012 period, when SGIP was organized as a public-private partnership. The documents included on this site reflect the work done during that period.

---

[89] http://collaborate.nist.gov/twiki-sggrid/bin/view/SmartGrid/WebHome

As part of its Charter objectives during this time period, the SGIP produced and maintained a Catalog of Standards (CoS). The CoS is a compendium of standards and practices considered to be relevant for the development and deployment of a robust and interoperable smart grid. The CoS provides a key—but not exclusive—source of input to the NIST process for coordinating the development of a framework of protocols and model standards for an interoperable smart grid. The extensive information included for each entry will also be a useful resource for utilities, manufacturers, regulators, consumers, and other smart grid stakeholders. The SGIP assembled this set of documents as a reference to the smart grid community, and it is not anticipated that the standards will be made mandatory. (For more information on the Catalog of Standards, see Section 3.5.)

During this highly productive three-year period, 2010-2012, the SGIP energized the smart grid stakeholder community to complete 11 Priority Action Plans, establish the Catalog of Standards (CoS), and approve 58 standards into the CoS. Two key publications released during this time period were NISTIR 7628: *Guidelines for Smart Grid Cyber Security* (released in August 2010)[90] and the *Interoperability Process Reference Manual* (IPRM) (released in January 2012).[91] Release 2.0 of the NIST Framework included detailed information on the wide range of work products and deliverables in key technical areas such as architecture (Chapter 3), cybersecurity (Chapter 6), and testing and certification (Chapter 7).

By the end of 2012, NIST had substantially completed Phases 2 and 3 of its three-phase plan (see Section 3.2).

In addition to the useful technical work products—such as the NISTIR 7628, the IPRM, and the Catalog of Standards—the SGIP provided one other important product—the stakeholder-engagement process itself. This process has been recognized within the federal government as an effective method by which the government can convene and engage key stakeholders to address important technical issues facing the nation. For example, the Cybersecurity Framework process that NIST is using to carry out Executive Order 13636, "Improving Critical Infrastructure Cybersecurity,"[92] draws heavily on the successful SGIP experience.[93]

Successful methodology implemented during the SGIP stakeholder-engagement process included the use of appropriate governance methods, a large stakeholder base, differing group structures ranging from tiger teams to the Governing Board, the use of technical champions, and the use of several collaborative tools, as described in the following list:

1. <u>Successful Governance Model.</u> The governance model was a key factor in the overall project success. NIST provided guidance and "behind-the-scenes" assistance that resulted

---

[90] See http://www.nist.gov/smartgrid/upload/nistir-7628_total.pdf

[91] See https://collaborate.nist.gov/twiki-sggrid/pub/SmartGrid/SmartGridTestingAndCertificationCommittee/IPRM_final_-_011612.pdf

[92] See http://www.nist.gov/itl/cyberframework.cfm

[93] See http://www.sgip.org/nist-to-play-major-role-in-administrations-executive-order-on-improving-critical-infrastructure-cybersecurity/#sthash.Q1Vv97Gy.dpbs

in tasks being accomplished in a prioritized way using NIST staff and funded contractors. Governance was provided by the Project Management Office (PMO), the Governing Board, and the Plenary Officers. The PMO was established and managed by the SGIP Administrator, and it functioned as a collaboration between NIST and the SGIP leadership, with inputs from the volunteer committee leads. The PMO ensured that priorities were addressed, that common processes were developed and used across the organization, and that regular status reporting occurred. The Governing Board was elected and attracted key leaders in the industry. The Plenary Officers helped to provide the day-to-day operational leadership and gave the volunteer members a voice in the organization.

2. Stakeholder Engagement. The SGIP featured many stakeholder categories, and despite concerns about managing such a large number of stakeholders, the large stakeholder group was effective. The SGIP had 22 stakeholder communities, with each community having one elected representative on the Governing Board. In addition, SGIP members elected three "At Large" Governing Board positions not tied to a particular stakeholder community but which were seen as cross-cutting. The large number of stakeholders gave many people the opportunity to run for the Governing Board and become active participants and proponents of the process.

3. Engaged Active Leadership. Strong and engaged leadership on committees/working groups encouraged volunteer participants to contribute. It was even more important that leadership was open, unbiased, and willing to listen to all views to facilitate consensus solutions. Committee leadership and program administrators who were very active communicators helped to maintain a strong engagement with volunteer participants.

4. Standardized Methodology. The development of standard documentation and processes was a key advantage. PMO guidance and diligence worked well to ensure consistent processes were used. Consistent processes allowed momentum to build throughout the SGIP.

5. The NIST Smart Grid Collaboration Wiki and the Information Knowledge Base (IKB). This Wiki served as the web-based repository for all SGIP-related information and was an important element in the overall success of the SGIP process. A key part of the Wiki was IKB, which served as a comprehensive library and repository for smart grid technical knowledge.

6. Priority Action Plans (PAPs). The PAPs were projects run under a common PMO-directed process that addressed standards gaps or harmonization needs. PAP working groups developed rich standards requirements across multiple stakeholder communities, which were then passed to the applicable SSOs. The PAPs then verified the SSO standards/guidelines output to ensure the requirements were met. Because the SSOs were involved in the PAPs, they made the PAP requirements priorities for their standards development activities within the SSO organizations.

7. Tiger Teams. Tiger Team meetings were an important tool for successfully resolving issues that arose. The Tiger Teams did not bypass the regular process but did allow key stakeholders to produce useful, publicly reviewable results.

8. Collaborative Tool Set. The NIST Smart Grid Collaboration Wiki, webinars, and mail lists supported the dispersed SGIP members by allowing all members quick access to the completed results as well as material under development. The online meeting tools helped participants collaborate during both virtual and Face-to-Face meetings.

9. Technical Champions. "Technical Champions" describe experts funded through a NIST contract to address a specific technical need. Technical champions contributed to the various SGIP committees, working groups, and PAP project efforts. They were instrumental in accelerating the work of the SGIP and were assigned based on priorities and budgeting realities. Technical champions not only advanced the technical work, but also served as group leaders and administrators.

10. Virtual and In-Person Meetings. Conference calls and Face-to-Face (F2F) meetings were both essential formats for exchanging information and reaching consensus. Conference calls succeeded in moving tasks forward between regular F2F meetings. Regularly scheduled meetings and ad-hoc meetings based upon known targets allowed teams to accomplish most tasks. F2F meetings provided a venue for working out agreements on topics not resolved or even addressed during conference calls.

11. Building Membership. During this period, the SGIP grew to be a forum with over 790 organizational members and over 1900 individual members. Because the SGIP was government-sponsored during this time period, there were no membership dues.

3.4. SGIP, the Industry-Led Non-Profit Organization: 2013 - Ongoing

In December 2012, the SGIP transitioned its functions from a government-funded public-private partnership to an industry-led non-profit organization. The organization, organized as a 501(c)(3) non-profit, is legally known as "Smart Grid Interoperability Panel 2.0, Inc."

Almost all elements of the purpose, structure, and processes of the government-funded organization were carried over to the industry-led organization. The PAPs, DEWGs, Standing Committees, Working Groups, and Catalog of Standards were all continued in the new organization. In a few cases, there were name changes (e.g., the Cybersecurity Working Group became the Smart Grid Cybersecurity Committee). The overall guidance of the organization is now provided by the Board of Directors, which assumed many functions of the Governing Board. For further details on SGIP's current structure, governance, and ongoing activities, please consult the organization's website (www.sgip.org).[94]

NIST continues to be an active member of the organization, providing active technical participation and leadership in committees and working groups. SGIP's relationship with NIST is expressed in a Memorandum of Understanding (MOU) signed by both parties in December 2012, in which NIST and the SGIP agree to work on "appropriate strategies for the success of the national goals for a smart grid interoperability standards framework." The MOU describes how the SGIP will cooperate with NIST to continue to evolve the framework, promote the

---

[94] See http://sgip.org

development of interoperability standards, and provide specific leadership roles for NIST in the SGIP.[95]

In December 2012, NIST posted an Announcement of Federal Funding Opportunity for a "Smart Grid Interoperability Standards Cooperative Agreement Program."[96] The announcement described the proposed program as follows:

> The project process, in which NIST will have substantial participation, coordinates all stakeholders of the smart grid to accelerate standards development and harmonization and advance the interoperability and security of smart grid devices and systems. This activity involves developing use cases, identifying gaps and overlaps in smart grid standards, developing requirements that address these gaps, and developing plans to achieve coordination with standards development organizations (SDOs) and standards setting organizations (SSOs) to incorporate these requirements into existing or new standards and guidelines in a timely way. The process involves interaction with the smart grid community using principles of transparency, accountability, inclusiveness and consensus.

> Specifically, the awardee will work cooperatively with NIST to:

> 1. Provide the technical guidance and coordination necessary to facilitate the development of secure and reliable standards for smart grid interoperability, including development of smart grid architectural principles and conceptual framework;

> 2. Identify and specify the necessary testing and certification requirements, including providing the underlying rationale and implementation guidance where appropriate, to assess the achievement of interoperability using smart grid standards;

> 3. Oversee the performance of these activities to achieve significant output and outcomes useful to the smart grid community, in order to maintain momentum and achievement;

> 4. Proactively inform and educate smart grid industry stakeholders on the definition of, and the benefits attributable to, interoperability; and

> 5. Conduct outreach to similar organizations in other countries to help establish global interoperability alignment.

Upon completion of a competitive solicitation and review process, SGIP ("Smart Grid Interoperability Panel 2.0, Inc.") was awarded the cooperative agreement in April 2013. The agreement, with a budget and performance period through the end of 2015, provides SGIP with up to $ 2.75 million, based on continued progress and subject to the availability of funds.

---

[95] http://members.sgip.org/apps/group_public/download.php/1162/Signed%20NIST%20-%20SGIP%20MOU.pdf

[96] http://www.nist.gov/smartgrid/upload/NIST-20121129-Smart-Grid-FFO.pdf

Throughout 2013, NIST and SGIP have worked together as outlined in the cooperative agreement. The substance of that ongoing work is described in the following chapters of this third release of the framework document (Release 3.0), which deal with the key technical areas involved with smart grid interoperability, including the following:

- Architecture (Chapter 5)

- Cybersecurity (Chapter 6)

- Testing and Certification (Chapter 7)

3.5. SGIP Catalog of Standards

As part of its Charter objectives, the SGIP produces and maintains a Catalog of Standards (CoS). More details on the CoS and on the standards currently listed in the CoS are available from the SGIP website.[97]

The CoS is a compendium of standards and practices considered to be relevant for the development and deployment of a robust and interoperable smart grid. The CoS provides a key—but not exclusive—source of input to the NIST process for coordinating the development of a framework of protocols and model standards for an interoperable smart grid. The extensive information included for each entry will also be a useful resource for utilities, manufacturers, regulators, consumers, and other smart grid stakeholders. The SGIP is assembling this set of documents as a reference to the smart grid community, and does not anticipate that the standards will be made mandatory.

The CoS review process evaluates smart grid interoperability standards against set criteria as determined by review teams from the architecture, cybersecurity, testing and certification working groups, and the Program Management Office. Individual SGIP members vote on whether to include the standard(s) in the CoS, with an affirmative vote from 75% of the voting pool needed for inclusion.

The CoS[98] was not designed to select favorites or to eliminate competition within the standards arena. Therefore, it could contain multiple standards or guidelines that accomplish similar interoperability goals and that have equivalent functionality. Some CoS standards entries contain optional elements that are not required for all implementations. The CoS makes no guarantees, and it does not warrant that compliance with the CoS standards will achieve interoperability. Rather, voting for inclusion in the CoS is based on five criteria:

1. Relevancy: The standard facilitates interoperability related to the integration of smart grid devices or systems. As defined by EISA, relevant smart grid capabilities are:

---

[97] http://www.sgip.org/catalog-of-standards/#sthash.grBvHQ9d.dpbs

[98] http://www.sgip.org/catalog-of-standards/#sthash.6eKlWM4k.dpbs

- o Improved reliability, security and efficiency of the smart grid;
- o Dynamic optimization of grid operations and resources, with full cybersecurity;
- o Deployment and integration of distributed resources and generation, including renewable resources;
- o Development and incorporation of demand response, demand-side resources, and energy-efficiency resources;
- o Deployment of "smart" technologies[99];
- o Integration of "smart" appliances and consumer devices
- o Deployment and integration of advanced electricity storage and peak-shaving technologies[100];
- o Provision to consumers of timely information and control;
- o Development of standards for communication and interoperability of appliances and equipment[101]; and
- o Lowering of unreasonable or unnecessary barriers to adoption of smart grid technologies, practices, and services.

2. Community Acceptance: The standard should be widely acknowledged as facilitating interoperability related to the integration of devices or systems that enable smart grid capabilities.

3. Deployment Suitability: The standard must demonstrate evidence of either having already been deployed or it must be expected to fulfill a smart grid deployment gap with demonstrated adequate performance capabilities in commercial (real-world) applications.

4. Interface Characterization: The relevant portions of the standard focus on requirements for integration and interaction through well-defined interfaces. The standard facilitates independence and flexibility in device or system design and implementation choices.

5. Document Maintenance: The standard is supported by a multi-member organization that will ensure that it can be unambiguously referenced, that it is regularly revised and improved to meet changing requirements, and that there is a strategy for ensuring its continued relevance.

Compliance with a standard does not guarantee interoperability. Though standards facilitate interoperability, they rarely, if ever, cover all levels of agreement and configuration required in practice. As a part of its work program, the SGIP has defined a testing and certification framework for test programs that may be applied to the equipment, devices, and systems built to

---

[99] Real-time, automated, interactive technologies that optimize the physical operation of appliances and consumer devices for metering, communications concerning grid operations and status, and distribution automation.

[100] Including plug-in electric and hybrid electric vehicles, and thermal-storage air conditioning.

[101] Connected to the electric grid, including the infrastructure serving the grid

the standards listed in the CoS. If these test programs are applied, they will substantiate that implementations designed to the respective standards not only have compliance with the standards, but are also interoperable with one another. The CoS entry will indicate when test profiles have been defined and testing organizations identified for a particular standard.

The SGIP PMO is responsible for the process of standards inclusion in the Catalog of Standards. During the original SGIP tenure (2009-2012), 58 Smart Grid standards underwent full independent reviews by SGIP experts in the areas of cybersecurity and architecture. Additionally, the standards underwent a Governing Board review and the SGIP plenary voting processes before being approved for inclusion within the CoS.

The CoS contains both standards and guidelines from smart grid areas including smart metering, substation automation, electric vehicle grid integration, internet and wireless protocol usage, precision time synchronization, synchrophasors, customer energy usage (e.g., Green Button), cybersecurity, calendaring/scheduling models, and pricing models.

Because of the large number of standards that might be considered for the CoS, it was necessary to streamline the review process by establishing a CoS review queue. As of September 2013, there are 82 standards and guidelines being actively tracked in the CoS review queue. These standards and guidelines are being reviewed by the SGIP team experts and will be voted on for inclusion in the CoS once the review process is completed. This process has been transferred to the industry-led SGIP essentially unchanged.

4. Standards Identified for Implementation

4.1. Guiding Principles and Process Used for Identifying Interoperability Standards

The Energy Independence and Security Act of 2007 (EISA) assigned the National Institute of Standards and Technology (NIST) the responsibility to coordinate the development of an interoperability framework including model standards and protocols.

Two lists of standards were presented in the original Framework Release 1.0 in January 2010:

> 1) Table 4-1 in Section 4.3, was a list of smart grid standards and specifications identified as important for the smart grid. Requirements documents and guidelines were also included in this table; and

> 2) Table 4-2 in Section 4.4, contained documents that have, or are likely to have, applicability to the smart grid, subject to further review and consensus development being carried out through plans identified in this roadmap.

Both of these tables were based on the outcomes of several workshops, individual stakeholder inputs, Domain Expert Working Group (DEWG) discussions and work products, and public comments solicited on both the standards and the first release of the framework document.

With the advent of the SGIP, changes were made in the list of identified standards as Priority Action Plan (PAP) tasks reached completion, and as cybersecurity, architecture, and other reviews were performed by SGIP committees. Standards were voted upon by the SGIP Plenary for inclusion in the Catalog of Standards (CoS). New smart grid standards were also identified for review through activities of the SGIP working groups. Tables 4-1 and 4-2 were updated in Framework Release 2.0, published in February 2012.

Release 3.0 of the NIST Framework includes additional standards in Table 4-1 that have also been added to the CoS through the SGIP process. NIST relies strongly upon the SGIP's CoS process, and its PAP, Working Group, and Committee activities to help fulfill the EISA mission and to continue to evolve the NIST Framework. These groups identify standards gaps, develop plans in coordination with SSOs to address standards issues, work with the SSOs to execute those plans, and perform standards reviews. Finally, the standards under consideration undergo the SGIP voting process for final consensus approval for the CoS. Once a standard has entered the SGIP CoS, a review by NIST and an opportunity for public comment will precede its addition to the list of identified standards in the NIST Framework.

The NIST list may differ from the SGIP CoS due to additional inputs used for the NIST Framework. There will also be additional gaps and standards that NIST identifies due to staff expertise and knowledge of the Smart Grid community and stakeholders.

The list of standards for further review, Table 4-2, which appeared in previous releases of the NIST Framework, has been removed from this chapter in Release 3.0. The SGIP has stated that it will continue to consider new candidate standards for possible inclusion in the CoS. This change was made because this second list will change more rapidly than Table 4-1, and it will therefore be more difficult to keep this second list up-to-date between releases of the Framework.

The lists of standards in this release of the NIST Framework document include a number of updates to those presented in Release 2.0. The changes are as follows:

- For Release 3.0, standards added to the list of NIST-identified standards, Table 4-1, have been reviewed and voted on according to the SGIP Catalog of Standards (CoS) process, recommended by the SGIP Governing Board (SGIP GB), and approved by the SGIP plenary. This process will continue as it is intended that all of the standards identified in Table 4-1 in Release 1.0 and Release 2.0 will be reviewed by the SGIP for the CoS. The CoS is further discussed in Section 3.5.

- Several standards that did not exist at the time Release 2.0 were completed in February 2012 have been added to the table. In some cases, the standards added to Table 4-1, which have been reviewed and approved for the CoS according to the SGIP process, are closely related to standards already included on the list.

Desirable and nonexclusive guiding principles used in the selection of standards for the framework are given in the inset frames in this section, entitled "Guiding Principles for Identifying Standards for Implementation" (at the end of section 4.1). NIST has used the criteria listed in these inset frames to evaluate standards, specifications, requirements, and guidelines for inclusion in all versions of the *NIST Framework and Roadmap for Smart Grid Interoperability Standards*. This set of criteria is extensive, and the complete list does not apply to each standard, specification, or guideline listed in Table 4-1. Judgments as to whether each item merits inclusion is made on the basis of combinations of relevant criteria.

The items included in Table 4-1 are, in most cases, voluntary consensus standards developed and maintained by American National Standards Institute (ANSI)-accredited and other standards development organizations (SDOs). The phrases "standards- or specification-setting organizations (SSOs)" and "SDOs" are used loosely and interchangeably within the standards-related literature. However, for the purpose of this document, NIST is using the term "SSOs" to define the broader universe of organizations and groups—formal or informal—that develop standards, specifications, user requirements, guidelines, etc. The term "SDOs" is used to define standards development organizations that develop standards in processes marked by openness, balance, and transparency, and characterized by due process to address negative comments. NIST uses the two terms, SSOs and SDOs, to address the wide variations in types of organizations that are developing standards, specifications, user guidelines, and other input, which are then being identified and considered for use in the Smart Grid Framework.

Also, in this document, NIST uses the definition of voluntary consensus standards from Office of Management and Budget (OMB) Circular A-119, *Federal Participation in the Development and Use of Voluntary Consensus Standards and in Conformity Assessment Activities,*[102] where such

---

[102] OMB Circular A-119, *Federal Participation in the Development and Use of Voluntary Consensus Standards and in Conformity Assessment Activities,* February 10, 1998, see http://standards.gov/a119.cfm

standards are defined as developed and adopted by voluntary consensus standards bodies. For these voluntary consensus standards, OMB Circular A-119 outlines provisions that require that the relevant intellectual property owners have agreed to make that intellectual property available on a non-discriminatory, royalty-free, or reasonable-royalty basis to all interested parties. As defined in the OMB document, voluntary consensus standards bodies are "domestic or international organizations which plan, develop, establish, or coordinate voluntary consensus standards using agreed-upon procedures,"[103] and have the following attributes: 1) openness, 2) balance of interest, 3) due process, 4) a process for appeals, and 5) consensus.

Consensus is defined as general agreement, but not necessarily unanimity. Consensus includes a process for attempting to resolve objections by interested parties. The process includes the following attributes:

- All comments are considered fairly.

- Each objector is advised of the disposition of his or her objection(s) and the reasons why.

- The consensus body members are given an opportunity to change their votes after reviewing the comments.

As a general rule, it is NIST's position that smart grid interoperability standards should be developed in processes that are open, transparent, balanced, and have due process, consistent with the decision of the World Trade Organization's Technical Barriers to Trade Committee Principles for the Development of International Standards.[104] That is, standards should be "developed and maintained through a collaborative, consensus-driven process that is open to participation by all relevant and materially affected parties and not dominated or under the control of a single organization or group of organizations, and readily and reasonably available to all for smart grid applications."[105] In addition, smart grid interoperability standards should be developed and implemented internationally, wherever practical.

Because of the massive investment and accelerated timeline for deployment of smart grid devices and systems, along with the consequent accelerated timetable for standards development and harmonization, NIST did not originally limit the lists of both identified and candidate standards to SDO-developed voluntary consensus standards. Rather, Table 4-1 also includes specifications, requirements, and guidelines developed by other SSOs. This was done to ensure that the interoperability framework would reflect the current state and anticipate the future of the smart grid. The SSO documents were developed by user groups, industry alliances, consortia, and other organizations. However, it is envisioned that ultimately these specifications and other

---

[103] Ibid.

[104] Annex 4, *Second Triennial Review of the Operation and Implementation of the Agreement on Technical Barriers to Trade, WTO G/TBT/9, November 13, 2000.*

[105] *ANSI Essential Requirements: Due process requirements for American National Standards*, Edition: January, 2009, see http://www.ansi.org/essentialrequirements/

documents will be used for development of standards by SDOs, and in several cases this has occurred.

In making the selections of SSO documents listed in this section, NIST attempted to ensure that documents were consistent with the guiding principles, including that they be open and accessible. This does not mean that all of the standards and specifications are available for free, or that access can be gained to them without joining an organization (including those organizations requiring a fee). It does mean that they will be made available under fair, reasonable, and nondiscriminatory terms and conditions, which may include monetary compensation. To facilitate the development of the smart grid and the interoperability framework, NIST has worked with SSOs to find ways to make the interoperability documents more accessible so that cost and other factors that may be a barrier to some stakeholders are made less burdensome. NIST, the SGIP, and ANSI have coordinated to make documentary standards available to SGIP working groups and other stakeholders for a limited time to support working group and PAP reviews and completion of the artifacts required for the CoS.

Guiding Principles for Identifying Standards for Implementation

For *the NIST Framework and Roadmap for Smart Grid Interoperability Standards, List of Identified Standards, Table 4-1,* a standard, specification, or guideline is evaluated on whether it:

- Is well-established and widely acknowledged as important to the smart grid.
- Is an open, stable, and mature industry-level standard developed in a consensus process from a standards development organization (SDO).
- Enables the transition of the legacy power grid to the smart grid.
- Has, or is expected to have, significant implementations, adoption, and use.
- Is supported by an SDO or standards- or specification-setting organization (SSO) such as a users group to ensure that it is regularly revised and improved to meet changing requirements and that there is a strategy for continued relevance.
- Is developed and adopted internationally, wherever practical.
- Is integrated and harmonized, or there is a plan to integrate and harmonize it with complementing standards across the utility enterprise through the use of an industry architecture that documents key points of interoperability and interfaces.
- Enables one or more of the framework characteristics as defined by EISA[*] or enables one or more of the six chief characteristics of the envisioned smart grid.[†]
- Addresses, or is likely to address, anticipated smart grid applications.
- Is applicable to one of the priority areas identified by FERC[‡] and NIST:
  - Demand Response and Consumer Energy Efficiency;
  - Wide Area Situational Awareness;
  - Integration of Distributed Renewable Generation and Storage;
  - Electric Transportation;
  - Advanced Metering Infrastructure;
  - Distribution Grid Management;
  - Cybersecurity; and
  - Network Communications.

[*]Energy Independence and Security Act of 2007 [Public Law No: 110-140] Title XIII, Sec. 1305.
[†] U.S. Department of Energy, Smart Grid System Report, July 2009.
[‡] Federal Energy Regulatory Commission, *Smart Grid Policy*, 128 FERC ¶ 61,060 [Docket No. PL09-4-000] July 16, 2009. See http://www.ferc.gov/whats-new/comm-meet/2009/071609/E-3.pdf

---

Guiding Principles for Identifying Standards for Implementation (cont'd)

- Focuses on the semantic understanding layer of the GWAC stack,[*] which has been identified as most critical to smart grid interoperability.
- Is openly available under fair, reasonable, and non-discriminatory terms.
- Has associated conformance tests or a strategy for achieving them.
- Accommodates legacy implementations.
- Allows for additional functionality and innovation through:
    - *Symmetry* – facilitates bidirectional flows of energy and information.
    - *Transparency* – supports a transparent and auditable chain of transactions.
    - *Composition* – facilitates building of complex interfaces from simpler ones.
    - *Extensibility* – enables adding new functions or modifying existing ones.
    - *Loose coupling* – helps to create a flexible platform that can support valid bilateral and multilateral transactions without elaborate prearrangement.[**]
    - *Layered systems* – separates functions, with each layer providing services to the layer above and receiving services from the layer below.
    - *Shallow integration* – does not require detailed mutual information to interact with other managed or configured components.

[*] GridWise Architecture Council, GridWise Interoperability Context-Setting Framework, March 2008.
[**] While loose coupling is desirable for general applications, tight coupling often will be required for critical infrastructure controls.

4.2. Overview of the Standards Identification Process

The process used to establish the list presented in Table 4-1 is described below.

During the first phase of the NIST three-phase plan for smart grid interoperability, NIST's approach to accelerate the development of standards was to 1) identify existing standards that could be immediately applied to meet smart grid needs, or were expected to be available in the near future, and 2) identify gaps and establish priorities and action plans to develop additional needed standards to fill these gaps.

After the publication of the NIST Framework, Release 1.0, and the establishment of the SGIP, NIST transitioned the standard identification process so that it now works through various SGIP venues and activities. These venues include the many SGIP committees, SGIP working groups, PAPs, and SGIP face-to-face meetings in conjunction with many industry conferences relevant to the smart grid, such as IEEE and IEC conferences and committee meetings. A summary description of the SGIP, the SGIP's Board of Directors, various committees, working groups, and PAPs can be found in Chapter 3 and Appendix D, and detailed information about them and their activities is given on the SGIP website.[106]

Priority Action Plans (PAPs) are established by the SGIP when there is a need for interoperability coordination on resolving urgent standards issues. The PAPs are executed within the scope of the SSOs that assume responsibility for the tasks that implement the plans. The role of the SGIP is to facilitate this process, to ensure that all PAP materials are available to SGIP members, and to provide guidance as needed when significant differences among the participants in the PAP occur, or there is uncertainty about the PAP goals. Once the issues are resolved, the standard resulting from the PAP and actions of the participating SSOs continues through the SGIP review and approval process and ultimately is listed in the SGIP CoS. The CoS is discussed in greater detail in Section 3.5, where the purpose and scope, as well as the process and procedures for its management are described. As mentioned earlier, the SGIP CoS is anticipated to be a key but not an exclusive source of input to the NIST process for coordinating the development of a framework of protocols and model standards for the smart grid under its EISA responsibilities.

The CoS is a compendium of standards and practices considered to be relevant for the development and deployment of a robust and interoperable smart grid. The CoS may contain multiple entries that may accomplish the same goals and are functionally equivalent; similarly, a single CoS entry may contain optional elements that need not be included in all implementations. In general, compliance with a standard does not guarantee interoperability because although standards facilitate interoperability, they rarely, if ever, cover all levels of agreement and configuration required in practice. As a part of its work program, the SGIP has defined a testing and certification framework for test programs that may be applied to the equipment, devices, and systems built to meet the requirements and specifications of the standards listed in the CoS. If these programs are applied, they will substantiate that implementations designed to the respective standards not only have compliance with the standards, but are also interoperable with one another.

The SGIP uses the process for adding standards to the CoS described in Section 3.5. This process includes review by the Standards Subgroup of the SGCC to determine if the standards have adequately addressed cybersecurity requirements, which are defined in the NIST Interagency Report (NISTIR) 7628, *Guidelines for Smart Grid Cyber Security.*[107] The SGIP Smart Grid Architecture Committee (SGAC), Smart Grid Testing and Certification Committee (SGTCC), and Smart Grid Implementation and Methods Committee (SGIMC) also perform reviews of the standard with respect to their requirements, and the Board of Directors votes to recommend the standard to the SGIP membership, which then votes on whether to approve the standard for the CoS.

Cybersecurity and architecture—and going forward, Testing and Certification reviews—will be applied to other standards identified in the table below, as well as those identified in future NIST

---

[106] http://sgip.org/

[107] http://csrc.nist.gov/publications/PubsNISTIRs.html#NIST-IR-7628

and SGIP activities.[108] The SGCC, SGAC, and TCC have assigned liaisons to other SGIP working groups, PAPs, DEWGs, as well as to SDOs and SSOs to participate in and support the review of the standards when needed.

4.3. Current List of Standards Identified by NIST

Table 4-1 contains the standards identified by NIST at the conclusion of the process described in Release 1.0,[109] which was a transparent and highly participatory public process, as well as those that were added following the establishment of the SGIP CoS and its subsequent expansion. These standards support interoperability of smart grid devices and systems. Table 4-1 groups the documents into families, such as the Internet Engineering Task Force (IETF) standards, and further identifies the families as standards and specifications, requirements, and guidelines. For Framework Release 3.0, these families of and individual standards are grouped according to the principal domain that they apply to. Cross-cutting standards, such as cybersecurity standards, are listed together as a group in the table. The table includes the names of the responsible standards bodies with links to the standard. Because all the standards in Table 4-1 were reviewed prior to when SGIP 2.0, Inc., became fully operational in April 2013, links are provided to the SGCC assessment, the SGIP Catalog of Standards information forms, and other artifacts on the NIST-maintained collaboration website[110]. A column is also provided to indicate whether a standard in Table 4-1 has been included in the SGIP CoS as of the time of this report's publication date.

All of the standards listed in Table 4-1 are subject to review—or have already been reviewed—by the SGIP SGCC Standards subgroup and the SGIP Smart Grid Architecture Committee (SGAC). Future standards reviewed by SGIP for the CoS will also be subject to review by the SGIP SGTCC) SGIMC.

Table 4-1 now identifies 71 smart grid-relevant standards. Many of the standards in Table 4-1 are undergoing development and require modifications, some of which are being addressed through the SGIP PAPs. The SGIP SGAC and SGCC, whose ongoing efforts are described in more detail in Chapters 5 and 6, respectively, are also addressing some of these needed modifications. As discussed further in Chapter 7, experience gained with devices designed to meet the requirements of the standards from interoperability testing and certification activities managed by Interoperability Testing and Certification Authorities (ITCAs) will also influence the changes to these standards.

---

[108] Results of these reviews will be available to SGIP members on the SGIP website: see http://sgip.org/

[109] See http://www.nist.gov/public_affairs/releases/upload/smartgrid_interoperability_final.pdf, p. 48

[110] See http://collaborate.nist.gov/twiki-sggrid/bin/view/SmartGrid/WebHome

Table 4-1. Identified Standards

#	Standard	Application	Comments	Included in SGIP Catalog of Standards?[111]	SG Conceptual Architecture Domains
	Standards and Specifications				
	ANSI C12 Suite :		Open, mostly mature standards developed and maintained by an SDO.		
1	ANSI C12.1 http://webstore.ansi.org/RecordDetail.aspx?sku=ANSI+C12.1-2008 CSWG Report : http://collaborate.nist.gov/twiki-sggrid/pub/SmartGrid/SGIPCosSIFANSIC1212008/CSWG_Standards_ANSI_C12.1_Review.pdf CoS : http://collaborate.nist.gov/twiki-sggrid/bin/view/SmartGrid/SGIPCosSIFANSIC1212008	Establishes acceptable performance criteria for new types of ac watt hour meters, demand meters, demand registers, pulse devices and auxiliary devices. Describes acceptable in-service performance levels for meters and devices used in revenue metering.	C12.1, 2008 is currently being revised. The revision will eventually include updates and corrections to the electromagnetic interference and compatibility test methods in section 4.7.3 as recommended by the SGIP EMII WG.	'	Customer, Service Providers
2	ANSI C12.18-2006: http://webstore.ansi.org/FindStandards.aspx?SearchString=c12.18&SearchOption=0&PageNum=0	Revenue metering End Device Tables.		Y	Customer, Service Providers

---

[111] **As of the draft publication date of this release of the NIST Framework, January, 2014**

#	Standard	Application	Comments	Included in SGIP Catalog of Standards?[111]	SG Conceptual Architecture Domains
	&SearchTermsArray=null|c12.18|null CSWG Report: http://collaborate.nist.gov/twiki-sggrid/pub/SmartGrid/CSCTGStandards/CSWG_Standards_ANSI_C12.18_Review_final.docx CoS : http://collaborate.nist.gov/twiki-sggrid/bin/view/SmartGrid/SGIPCosSIFANSIC12182006				
3	ANSI C12.19-2008 http://webstore.ansi.org/RecordDetail.aspx?sku=ANSI+C12.19-2008 CSWG Report http://collaborate.nist.gov/twiki-sggrid/pub/SmartGrid/CSCTGStandards/CSWG_Standards_ANSI_C12.19_Review_final.docx CoS :	Electricity Meters - 0.2 and 0.5 Accuracy Classes	It is recognized that ANSI C12.19 version 2, and correspondingly IEEE 1377 version 2, are extremely flexible metering data and information models that provide a wide range of functions and capabilities for delivery of actionable information, such as energy usage in kilowatt hours from a meter, load profiles and control information, such as load control, programming and firmware management. These capabilities call complex programming to secure the control and	Y	Customer, Service Providers

#	Standard	Application	Comments	Included in SGIP Catalog of Standards?[111]	SG Conceptual Architecture Domains
	http://collaborate.nist.gov/twiki-sggrid/bin/view/SmartGrid/SGIP CosSIFANSIC12192008		the information. ANSI C12.19 version 2 implements a comprehensive information class model by which the table and proc0dures classes and their class attributes are modeled using an extensible XML-based Table Definition Language (TDL). The instances of the data model (TDL classes) can be described in terms of the XML-based Exchange Data Language (EDL) that can be used to constrain oft-utilized information into a well-known form. The model and element instance information can be used by head end systems that implement ANSI C12.19 interoperable to communicate and manage any end device produced by any vendor company. PAP05 has been set up to establish consistent sets of commonly used data tables, procedures and services for meter information communication that will greatly reduce the time for utilities		

#	Standard	Application	Comments	Included in SGIP Catalog of Standards?[111]	SG Conceptual Architecture Domains
			and others requiring to implement smart grid functions, such as demand response and real-time usage information (PAP05: Standard Meter Data Profiles). The task was undertaken by the Association of Edison Illuminating Companies (AEIC). AEIC completed a new interoperability standard on November 19, 2010, "Smart Grid/AEIC AMI Interoperability Standard Guidelines for ANSI C12.19 / IEEE 1377 / MC12.19 End Device Communications and Supporting Enterprise Devices, Networks and Related Accessories, Version 2.0." The interoperability standard is also included in this table.		
4	ANSI C12.20 http://webstore.ansi.org/FindStandards.aspx?SearchString=c12.20&SearchOption=0&PageNum=0&SearchTermsArray=null|c12.20|null CSWG:	Transport of measurement device data over telephone networks.	Establishes the physical aspects and acceptable performance criteria for 0.2 and 0.5 accuracy class electricity meters meeting Blondel's Theorem.	Y	Customer, Service Providers

62

#	Standard	Application	Comments	Included in SGIP Catalog of Standards?[111]	SG Conceptual Architecture Domains
	http://collaborate.nist.gov/twiki-sggrid/bin/view/SmartGrid/SGIPCosSIFANSIC12202010 CoS : http://collaborate.nist.gov/twiki-sggrid/bin/view/SmartGrid/SGIPCosSIFANSIC12202010				
5	ANSI C12.21/IEEE P1702/MC1221 http://webstore.ansi.org/FindStandards.aspx?SearchString=c12.21&SearchOption=0&PageNum=0&SearchTermsArray=null|c12.21|null CSWG Report http://collaborate.nist.gov/twiki-sggrid/pub/SmartGrid/CSCTGStandards_ANS1_C12.21_Review_final.docx CoS : http://collaborate.nist.gov/twiki-sggrid/bin/view/SmartGrid/SGIPCosSIFANSIC12212006	Protocol and optical interface for measurement devices.	Details the criteria required for communications between a C12.21 device and a C12.21 client via a modem connected to the switched telephone network. The C12.21 client could be a laptop or portable computer, a master station system or another electronic communications device.	Y	Customer, Service Providers
6	ANSI/American Society of Heating, Refrigeration, and Air	BACnet defines an information model and	Open, mature standard with conformance testing developed and	Y	Customer

#	Standard	Application	Comments	Included in SGIP Catalog of Standards?[111]	SG Conceptual Architecture Domains
	Conditioning Engineers (ASHRAE) 135-2012/ISO 16484-5 BACnet http://www.techstreet.com/products/1852610 A Data Communication Protocol for Building Automation and Control Networks CoS: http://collaborate.nist.gov/twiki-sggrid/bin/view/SmartGrid/SGIPCosSIFASHRAE1352010	messages for building system communications at a customer's site. BACnet incorporates a range of networking technologies, using IP protocols, to provide scalability from very small systems to multi-building operations that span wide geographic areas.	maintained by an SDO. BACnet is adopted internationally as EN ISO 16484-5 and used in more than 80 countries. BACnet serves as a customer domain communication protocol and is relevant to the Price, DR/DER, Energy Usage, and Facility Smart Grid Information Model PAPs (PAP03: Develop Common Specification for Price and Product Definition - http://collaborate.nist.gov/twiki-sggrid/bin/view/SmartGrid/PAP03PriceProduct, PAP09: Standard DR and DER Signals - http://collaborate.nist.gov/twiki-sggrid/bin/view/SmartGrid/PAP09DRDER, PAP10: Standard Energy Usage Information - http://collaborate.nist.gov/twiki-sggrid/bin/view/SmartGrid/PAP10EnergyUsagetoEMS, and PAP17 Facility Smart Grid Information Standard - http://collaborate.nist.gov/twiki-		

#	Standard	Application	Comments	Included in SGIP Catalog of Standards?[111]	SG Conceptual Architecture Domains
			sgrid/bin/view/SmartGrid/PAP17Fac ilitySmartGridInformationStandard). Widely used in commercial, industrial and institutional buildings.		
7	ANSI/CEA 709 and Consumer Electronics Association (CEA) 852.1 LON Protocol Suite: http://www.lonmark.org/technica l_resources/standards http://www.ce.org/Standards/Sta ndard-Listings/R7-Home-Network-Committee	This is a general purpose local area networking protocol in use for various applications including electric meters, street lighting, home automation, and building automation.	Widely used, mature standards, supported by the LonMark International users group. These standards are also adopted internationally as ISO/IEC 14908, Parts 1, 2, 3, and 4. These standards serve on the customer side of the facility interface and are relevant to the Price, Demand Response (DR)/Distributed Energy Resource (DER), and Energy Usage PAPs (PAP03: Develop Common Specification for Price and Product Definition - http://collaborate.nist.gov/twiki-sgrid/bin/view/SmartGrid/PAP03Pric eProduct, PAP09: Standard DR and DER Signals - http://collaborate.nist.gov/twiki-sgrid/bin/view/SmartGrid/PAP09DR DER, and PAP10: Standard Energy	N	Customer, Service Providers

#	Standard	Application	Comments	Included in SGIP Catalog of Standards?[111]	SG Conceptual Architecture Domains
			Usage Information - http://collaborate.nist.gov/twiki-sggrid/bin/view/SmartGrid/PAP10EnergyUsagetoEMS)		
8	IEC 60870-6 -503 Telecontrol Application Service Element 2 (TASE.2) http://webstore.iec.ch/webstore/webstore.nsf/artnum/034806 CSWG Report http://collaborate.nist.gov/twiki-sggrid/pub/SmartGrid/CSCTGStandards/StandardsReviewPhase-1Report.pdf Narrative http://collaborate.nist.gov/twiki-sggrid/pub/SmartGrid/NISTStandardsSummaries/IEC_60870_Narrative_10-6-2010.doc CoS: http://collaborate.nist.gov/twiki-sggrid/bin/view/SmartGrid/SGIPCosSIFIEC608706503	This standard defines the messages sent between control centers of different utilities.	Open, mature standard developed and maintained by an SDO. It is widely implemented with compliance testing. This is part of the IEC 60870 Suite of standards. It is used in almost every utility for inter-control center communications between SCADA and/or Energy Management System (EMS) systems. It is supported by most vendors of SCADA and EMS systems.	Y	Transmission, Distribution

#	Standard	Application	Comments	Included in SGIP Catalog of Standards?[111]	SG Conceptual Architecture Domains
9	IEC 60870-6-702 Telecontrol Equipment and SystmsSystems - Part 6: Telecontrol protocols compatible with ISO standards and ITU-T recommendations - Section 702: Functional profile for providing the TASE.2 application service in end systems CoS: http://collaborate.nist.gov/twiki-sggrid/bin/view/SmartGrid/SGIP CosSIFIEC608706702	This section of the standard, IEC 60870-6-702, defines a standard profile, or set of options for implementing the application, presentation, and session layers. This is known as an A-profile. For a complete protocol implementation of TASE.2, this A-profile must interface to a connection-oriented transport profile, or T-profile that specifies the transport, network and possibly data link layers. A T-profile that is commonly used with this standard includes RFC1006, TCP, IP, and Ethernet. This section of the standard defines the Protocol Implementation Conformance Statements (PICS) for TASE.2, including tables specifying which services and objects are mandatory and		Y	Transmission

67

#	Standard	Application	Comments	Included in SGIP Catalog of Standards?[111]	SG Conceptual Architecture Domains
		optional for compliance with the standard.			
10	IEC 60870-6-802 Telecontrol Equipment and Systms - Part 6: Telecontrol protocols compatible with ISO standards and ITU-T recommendations - Section 802: TASE.2 Object Models CoS: http://collaborate.nist.gov/twiki-sggrid/bin/view/SmartGrid/SGIP CosSIFIEC60870680802	Standard for Communications between electric power control centers. Formerly known as Inter Control Center Protocol (ICCP), the standard is used for communication of electric power system status and control messages between power control centers.	This part of the standard defines the object models used at the application layer of the protocol. It includes data objects for basic Supervisory Control and Data Acquisition (SCADA) as well as specific objects for control center concepts such as Transfer Accounts, Device Outages, and Power Plants.	Y	Transmission
	IEC 61850 Suite: Communication networks and systems in substations (Only individual parts are being numbered) http://webstore.iec.ch/webstore/websto re.nsf/artnum/033549!opendocument CSWG Report	This standard defines communications within transmission and distribution substations for automation and protection. It is being extended to cover communications beyond the substation to integration of distributed resources and between substations.	Open standard with conformance testing that is developed and maintained by an SDO. It has been widely adopted world-wide and is starting to be adopted in North America. Developed initially for field device communications within substations, this set of standards is now being extended to communications between substations,	Y	Transmission, Distribution

#	Standard	Application	Comments	Included in SGIP Catalog of Standards?[111]	SG Conceptual Architecture Domains
	http://collaborate.nist.gov/twiki-sggrid/pub/SmartGrid/CSCTGStandards/StandardsReviewPhase-1Report.pdf Narrative http://collaborate.nist.gov/twiki-sggrid/pub/SmartGrid/NISTStandards Summaries/IEC_61850_Narrative_10-6-2010.doc http://collaborate.nist.gov/twiki-sggrid/bin/view/SmartGrid/SGIPCoSS tandardsInformationLibrary		between substations and control centers, and including hydroelectric plants, DER, and synchrophasors. It is also adapted for use in wind turbines (IEC 61400-25) and switchgears (IEC 62271-3). Several PAPs (PAP07, PAP08, PAP12, and PAP13) are dedicated to further development work in various areas. PAP07 has developed requirements to update IEC 61850-7-420 Distributed Energy Resource (DER) Information Models to include storage devices and Smart Grid functionality necessary to support high penetration of DER. PAP07 is also mapping the information models to application protocols including Smart Energy Profile (SEP2) and DNP3. The new information models requirements are included in the IEC Technical Report, IEC 61850-90-7 published in February 2013 and will also be		

#	Standard	Application	Comments	Included in SGIP Catalog of Standards?[111]	SG Conceptual Architecture Domains
			included in the modified normative standard that will follow. (PAP07: Energy Storage Interconnection Guidelines - http://collaborate.nist.gov/twiki-sggrid/bin/view/SmartGrid/PAP07Storage) PAP12 has been working on the mapping of IEEE 1815 (DNP3) to IEC 61850 objects, and it has resulted in a draft IEEE standard P1815.1 being completed in early 2011 for adoption by IEEE around mid-2011. (PAP12: Mapping IEEE 1815 (DNP3) to IEC 61850 Objects - http://collaborate.nist.gov/twiki-sggrid/bin/view/SmartGrid/PAP12DNP361850) PAP13 was established to assist and accelerate the integration of standards (IEEE C37.118 and IEC 61850) that impact phasor measurement systems and applications that use synchrophasor data, as well as implementation profiles for IEEE Std		

70

#	Standard	Application	Comments	Included in SGIP Catalog of Standards?[111]	SG Conceptual Architecture Domains
			1588 for precision time synchronization. (PAP13: Harmonization of IEEE C37.118 with IEC 61850 and Precision Time Synchronization - http://collaborate.nist.gov/twiki-sggrid/bin/view/SmartGrid/PAP13618 50C27118HarmSynch) IEEE will split current IEEE C37.118-2005 into two parts in its new revision to facilitate the harmonization with IEC standards: C37.118.1 Standard for synchrophasor measurements for power systems aimed to become an IEEE/IEC dual-logo standard, and C37.118.2, Standard for synchrophasor data transfer for power systems to be harmonized with / transitioned to IEC 61850-90-5, which was published in May 2012. PAP8 is working on harmonizing this family of standards, the IEC 61970 family of standards (Common Information Model or CIM), and		

71

#	Standard	Application	Comments	Included in SGIP Catalog of Standards?[111]	SG Conceptual Architecture Domains
			MultiSpeak for distribution grid management (PAP08: CIM/61850 for Distribution Grid Management - http://collaborate.nist.gov/twiki-sggrid/bin/view/SmartGrid/PAP08DistrObjMultispeak).		
11	IEC 61850-1 CoS: http://collaborate.nist.gov/twiki-sggrid/bin/view/SmartGrid/SGIPCosSIFIECTR618501		This document, Part 1 of the standard, provides an overview of the other parts of the standard and an introduction to key concepts used in the rest of the standard, such as logical nodes.	Y	Transmission, Distribution
12	IEC61850-2 CoS: http://collaborate.nist.gov/twiki-sggrid/bin/view/SmartGrid/SGIPCosSIFIECTS618502		This document, Part 2 of the standard, is the glossary.	Y	Transmission, Distribution
13	IEC61850-3 CoS: http://collaborate.nist.gov/twiki-sggrid/bin/view/SmartGrid/SGIPCosSIFIEC618503		This document, Part 3 of IEC 61850 applies to substation automation systems (SAS). It describes the communication between intelligent electronic devices (IEDs) in the substation and the related system requirements. The specifications of	Y	Transmission, Distribution

#	Standard	Application	Comments	Included in SGIP Catalog of Standards?[111]	SG Conceptual Architecture Domains
			this part pertain to the general requirements of the communication network, with emphasis on the quality requirements. It also deals with guidelines for environmental conditions and auxiliary services, with recommendations on the relevance of specific requirements from other standards and specifications.		
14	IEC61850-4 CoS: http://collaborate.nist.gov/twiki-sggrid/bin/view/SmartGrid/SGIPCosSIFIEC618504		The specifications of this part pertain to the system and project management with respect to: • the engineering process and its supporting tools; • the life cycle of the overall system and its IEDs; • the quality assurance beginning with the development stage and ending with discontinuation and decommissioning of the SAS and its IEDs. The requirements of the system and project management process and of special supporting tools for engineering and testing are described.	Y	Transmission, Distribution

73

#	Standard	Application	Comments	Included in SGIP Catalog of Standards?[111]	SG Conceptual Architecture Domains
			The IEC 61850-4 covers system and project management requirements for Utility Automation Systems, which implies a broader scope than the substation automation communication equipment only. However, the language in the document is heavily based on Substation Automation.		
15	IEC61850-5 CoS: http://collaborate.nist.gov/twiki-sggrid/bin/view/SmartGrid/SGIP CosSIFIEC618505		This part of IEC 61850 applies to Substation Automation Systems (SAS). It standardizes the communication between intelligent electronic devices (IEDs) and the related system requirements. The specifications of this part refer to the communication requirements of the functions being performed in the substation automation system and to device models. All known functions and their communication requirements are identified.	Y	Transmission, Distribution
16	IEC61850-6 CoS:		This part of IEC 61850 specifies a file format for describing communication-	Y	Transmission, Distribution

74

#	Standard	Application	Comments	Included in SGIP Catalog of Standards?[111]	SG Conceptual Architecture Domains
	http://collaborate.nist.gov/twiki-sggrid/bin/view/SmartGrid/SGIPCosSIFIEC618506		related IED (Intelligent Electronic Device) configurations and IED parameters, communication system configurations, switch yard (function) structures, and the relations between them. The main purpose of this format is to exchange IED capability descriptions, and SA system descriptions between IED engineering tools and the system engineering tool(s) of different manufacturers in a compatible way. The defined language is called System Configuration description Language (SCL). The IED and communication system model in SCL is according to IEC 61850-5 and IEC 1850-7-x. SCSM specific extensions or usage rules may be required in the appropriate parts. The configuration language is based on the Extensible Markup Language (XML) version 1.0 (see XML references in Clause 2). This standard does not specify individual implementations or		

#	Standard	Application	Comments	Included in SGIP Catalog of Standards?[111]	SG Conceptual Architecture Domains
			products using the language, nor does it constrain the implementation of entities and interfaces within a computer system. This part of the standard does not specify the download format of configuration data to an IED, although it could be used for part of the configuration data.		
17	IEC61850-7-1 CoS: http://collaborate.nist.gov/twiki-sggrid/bin/view/SmartGrid/SGIP CosSIFIEC6185071		The purpose of this part of the IEC 61850 series is to provide – from a conceptual point of view – assistance to understand the basic modelling concepts and description methods for: • substation-specific information models for power utility automation systems, • device functions used for power utility automation purposes, and • communication systems to provide interoperability within power utility facilities

Furthermore, this part of the IEC 61850 series provides explanations and provides detailed requirements relating to the relation between IEC | Y | Transmission, Distribution |

76

#	Standard	Application	Comments	Included in SGIP Catalog of Standards?[111]	SG Conceptual Architecture Domains
			61850-7-4, IEC 61850-7-3, IEC 61850-7-2 and IEC 61850-5. This part explains how the abstract services and models of the IEC 61850-7-x series are mapped to concrete communication protocols as defined in IEC 61850-8-1.		
18	IEC61850-7-2 CoS: http://collaborate.nist.gov/twiki-sggrid/bin/view/SmartGrid/SGIPCosSIFIEC6185072		This part of IEC 61850 applies to the ACSI communication for utility automation. The ACSI provides the following abstract communication service interfaces. a) Abstract interface describing communications between a client and a remote server for – real-time data access and retrieval, – device control, – event reporting and logging, – setting group control, – self-description of devices (device data dictionary), – data typing and discovery of data types, and – file transfer. b) Abstract interface for fast and reliable system-wide event	Y	Transmission, Distribution

#	Standard	Application	Comments	Included in SGIP Catalog of Standards?[111]	SG Conceptual Architecture Domains
			distribution between an application in one device and many remote applications in different devices (publisher/sub-scribersubscriber) and for transmission of sampled measured values (publisher/subscriber).		
19	IEC61850-7-3 CoS: http://collaborate.nist.gov/twiki-sggrid/bin/view/SmartGrid/SGIP CosSIFIEC6185073		This part of IEC 61850 specifies constructed attribute classes and common data classes related to substation applications. In particular, it specifies: · common data classes for status information, · common data classes for measured information, · common data classes for control, · common data classes for status settings, · common data classes for analogue settings and · attribute types used in these common data classes. This International Standard is applicable to the description of device models and functions of substations and feeder equipment.	Y	Transmission, Distribution

#	Standard	Application	Comments	Included in SGIP Catalog of Standards?[111]	SG Conceptual Architecture Domains
20	IEC 61850-7-4 CoS: http://members.sgip.org/apps/group_public/document.php?document_id=2586&wg_abbrev=cosd		This part specifies the abstract information model of devices and functions, consisting of data objects contained in Logical Nodes (LNs). This part was initially just for substation automation, but has been expanded to include the common Logical Nodes used in many different domains, including: • Intra-substation information exchanges • Substation-to-substation information exchanges • Substation-to-control center information exchanges • Power plant-to-control center information exchanges • Information exchange for distributed generations • Information exchange for distributed automations • Information exchange for metering. This part also specifies normative naming rules for multiple instances and private, compatible extensions of logical node (LN) classes and data object (DO) names.	Y	Transmission, Distribution
21	IEC61850-7-410 CoS: http://collaborate.nist.gov/twiki-sggrid/bin/view/SmartGrid/SGIPCosSIFIEC618507410		IEC 61850-7-410 is part of the IEC 61850 series. This part of IEC 61850 specifies the additional common data classes, logical nodes and data objects required for the use of IEC 61850 in a	Y	Transmission, Distribution

79

#	Standard	Application	Comments	Included in SGIP Catalog of Standards?[111]	SG Conceptual Architecture Domains
			hydropower plant. The Logical Nodes and Data Objects defined in this part of IEC 61850 belong to the following fields of use: • Electrical functions. This group includes LN and DO used for various control functions, essentially related to the excitation of the generator. New LN and DO defined within this group are not specific to hydropower plants; they are more or less general for all types of larger power plants. • Mechanical functions. This group includes functions related to the turbine and associated equipment. The specifications of this document are intended for hydropower plants, modifications might be required for application to other types of generating plants. Some more generic functions are defined under Logical Node group K. • Hydrological functions. This group of functions includes objects related to water flow, control and management of reservoirs and dams. Although specific for hydropower plants, the LN and DO defined here can also be		

#	Standard	Application	Comments	Included in SGIP Catalog of Standards?[111]	SG Conceptual Architecture Domains
			used for other types of utility water management systems. • Sensors. A power plant will need sensors providing measurements of other than electrical data. With a few exceptions, such sensors are of general nature and not specific for hydropower plants.		
22	IEC61850-7-420 CoS: http://collaborate.nist.gov/twiki-sggrid/bin/view/SmartGrid/SGIP CosSIFIEC618507420		This International Standard defines the IEC 61850 information models to be used in the exchange of information with distributed energy resources (DER), which comprise dispersed generation devices and dispersed storage devices, including reciprocating engines, fuel cells, microturbines, photovoltaics, combined heat and power, and energy storage. The IEC 61850 DER information model standard utilizes existing IEC 61850-7-4 logical nodes where possible, but also defines DER-specific logical nodes where needed.	Y	Transmission, Distribution
23	IEC61850-8-1 CoS: http://collaborate.nist.gov/twiki-sggrid/bin/view/SmartGrid/SGIP CosSIFIEC618508l		IEC 61850-8-1 maps the: • Abstract service models defined in IEC 61850-7-2 as "Abstract Communication Services Interface (ACSI)", including the Generic	Y	Transmission, Distribution

81

#	Standard	Application	Comments	Included in SGIP Catalog of Standards?[111]	SG Conceptual Architecture Domains
			Object-Oriented Substation Event (GOOSE) and Sampled Values (SV) messages • Common data classes (CDCs) defined in IEC 61850-7-3 • Data objects in Logical Nodes (LNs) defined in the IEC 61850-7-4, 7-410, and 7-420 to the "bits and bytes" protocols of the Manufacturing Message Specification (MMS) at the ISO/OSI Application Layer, that runs over IEC 8802-3 (commonly referred to as Ethernet) at the ISO/OSI Data Link Layer. • Time synchronization uses the Simple Network Time Protocols (SNTP) protocol. • Different profiles are established for different types of messages, ranging from the very fast GOOSE event messages and rapid continuous sampled values messages running directly over Ethernet, to special time synchronization interactions over UDP, to the normal information exchange messages running over TCP/IP.		

82

#	Standard	Application	Comments	Included in SGIP Catalog of Standards?[111]	SG Conceptual Architecture Domains
			• The standard also addresses additional mapping issues, including file transfers, the system configuration language, conformance, multicast, and timing issues.		
24	IEC61850-9-2 CoS: http://collaborate.nist.gov/twiki-sggrid/bin/view/SmartGrid/SGIP CosSIFIEC6185092		IEC 61850 supports "sampled values" which are continuously streaming raw measurements from sensors, e.g. voltage measurements from Potential Transformers (PTs) or water flow measurements in hydro plants. This standard maps the abstract services defined in IEC 61850-7-2 for retrieving these sampled values to the (A-Profile) Manufacturing Message Specification (MMS) as standardized in IEC 61850-8-1 and to (T-Profile) TCP/IP over (essentially) Ethernet over fiber optic media. Other media may also be used, but are not specified in this document.	Y	Transmission, Distribution
25	IEC61850-10 CoS:		IEC 61850 was originally focused on substation automation. This part defines the conformance testing	Y	Transmission, Distribution

83

#	Standard	Application	Comments	Included in SGIP Catalog of Standards?[111]	SG Conceptual Architecture Domains
	http://collaborate.nist.gov/twiki-sggrid/bin/view/SmartGrid/SGIPCosSIFIEC6185010		requirements and measurement techniques for ensuring optimal performance for implementations of substation automation using IEC 61850. The testing covers: • General testing plan and procedure requirements • Quality assurance requirements • Use of SCL files • Documentation and test reports • Positive and negative test cases for the services defined in IEC 61850-7-2 • Accuracy of time synchronization • Performance tests		
26	IEC61850-90-5 CoS: http://collaborate.nist.gov/twiki-sggrid/bin/view/SmartGrid/SGIPCosSIFIECTR61850905		IEC 61850-90-5: This technical report is a part of the IEC 61850 series of standards that adds a method for exchanging synchrophasor data between PMUs, PDCs, WAMPAC (Wide Area Monitoring, Protection, and Control) systems, and between control center applications. The data, to the extent	Y	Transmission, Distribution

#	Standard	Application	Comments	Included in SGIP Catalog of Standards?[111]	SG Conceptual Architecture Domains
			covered in IEEE C37.118.2 - 2011, is transported in a way that is compliant to the concepts of IEC 61850. This document also provides routable profiles for IEC 61850-8-1 GOOSE and IEC 61850-9-2 SV packets. These routable packets can be utilized to transport general IEC 61850 data as well as synchrophasor data.		
27	IEC 61968/61970 Suites http://webstore.iec.ch/webstore/webstore.nsf/mysearchajax?Openform&key=61968&sorting=&start=1&onglet=1 CSWG Report http://collaborate.nist.gov/twiki-sggrid/pub/SmartGrid/CSCTGStandards/StandardsReviewPhase-1Report.pdf Narrative IEC 61968 http://collaborate.nist.gov/twiki-sggrid/pub/SmartGrid/NISTStandardsSummaries/IEC_61968_Narrative_10-6-2010.doc	These families of standards define information exchanged among control center systems using common information models. They define application-level energy management system interfaces and messaging for distribution grid management in the utility space.	Open standards that are starting to become more widely implemented, developed and maintained by an SDO with support from a users group. They are part of PAP08 activities relating to integration with IEC 61850 and MultiSpeak (PAP08: CIM/61850 for Distribution Grid Management - http://collaborate.nist.gov/twiki-sggrid/bin/view/SmartGrid/PAP08DistrObjMultispeak). Work is continuing to add extensions to the CIM for new Smart Grid functionality, and it is expected have more complete	N	Operations

85

#	Standard	Application	Comments	Included in SGIP Catalog of Standards?[111]	SG Conceptual Architecture Domains
	Narrative IEC 61970 http://collaborate.nist.gov/twiki-sggrid/pub/SmartGrid/NISTStandardsSummaries/IEC_61970_Narrative_10-6-2010.doc		coverage of distribution automation devices and systems in the future.		
28	IEEE 1815 (DNP3) IEEE Xplore - IEEE Std 1815-2012 http://standards.ieee.org/findstds/standard/1815-2012.html http://collaborate.nist.gov/twiki-sggrid/bin/view/SmartGrid/SGIPCosSIFIEEE181	This standard is used for substation and feeder device automation, as well as for communications between control centers and substations.	An open, mature, widely implemented specification initially developed and supported by a group of vendors, utilities, and other users, and now maintained by an SDO. IEEE has adopted it as an IEEE standard, IEEE Std 1815-2010, excluding the cybersecurity part which is being updated by IEEE Substation Committee Working Group (WG) C12. A Priority Action Plan (PAP12) was established to support transport of smart grid data and management functions between networks implementing IEEE 1815 and IEC 61850. PAP12 has coordinated actions on the development of mapping between IEC 61850 and IEEE 1815 (DNP3) objects	Y	Generation, Transmission, Distribution, Operations, Service Provider

#	Standard	Application	Comments	Included in SGIP Catalog of Standards?[111]	SG Conceptual Architecture Domains
			that will allow presently communicated supervisory control and data acquisition (SCADA) information to be used in new ways, while also providing the ability to create new applications using the existing DNP3 infrastructure. A draft IEEE 1815.1 mapping standard has been developed, and a new working group C14 under IEEE substation committee has been established to adopt it as a formal IEEE standard. It is also anticipated to be adopted later by IEC as a dual-logo IEEE/IEC standard. (PAP12: Mapping IEEE 1815 (DNP3) to IEC 61850 Objects - http://collaborate.nist.gov/twiki-sggrid/bin/view/SmartGrid/PAP12DN P361850).		
29	IEEE C37.118.1-2011 IEEE Standard for Synchrophasor Measurements for Power Systems http://standards.ieee.org/develop/ wg/C37.118.1_WG.html	This standard defines phasor measurement unit (PMU) performance specifications	Open standard, widely implemented, developed and maintained by an SDO. Standard is overseen by the IEEE Power System Relaying Committee (PSRC) Relaying Communications Subcommittee Working Groups H11	N	Transmission, Distribution

87

#	Standard	Application	Comments	Included in SGIP Catalog of Standards?[111]	SG Conceptual Architecture Domains
			and H19. This standard is intended to become an IEEE/IEC dual-logo standard.		
30	IEEE C37.118.2 Standard for synchrophasor data transfer for power systems http://standards.ieee.org/develop/wg/C37.118.2_WG.html	This standard defines communications for phasor measurement units (PMUs).	Some items not covered in C37.118-2005 include communication service modes, remote device configuration, dynamic measurement performance, and security IEEE PSRC WG C5 has developed a "Guide for Synchronization, Calibration, Testing, and Installation of Phasor Measurement Units (PMU) applied in Power System Protection and Control" based on the C37.118 standards and previous publications by North American Synchro-Phasor Initiative (NASPI) in these areas. They are part of PAP13 relating to harmonization of IEC 61850 and IEEE C37.118 standards (PAP13: Harmonization of IEEE C37.118 with IEC 61850 and Precision Time Synchronization - http://collaborate.nist.gov/twiki-	N	Transmission, Distribution

88

#	Standard	Application	Comments	Included in SGIP Catalog of Standards?[111]	SG Conceptual Architecture Domains
			sgrid/bin/view/SmartGrid/PAP13618 50C27118HarmSynch).		
31	IEEE C37.238 -2011 IEEE Standard Profile for Use of IEEE 1588 Precision Time Protocol in Power System Applications http://standards.ieee.org/findstds/ standard/C37.238-2011.html http://collaborate.nist.gov/twiki-sgrid/bin/view/SmartGrid/SGIP CosSIFIEEEC372382011	Ethernet communications for power systems	This standard specifies a common profile for use of IEEE 1588-2008 Precision Time Protocol (PTP) in power system protection, control, automation and data communication applications utilizing an Ethernet communications architecture. The profile specifies a well-defined subset of IEEE 1588-2008 mechanisms and settings aimed at enabling device interoperability, robust response to network failures, and deterministic control of delivered time quality. It specifies the preferred physical layer (Ethernet), higher level protocol used for PTP message exchange and the PTP protocol configuration parameters. Special attention is given to ensuring consistent and reliable time distribution within substations, between substations, and across wide	Y	Transmission, Distribution

#	Standard	Application	Comments	Included in SGIP Catalog of Standards?[111]	SG Conceptual Architecture Domains
			geographic areas. (Source: IEEE PC37.238 D4.0 – Scope Statement)		
32	IEEE C37.239-2010 Standard for Common Format for Event Data Exchange (COMFEDE) for Power Systems http://www.pes-psrc.org/h/ http://ieeexplore.ieee.org/xpl/login.jsp?tp=&arnumber=5638582& url=http%3A%2F%2Fieeexplore. ieee.org%2Fxpls%2Fabs_all.jsp %3Farnumber%3D5638582 http://collaborate.nist.gov/twiki-sggrid/bin/view/SmartGrid/SGIP CosSIFIEEEC372392010	Interchange of power system event data	A common format for data files used for the interchange of various types of event data collected from electrical power systems or power system models is defined. Extensibility, extension mechanisms, and compatibility of future versions of the format are discussed. An XML schema is defined. A sample file is given. It doesn't define what is transferred via communications. It is only a file format for offline analysis and data exchange.	Y	Transmission, Distribution
33	IEEE 1547 Suite: Standard for Interconnecting Distributed Resources with Electric Power Systems https://sbwsweb.ieee.org/ecusto mercme_enu/start.swe?SWECmd =GotoView&SWEView=Catalog +View+(eSales)_Standards_IEE E&mem_type=Customer&SWE	This family of standards defines physical and electrical interconnections between the grid and distributed generation (DG) and storage.	Open standards developed and maintained by an SDO with significant implementation for the parts covering physical/electrical connections. The parts of this suite of standards that describe messages are not as widely deployed as the parts that specify the physical interconnections. Many utilities and	N	Transmission, Distribution, Customer

90

#	Standard	Application	Comments	Included in SGIP Catalog of Standards?[111]	SG Conceptual Architecture Domains
	Ho=sbwsweb.ieee.org&SWETS =192713657 http://www.sgiclearinghouse.org/ ?q=node/1116&lb=1		regulators require their use in systems. Revising and extending the IEEE 1547 family is a focus of PAP07, covering energy storage interconnections (PAP07: Energy Storage Interconnection Guidelines - http://collaborate.nist.gov/twiki-sggrid/bin/view/SmartGrid/PAP07Storage).). When applied to utility-interactive equipment, Underwriters Laboratories (UL) 1741, "Standard for Safety Inverters, Converters, Controllers and Interconnection System Equipment for Use With Distributed Energy Resources," should be used in conjunction with 1547 and 1547.1 standards which supplement them. The products covered by these requirements are intended to be installed in accordance with the National Electrical Code, National Fire Protection Association (NFPA) 70.		

#	Standard	Application	Comments	Included in SGIP Catalog of Standards?[111]	SG Conceptual Architecture Domains
34	IEEE 1588: The Precise Networked Clock Synchronization http://www.nist.gov/el/isd/ieee/intro1588.cfm	Standard for time management and clock synchronization across the Smart Grid for equipment needing consistent time management.	Open standard. Version 2 is not widely implemented for power applications. Developed and maintained by an SDO.	N	Transmission, Distribution
		Profile of IEEE 1588 for electric power systems.	IEEE PSRC Subcommittee Working Group H7 is developing a new standard C37.238 (IEEE Standard Profile for use of IEEE Std. 1588 Precision Time Protocol in Power System Applications). See #31 in this table, IEEE C37.238 - 2011 - IEEE Standard Profile for Use of IEEE 1588 Precision Time Protocol in Power System Applications. This standard was part of PAP13, which covered incorporating precision time synchronization with harmonization of IEEE and IEC standards for communications of phasor data (http://collaborate.nist.gov/twiki-sggrid/bin/view/SmartGrid/PAP13618 50C27118HarmSynch).		Transmission, Distribution

#	Standard	Application	Comments	Included in SGIP Catalog of Standards?[111]	SG Conceptual Architecture Domains
35	Inter-System Protocol(ISP)-based Broadband-Power Line Carrier (PLC) coexistence mechanism: (Portion of) IEEE 1901-2010 (ISP) and International Telecommunications Union Telecommunication Standardization Sector (ITU-T) G.9972 (06/2010) IEEE 1901-2010 http://standards.ieee.org/findstds/standard/1901-2010.html ITU-T G.9972 http://www.itu.int/rec/T-REC-G.9972-201006-P/en	Both IEEE 1901-2010, "IEEE Standard for Broadband over Power Line Networks: Medium Access Control and Physical Layer Specifications," and ITU-T G.9972 (06/2010), "Coexistence mechanism for wireline home networking transceivers," specify Inter-System Protocol (ISP) based Broadband (> 1.8 MHz) PLC (BB-PLC) coexistence mechanisms to enable the coexistence of different BB PLC protocols for home networking.	Open standards developed and maintained by SDOs. Both IEEE 1901 and ITU-T G.9972 are developed and maintained by SDOs. Through coordination by PAP15 (PAP15: Harmonize Power Line Carrier Standards for Appliance Communications in the Home - http://collaborate.nist.gov/twiki-sggrid/bin/view/SmartGrid/PAP15PLCForLowBitRates), the divergence between the two standards has been successfully eliminated before ratification. IEEE 1901-compliant devices implementing either one of the two IEEE 1901 Physical (PHY)/ Media Access Control (MAC) Layers can coexist with each other. Likewise, ITU-T G.9960/9961 devices that implement ITU-T G.9972 can coexist	Y[112]	Customer

[112] IEEE 1901-2010 and the ITU-T G.99xx series of standards appear on the CoS in their entirety. Only the coexistence portion of IEEE 1901-2010 and ITU-T G.9972 are included in this table because of incompatibilities with the other parts of the standard and series. See the PAP 15 document, NISTIR 7862 "Guideline for the Implementation of Coexistence for Broadband Power Line Communication Standards" for further guidance (http://nvlpubs.nist.gov/nistpubs/ir/2012/NIST.IR.7862.pdf).

#	Standard	Application	Comments	Included in SGIP Catalog of Standards?[111]	SG Conceptual Architecture Domains
			with IEEE 1901-compliant devices implementing either one of the two IEEE P1901 PHY/MACs, and vice versa.		
36	MultiSpeak http://www.nreca.coop/what-we do/multispeak/aboutmultispeak/	A specification for application software integration within the utility operations domain; a candidate for use in an Enterprise Service Bus.	An open, mature specification developed and maintained by a consortium of electric utilities and industry vendors, with an interoperability testing program. It is part of PAP08's task for harmonization of IEC 61850/CIM and MultiSpeak (PAP08: CIM/61850 for Distribution Grid Management - http://collaborate.nist.gov/twiki-sggrid/bin/view/SmartGrid/PAP08DistrObjMultispeak).	N	Distribution
37	NAESB REQ18, WEQ19 Energy Usage Information http://www.naesb.org/member_login_check.asp?doc=weq_rat102910_weq_2010_ap_6d_rec.doc, http://www.naesb.org/member_login_check.asp?doc=req_rat102910_req_2010_ap_9d_rec.doc	The standards specify two-way flows of energy usage information based on a standardized information model.	Open standards, developed and maintained by an SDO. These are new standards to be adopted and deployed. It will be a basis for additional standards and recommendations including those from PAP17; also used as input for Energy Interoperation.	Y	Customer, Service Provider

#	Standard	Application	Comments	Included in SGIP Catalog of Standards?[111]	SG Conceptual Architecture Domains
	CoS Web page: http://collaborate.nist.gov/twiki-sggrid/bin/view/SmartGrid/SGIPCosSIFNAESBREQ18WEQ19		The standards have been reviewed by PAP10 (PAP10: Standard Energy Usage Information - http://collaborate.nist.gov/twiki-sggrid/bin/view/SmartGrid/PAP10EnergyUsagetoEMS) and SGAC. It has been recommended by the SGIP Governing Board and approved by the SGIP Plenary for inclusion in the Catalog of Standards.

In related work, the NAESB Energy Services Provider Interface (ESPI) Task Force is developing a Req.21, ESPI. See http://www.naesb.org/espi_task_force.asp for further information.

Customers will benefit from energy usage information that enables them to make better decisions and take other actions consistent with the goals of Sections 1301 and 1305 of EISA. An understanding of energy usage informs better decisions about energy | | |

#	Standard	Application	Comments	Included in SGIP Catalog of Standards?[111]	SG Conceptual Architecture Domains
			use and conservation, and is the basis for performance feedback on the operation of customerowned energy management systems and understanding device energy usage and management. This standard defines an information model of semantics for the definition and exchange of customer energy usage information. The actual exchange standards are anticipated to be derivative from this seed standard. A revision of this standard has been approved through the NAESB process but has not yet been re-evaluated by SGIP for the CoS.		
38	NAESB REQ-21 Energy Services Provider Interface (ESPI) CoS: http://collaborate.nist.gov/twiki-sggrid/bin/view/SmartGrid/SGIP CosSIFNAESBREQ21	ESPI builds on the NAESB Energy Usage Information (EUI) Model and, subject to the governing documents and any requirements of the applicable regulatory authority, will help enable retail customers to share	ESPI applies to customer interaction systems of utilities, third party service providers, and customers and their devices such as handheld and desktop computers, thermostats, electricity meters, etc.	Y	Customer, Service Provider

#	Standard	Application	Comments	Included in SGIP Catalog of Standards?[111]	SG Conceptual Architecture Domains
		energy usage information with third parties who have acquired the right to act in this role. ESPI will provide a consistent method for retail customers to authorize a third party to gain access to energy usage information. Doing so will help enable retail customers to choose third party products to assist them to better understand their energy usage and to make more economical decisions about their usage. ESPI will contribute to the development of an open and interoperable method for third party authorization and machine-to-machine exchange of retail customer energy usage information.			
39	NAESB REQ-22	The NAESB REQ.22 document "establishes voluntary Model Business	REQ.22 provides guidelines for the privacy business practices for Distribution Companies and Third	Y	Customer, Service Provider

#	Standard	Application	Comments	Included in SGIP Catalog of Standards?[111]	SG Conceptual Architecture Domains
	Third Party Access to Smart Meter-based Information Business Model Practices CoS: http://collaborate.nist.gov/twiki-sggrid/bin/view/SmartGrid/SGIPCosSIFNAESBREQ22	Practices for Third Party access to Smart Meter-based information." These business practices are intended only to serve as flexible guidelines rather than requirements, with the onus on regulatory authorities or similar bodies to establish the actual requirements. They are also not intended for any billing or collection activities.	Parties when managing private customer Smart Meter information. ESPI applies to customer interaction systems of utilities, third party service providers, and customers and their devices such as handheld and desktop computers, thermostats, electricity meters, etc. SGIP PAP 20, Green Button EPSI Evolution, is building on this work. Additionally, open source implementations for ESPI and related testing tools are being developed.		
40	NEMA Smart Grid Standards Publication SG-AMI 1-2009 – Requirements for Smart Meter Upgradeability http://www.nema.org/Standards/Pages/Requirements-for-Smart-Meter-Upgradeability.aspx CoS Web page:	This standard will be used by smart meter suppliers, utility customers, and key constituents, such as regulators, to guide both development and decision making as related to smart meter upgradeability.	This standard serves as a key set of requirements for smart meter upgradeability. These requirements should be used by smart meter suppliers, utility customers, and key constituents, such as regulators, to guide both development and decision making as related to smart meter upgradeability. The purpose of this document is to define requirements for smart meter firmware upgradeability in the context	Y	Customer, Distribution

#	Standard	Application	Comments	Included in SGIP Catalog of Standards?[111]	SG Conceptual Architecture Domains
	http://collaborate.nist.gov/twiki sggrid/bin/view/SmartGrid/SGIP CosSIFNEMASGAMI1		of an AMI system for industry stakeholders such as regulators, utilities, and vendors. This standard was coordinated by PAP00 Meter Upgradeability Standard - http://collaborate.nist.gov/twiki-sggrid/bin/view/SmartGrid/PAP00Met erUpgradability and has been recommended by the SGIP Governing Board and approved by the SGIP Plenary for the CoS.		
41	OPC-UA Industrial http://www.opcfoundation.org/D ownloads.aspx?CM=1&CN=KE Y&CI=283	A platform-independent specification for a secure, reliable, high-speed data exchange based on a publish/subscribe mechanism. Modern service-oriented architecture (SOA) designed to expose complex data and metadata defined by other information model specifications (e.g. IEC 61850, BACnet, OpenADR). Works with existing binary and	Widely supported open standard, with compliance testing program.	N	Customer

#	Standard	Application	Comments	Included in SGIP Catalog of Standards?[111]	SG Conceptual Architecture Domains
		eXtensible Markup Language (XML) schema defined data.			
42	Open Automated Demand 2.0 Response (OpenADR) http://www.openadr.org/specification Cos: OpenADR Profile A http://members.sgip.org/apps/org/workgroup/chairs/download.php/2224 OpenADR Profile B http://members.sgip.org/apps/org/workgroup/chairs/download.php/2224	The specification defines messages exchanged between the Demand Response (DR) Service Providers (e.g., utilities, independent system operators (ISOs) and customers for price-responsive and reliability-based DR.	Developed by Lawrence Berkeley National Laboratory and California Energy Commission and is currently supported by the OpenADR Alliance. Demand response signals are currently being standardized in OASIS Energy Interoperation. The Organization for the Advancement of Structured Information Standard (OASIS) is the SDO that created and published the OpenADR 2.0 Profile as a subset of the Energy Interoperation (EI) standard. The OpenADR Alliance maintains the standard and is recognized as the ITCA by SGIP. (PAP09: Standard DR and DER Signals - http://collaborate.nist.gov/twiki-sggrid/bin/view/SmartGrid/PAP09DR DER).http://collaborate.nist.gov/twiki-sggrid/bin/view/SmartGrid/PAP09DR DER). OpenADR 2.0 profile is a	Y	Operations, Service Providers

#	Standard	Application	Comments	Included in SGIP Catalog of Standards?[111]	SG Conceptual Architecture Domains
			profile (subset) of the Energy Interoperation standard.		
43	Open Geospatial Consortium Geography Markup Language (GML) http://www.opengeospatial.org/standards/gml	A standard for exchange of location-based information addressing geographic data requirements for many Smart Grid applications.	An open standard, GML encoding is in compliance with International Organization for Standardization (ISO) 19118 for the transport and storage of geographic information modeled according to the conceptual modeling framework used in the ISO 19100 series of International Standards and is in wide use with supporting open source software. Also used in Emergency Management, building, facility, and equipment location information bases (http://www.iso.org/iso/iso_catalogue/catalogue_tc/catalogue_detail.htm?csnumber=32554). Various profiles of GML are in common use in emergency management, EMIX, Energy Interoperation/OpenADR 2, and other specifications.	N	Transmission, Distribution

101

#	Standard	Application	Comments	Included in SGIP Catalog of Standards?[111]	SG Conceptual Architecture Domains
44	Organization for the Advancement of Structured Information Standard (OASIS) Energy Interoperation (EI) http://docs.oasis-open.org/energyinterop/ei/v1.0/energyinterop-v1.0.html CoS: http://collaborate.nist.gov/twiki-sggrid/bin/view/SmartGrid/SGIPCosSIFOASISEnergyInterop	Energy interoperation describes an information model and a communication model to enable demand response and energy transactions. XML vocabularies provide for the interoperable and standard exchange of: DR and price signals, bids, transactions and options, and customer feedback on load predictability and generation information.	This standard uses the EMIX information model for price and product as payload information. The DR specification is built on a unified model of retail (OpenADR) and wholesale (input from the ISO/RTO Council) DR. OpenADR 2.0 is a profile on EI. Energy Interop was developed as part of PAP09 (PAP09: Standard DR and DER Signals - http://collaborate.nist.gov/twiki-sggrid/bin/view/SmartGrid/PAP09DRDER).	Y	Markets
45	Organization for the Advancement of Structured Information Standard (OASIS) EMIX (Energy Market Information eXchange) CoS: http://collaborate.nist.gov/twiki-sggrid/bin/view/SmartGrid/SGIPCosSIFOASISEMIX	EMIX provides an information model to enable the exchange of energy price, characteristics, time, and related information for wholesale energy markets, including market makers, market participants, quote streams, premises automation, and devices.	EMIX has been developed as part of PAP03. (PAP03: Develop Common Specification for Price and Product Definition - http://collaborate.nist.gov/twiki-sggrid/bin/view/SmartGrid/PAP03PriceProduct This standard has been approved by the SGIP for the Catalog of Standards (see http://collaborate.nist.gov/twiki-	Y	Markets

#	Standard	Application	Comments	Included in SGIP Catalog of Standards?[111]	SG Conceptual Architecture Domains
			sgrid/bin/view/SmartGrid/SGIPCosS IFOASISEMIX)		
46	Smart Energy Profile 2.0 http://www.zigbee.org/Standards /ZigBeeSmartEnergy/SmartEner gyProfile2.aspx CSWG Report on Draft Technical Requirements Document 0.7 http://collaborate.nist.gov/twiki-sggrid/pub/SmartGrid/CSCTGSt andards/CSWG_Standards_SEP 2.0_Tech_Requirements_TRD_R eview_v10.pdf	Home Area Network (HAN) Device Communications and Information Model.	A profile has been developed to be technology-independent and useful for many Smart Grid applications. PAP 18 focused on developing specific requirements to allow the coexistence of SEP 1.x and 2.0 and to support the migration of 1.x implementations to 2.0. The PAP has produced a white paper summarizing the key issues with migration and making specific recommendations and a requirements document to be submitted to the ZigBee Alliance for consideration in developing the technology-specific recommendations, solutions, and any required changes to the SEP 2.0 specifications themselves. PAP18: SEP 1.x to SEP 2 Transition and Coexistence - http://collaborate.nist.gov/twiki-sggrid/bin/view/SmartGrid/PAP18SE P1To2TransitionAndCoexistence).	N	Customer

#	Standard	Application	Comments	Included in SGIP Catalog of Standards?[111]	SG Conceptual Architecture Domains
	Cross-cutting Standards				
47	Internet Protocol Suite, Request for Comments (RFC) 6272, Internet Protocols for the Smart Grid. CoS Web page: http://collaborate.nist.gov/twiki-sggrid/bin/view/SmartGrid/SGIPCosSIFIETFRFC6272	Internet Protocols for IP-based Smart Grid Networks IPv4/IPv6 are the foundation protocol for delivery of packets in the Internet network. Internet Protocol version 6 (IPv6) is a new version of the Internet Protocol that provides enhancements to Internet Protocol version 4 (IPv4) and allows a larger address space.	A set of open, mature standards produced by IETF for Internet technologies. As part of the tasks for PAP01 (PAP01: Role of IP in the Smart Grid - http://collaborate.nist.gov/twiki-sggrid/bin/view/SmartGrid/PAP01InternetProfile), a core set of IP protocols has been identified for smart grid. After review by PAP01, CSWG, and SGAC, it has been recommended by the SGIP Governing Board (SGIPGB) and approved by the SGIP Plenary for inclusion in the SGIP Catalog of Standards. The list has been published by the IETF as RFC6272, which identifies the key protocols of the Internet Protocol Suite for use in the smart grid. The target audience is those people seeking guidance on how to construct an appropriate Internet Protocol Suite profile for the smart grid.	Y	Cross-cutting

104

#	Standard	Application	Comments	Included in SGIP Catalog of Standards?[111]	SG Conceptual Architecture Domains
48	OASIS WS-Calendar http://docs.oasis-open.org/ws-calendar/ws-calendar-spec/v1.0/csprd03/ws-calendar-spec-v1.0-csprd03.html CoS: http://collaborate.nist.gov/twiki-sggrid/bin/view/SmartGrid/SGIPCosSIFOASISWSCalendar	XML serialization of IETF iCalendar for use in calendars, buildings, pricing, markets, and other environments. A communication specification used to specify schedule and interval between domains.	WS-Calendar describes a limited set of message components and interactions providing a common basis for specifying schedules and intervals to coordinate activities between services. The specification includes service definitions consistent with the OASIS SOA Reference Model and XML vocabularies for the interoperable and standard exchange of: • Schedules, including sequences of schedules • Intervals, including sequences of intervals This standard is the primary deliverable of the common schedules PAP04. (see PAP04: Develop Common Schedule Communication Mechanism for Energy Transactions - http://collaborate.nist.gov/twiki-sggrid/bin/view/SmartGrid/PAP04Sch edules) This standard has been approved by the SGIP for the Catalog of Standards (see http://collaborate.nist.gov/twiki-	Y	Cross-cutting

#	Standard	Application	Comments	Included in SGIP Catalog of Standards?[111]	SG Conceptual Architecture Domains
			sgrid/bin/view/SmartGrid/SGIPCosSIFOASISWSCalendar) This specification is used by EMIX (see PAP03: Develop Common Specification for Price and Product Definition - http://collaborate.nist.gov/twiki-sgrid/bin/view/SmartGrid/PAP03PriceProduct) and Energy Interoperation (see PAP09: Standard DR and DER Signals - http://collaborate.nist.gov/twiki-sgrid/bin/view/SmartGrid/PAP09DRDER)		

Requirements and Guidelines

#	Standard	Application	Comments	Included in SGIP Catalog of Standards?[111]	SG Conceptual Architecture Domains
49	NISTIR 7761v1, NIST Guidelines for Assessing Wireless Standards for Smart Grid Applications http://collaborate.nist.gov/twiki-sgrid/pub/SmartGrid/PAP02Objective3/NIST_PAP2_Guidelines_for_Assessing_Wireless_Standa	This report is a draft of key tools and methods to assist smart grid system designers in making informed decisions about existing and emerging wireless technologies. An initial set of quantified requirements have been	The wireless technologies presented here encompass different technologies that range in capabilities, cost, and ability to meet different requirements for advanced power systems applications. System designers are further assisted by the presentation of a set of wireless functionality and characteristics captured in a matrix for existing and emerging standards-based	Y	Guideline

#	Standard	Application	Comments	Included in SGIP Catalog of Standards?[111]	SG Conceptual Architecture Domains
	rds_for_Smart_Grid_Application s_1.0.pdf CoS: http://collaborate.nist.gov/twiki-sggrid/bin/view/SmartGrid/SGIP CosSIFNISTIR7761	brought together for advanced metering infrastructure (AMI) and initial Distribution Automation (DA) communications. These two areas present technological challenges due to their scope and scale. These systems will span widely diverse geographic areas and operating environments and population densities ranging from urban to rural.	wireless technologies. Details of the capabilities are presented in this report as a way for designers to initially sort through the available wireless technology options. To further assist decision making, the document presents a set of tools in the form of models that can be used for parametric analyses of the various wireless technologies.		
50	NISTIR 7862 – Guideline for the Implementation of Coexistence for Broadband Power Line Communication Standards http://dx.doi.org/10.6028/NIST.I R.7862 CoS: http://collaborate.nist.gov/twiki-sggrid/bin/view/SmartGrid/SGIP CosSIFNISTIR7862		This guideline provides an overview of broadband Power line communication (BB PLC) standards and their coexistence mechanism; the main purpose was to give a clear view of BB PLC standards and their relationships. The document also contains the most important result of SGIP Priority Action Plan 15, an industry agreement that all devices implementing any BB PLC standards must also implement the coexistence	Y	Guideline

107

#	Standard	Application	Comments	Included in SGIP Catalog of Standards?[111]	SG Conceptual Architecture Domains
			mechanism so that they will not interfere with each other.		
51	OpenHAN http://osgug.ucaiug.org/sgsystems/openhan/HAN%20Requirements/Forms/AllItems.aspx	A specification for home area network (HAN) to connect to the utility advanced metering system including device communication, measurement, and control.	A specification developed by a users group, Utility Communications Architecture International Users Group (UCAIug), that contains a "checklist" of requirements that enables utilities to compare the many available HANs.	N	Requirements
52	SAE J1772: SAE Electric Vehicle and Plug in Hybrid Electric Vehicle Conductive Charge Coupler SAE J1772: SAE Electric Vehicle and Plug in Hybrid Electric Vehicle Conductive Charge Coupler CoS Web page: http://collaborate.nist.gov/twiki-sggrid/bin/view/SmartGrid/SGIPCossSIFSAEJ1772	A recommended practice covering the general physical, electrical, functional, and performance requirements to facilitate conductive charging of Electric Vehicle (EV)/Plug-in Hybrid Electric Vehicle (PHEV) vehicles in North America.	This recommended practice responds to a need for a coupling device identified very early on in the EV industry and meets new interoperability and communications requirements. After review by PAP11 (PAP11: Common Object Models for Electric Transportation - http://collaborate.nist.gov/twiki-sggrid/bin/view/SmartGrid/PAP11PEV), CSWG, and SGAC, it has been recommended by the SGIPGB and approved by the SGIP Plenary for inclusion in the SGIP Catalog of Standards.	Y	Requirements

#	Standard	Application	Comments	Included in SGIP Catalog of Standards?[111]	SG Conceptual Architecture Domains
53	SAE J2836/1: Use Cases for Communication Between Plug-in Vehicles and the Utility Grid http://standards.sae.org/j2836/1_201004 CoS Web page: http://collaborate.nist.gov/twiki sggrid/bin/view/SmartGrid/SGIP CosSIFSAEJ283613	This document establishes use cases for communication between plug-in electric vehicles and the electric power grid, for energy transfer and other applications.	This document responds to a need by system designers for documentation of use cases as inputs to creation of end-to-end system solutions between EVs and utilities. After review by PAP11 (PAP11: Common Object Models for Electric Transportation - http://collaborate.nist.gov/twiki-sggrid/bin/view/SmartGrid/PAP11PEV), CSWG and SGAC, it has been recommended to and approved by the SGIPGB for inclusion in the SGIP Catalog of Standards.	Y	Requirements
54	SAE J2847/1: Communication between Plug-in Vehicles and the Utility Grid. http://standards.sae.org/j2847/1_201006		After review by PAP11 (PAP11: Common Object Models for Electric Transportation - http://collaborate.nist.gov/twiki-sggrid/bin/view/SmartGrid/PAP11PEV), CSWG and SGAC, it has been recommended to and approved by the SGIPGB for inclusion in the SGIP Catalog of Standards (http://collaborate.nist.gov/twiki-	Y	Requirements

#	Standard	Application	Comments	Included in SGIP Catalog of Standards?[111]	SG Conceptual Architecture Domains
			sggrid/bin/view/SmartGrid/SGIPCosSIFS AEJ28471).		
55	SGTCC Interoperability Process Reference Manual (IPRM) http://collaborate.nist.gov/twiki-sggrid/pub/SmartGrid/SGTCCIP RM/SGTCC_IPRM_Version_1_0_Updated.pdf	The Interoperability Process Reference Manual (IPRM) developed by SGIP's Smart Grid Testing and Certification Committee (SGTCC) outlines the conformance, interoperability, and cybersecurity testing and certification requirements for SGIP-recommended Smart Grid standards.	A guide developed and maintained by the SGIP's SGTCC. The IPRM has been designed to capture testing and certification processes and best practices needed to verify product interoperability amongst two or more products using the same standards-based communications technology. These processes and best practices are intended for use by an Interoperability Testing and Certification Authority (ITCA) in the design and management of a testing and certification program.	N	Guideline
56	SGIP 2011-0008-1 PAP 18 Transition from SEP 1 to SEP 2.0 http://collaborate.nist.gov/twiki-sggrid/pub/SmartGrid/SEPTransi tionAndCoexistenceWP/PAP_18_SEP_Migration_Guidelines_an d_Best_Practices_ver_1_03.docx		The SGIP Priority Action Plan 18: SEP 1.x to SEP 2.0 Transition and Coexistence was created to specifically address SEP 1.x to SEP 2.0 migration and coexistence. SEP 1.0 provides a set of functionality for HANs designed to meet the requirements established in the OpenHAN System Requirements	Y	Guideline

#	Standard	Application	Comments	Included in SGIP Catalog of Standards?[111]	SG Conceptual Architecture Domains
	CoS: http://collaborate.nist.gov/twiki-sggrid/bin/view/SmartGrid/SGIP CosSIFSGIP20110008_1		Specification v1.0 (produced by the Utility Communications Architecture International Users Group (UCAIug)). SEP 1.0 provides pricing support and consumption for multiple commodities (electric, gas, water), text messaging, direct load control, and demand response capability. SEP 2.0 is IP based; as such it will more easily integrate with existing IP-based systems and protocols and operate over alternative MAC/PHY layers to provide more system flexibility. As a result of significant architectural changes and feature upgrades, SEP 2.0 is not backwards compatible with SEP 1.x neither at the network and application layers nor in the security architecture. Therefore, use cases covering multiple SEP 1.x to SEP 2.0 migration scenarios were constructed and analyzed to determine requirements and best practices to		

#	Standard	Application	Comments	Included in SGIP Catalog of Standards?[111]	SG Conceptual Architecture Domains
			enable successful migrations and/or network coexistence.		
Cybersecurity					
57	Security Profile for Advanced Metering Infrastructure, v 1.0, Advanced Security Acceleration Project – Smart Grid, December 10, 2009 http://osgug.ucaiug.org/utilisec/amisec/Shared%20Documents/AMI%20Security%20Profile%20(ASAP SG)/AMI%20Security%20Profile%20-%20v1_0.pdf	This document provides guidance and security controls to organizations developing or implementing AMI solutions. This includes the meter data management system (MDMS) up to and including the HAN interface of the smart meter.	The Advanced Metering Infrastructure Security (AMI-SEC) Task Force was established under the Utility Communications Architecture International Users Group (UCAIug) to develop consistent security guidelines for AMI.	N	Cybersecurity
58	Department of Homeland Security (DHS), National Cyber Security Division. 2009, September. Catalog of Control Systems Security: Recommendations for Standards Developers.	The catalog presents a compilation of practices that various industry bodies have recommended to increase the security of control systems from both physical and cyber attacks.	This is a source document for the NIST Interagency Report NISTIR 7628, *Guidelines for Smart Grid Cyber Security* (http://csrc.nist.gov/publications/nistir/ir7628/introduction-to-nistir-7628.pdf http://csrc.nist.gov/publications/nistir/ir7628/nistir-7628_vol1.pdf	N	Cybersecurity

#	Standard	Application	Comments	Included in SGIP Catalog of Standards?[111]	SG Conceptual Architecture Domains
	https://www.smartgrid.gov/document/dhs_national_cyber_security_division_catalog_control_systems_security_recommendations_stand		http://csrc.nist.gov/publications/nistir/r7628/nistir-7628_vol2.pdf http://csrc.nist.gov/publications/nistir/r7628/nistir-7628_vol3.pdf).		
59	DHS Cyber Security Procurement Language for Control Systems https://www.smartgrid.gov/sites/default/files/doc/files/DHS_National_Cyber_Security_Division_Cyber_Security_Procurem.pdf	The National Cyber Security Division of the Department of Homeland Security (DHS) developed this document to provide guidance to procuring cybersecurity technologies for control systems products and services. It is not intended as policy or standard. Because it speaks to control systems, its methodology can be used with those aspects of Smart Grid systems.	This is a source document for the NIST Interagency Report NISTIR 7628, *Guidelines for Smart Grid Cyber Security* (http://csrc.nist.gov/publications/nistir/ir7628/introduction-to-nistir-7628.pdf /ir7628/introduction-to-nistir-7628.pdf http://csrc.nist.gov/publications/nistir/r7628/nistir-7628_vol1.pdf http://csrc.nist.gov/publications/nistir/r7628/nistir-7628_vol2.pdf http://csrc.nist.gov/publications/nistir/r7628/nistir-7628_vol3.pdf).	N	Cybersecurity
60	IEC 61851: Electric vehicle conductive charging system - Part 1: General requirements http://webstore.iec.ch/webstore/webstore.nsf/Artnum_PK/44636	Applies to equipment for charging electric road vehicles at standard alternating current (ac) supply voltages (as per IEC 60038) up to 690 V and at direct current (dc) voltages up to 1 000 V, and for providing		N	Requirement

113

#	Standard	Application	Comments	Included in SGIP Catalog of Standards?[111]	SG Conceptual Architecture Domains
		electrical power for any additional services on the vehicle if required when connected to the supply network.			
	IEC 62351 Family: Power systems management and associated information exchange - Data and communications security (Only individual parts are being numbered) http://webstore.iec.ch/webstore/websto re.nsf/artnum/037996!opendocument CSWG Report http://collaborate.nist.gov/twiki-sggrid/pub/SmartGrid/CSCTGStandar ds/StandardsReviewPhase-1Report.pdf Narrative http://collaborate.nist.gov/twiki-sggrid/pub/SmartGrid/NISTStandards Summaries/IEC_62351_Narrative_10-6-2010.doc CoS :	Open standard, developed and maintained by an SDO. Defines security requirements for power system management and information exchange, including communications network and system security issues, Transmission Control Protocol (TCP) and Manufacturing Messaging Specification (MMS) profiles, and security for Inter-Control Center Protocol (ICCP) and substation automation and protection. It is for use in conjunction with related IEC standards, but has not been widely adopted yet.		Y	Cybersecurity

#	Standard	Application	Comments	Included in SGIP Catalog of Standards?[111]	SG Conceptual Architecture Domains
	http://collaborate.nist.gov/twiki-sggrid/bin/view/SmartGrid/SGIPCoSStandardsInformationLibrary				
61	IEC 62351-1 CoS: http://collaborate.nist.gov/twiki-sggrid/bin/view/SmartGrid/SGIPCosSIFIECTS623511		Provides an introduction to the remaining parts of the IEC 62351 series, primarily to introduce the reader to various aspects of information security as applied to power system operations. The scope of the IEC 62351 series is information security for power system control operations.	Y	Cybersecurity
62	IEC 62351-2 CoS: http://collaborate.nist.gov/twiki-sggrid/bin/view/SmartGrid/SGIPCosSIFIECTS623512		Part 2 of the IEC 62351 series covers the key terms used in the series, including references to original definitions of cyber security terms and communications terms. The glossary can be found on the IEC website at: http://std.iec.ch/terms/terms.nsf/ByPub b?OpenView&Count=1&RestrictToC ategory=IEC%2062351-2	Y	Cybersecurity
63	IEC 62351-3 CoS:		Part 3 of the IEC 62351 series provides technical specifications on ensuring the confidentiality, tamper	Y	Cybersecurity

#	Standard	Application	Comments	Included in SGIP Catalog of Standards?[111]	SG Conceptual Architecture Domains
	http://collaborate.nist.gov/twiki-sggrid/bin/view/SmartGrid/SGIPCosSIFIECTS623513		detection, and message level authentication for SCADA and other telecontrol protocols which use TCP/IP as a message transport layer between communicating entities. TCP/IP-based protocols are secured through specification of the messages, procedures, and algorithms of Transport Layer Security (TLS).		
64	IEC 62351-4 CoS: http://collaborate.nist.gov/twiki-sggrid/bin/view/SmartGrid/SGIPCosSIFIECTS623514		Part 4 of the IEC 62351 series provides specifications to secure information transferred when using ISO 9506, Manufacturing Message Specification (MMS)-based applications; specifying which procedures, protocol extensions, and algorithms to use in MMS to provide security.	Y	Cybersecurity
65	IEC 62351-5 CoS: http://collaborate.nist.gov/twiki-sggrid/bin/view/SmartGrid/SGIPCosSIFIECTS623515		Part 5 of the IEC 62351 series specifies messages, procedures, and algorithms that apply to the operation of all protocols based on/derived from IEC 60870-5, Telecontrol equipment and systems-Part 5: Transmission protocols. The focus of this 62351-5 is	Y	Cybersecurity

#	Standard	Application	Comments	Included in SGIP Catalog of Standards?[111]	SG Conceptual Architecture Domains
			on the application layer authentication and security-issues that are a result of application layer authentication. While authentication of sources and receivers is considered the most important requirement and confidentiality is not considered important, encryption can be included by combining this standard with other security standards, such as IEC 62351-3, TLS.		
66	IEC 62351-6 CoS: http://collaborate.nist.gov/twiki-sggrid/bin/view/SmartGrid/SGIP CosSIFIECTS623516		Part 6 of the IEC 62351 series addresses security for IEC 61850 profiles through specification of messages, procedures, and algorithms. IEC 61850 specifies a number of different profiles which have different constraints, performance requirements, and security needs, but the primary requirement is for authentication of sources of data, receivers of data, and data integrity. Therefore, different security options are specified.	Y	Cybersecurity

117

#	Standard	Application	Comments	Included in SGIP Catalog of Standards?[111]	SG Conceptual Architecture Domains
67	IEC 62351-7 CoS: http://collaborate.nist.gov/twiki-sggrid/bin/view/SmartGrid/SGIPCosSIFIECTS623517		Part 7 of the IEC 62351 series provides an abstract model of network and system data elements that should be monitored and controlled. Its focus is network and system management, one area among many possible areas of end-to-end information security. The primary focus is the enhancement of overall management of the communications networks supporting power system operations, by specifying monitoring and control of communication networks and systems. Intrusion detection and intrusion prevention are addressed.	Y	Cybersecurity
68	IEC 62351-8 CoS: http://collaborate.nist.gov/twiki-sggrid/bin/view/SmartGrid/SGIPCosSIFIECTS623518		Part 8 of the IEC 62351 series specifies role-based access control (RBAC) requirements. RBAC is an alternative to the all-or-nothing super user model. RBAC is in keeping with the security principle of least privilege, which states that no subject should be given more rights than necessary for performing that subject's job. RBAC enables an	Y	Cybersecurity

#	Standard	Application	Comments	Included in SGIP Catalog of Standards?[111]	SG Conceptual Architecture Domains
			organization to separate super-user capabilities and package them into special user accounts termed roles for assignment to specific individuals according to their job needs.		
69	IEEE 1686-2007 http://standards.ieee.org/findstds/standard/1686-2007.html	The IEEE 1686-2007 is a standard that defines functions and features to be provided in substation intelligent electronic devices (IEDs) for critical infrastructure protection programs. The standard covers IED security capabilities including the access, operation, configuration, firmware revision, and data retrieval.	Open standard, developed and maintained by an SDO. Not widely implemented yet.	N	Cybersecurity
70	NERC Critical Infrastructure Protection (CIP) 002-009 http://www.nerc.com/page.php?cid=2|20	These standards cover organizational, processes, physical, and cybersecurity standards for the bulk power system.	Mandatory standards for the bulk electric system. Currently being revised by the North American Electric Reliability Corporation (NERC).	N	Cybersecurity
71	NIST Special Publication (SP) 800-53	These standards cover cybersecurity standards and	Open standards developed by NIST. SP 800-53 defines security measures	N	Cybersecurity

#	Standard	Application	Comments	Included in SGIP Catalog of Standards?[111]	SG Conceptual Architecture Domains
	http://dx.doi.org/10.6028/NIST.SP.800-53r4, NIST SP 800-82	guidelines for federal information systems, including those for the bulk power system.	required for all U.S. government computers. SP800-82 defines security specifically for industrial control systems, including the power grid.		
72	NISTIR 7628 Introduction to NISTIR 7628 Guidelines for Smart Grid Cyber Security http://csrc.nist.gov/publications/nistir7628/introduction-to-nistir-7628.pdf http://collaborate.nist.gov/twiki-sggrid/bin/view/SmartGrid/SGIPCosSIFNISTIR7628 Vol 1 http://csrc.nist.gov/publications/nistir/ir7628/nistir-7628_vol1.pdf Vol 2 http://csrc.nist.gov/publications/nistir/ir7628/nistir-7628_vol2.pdf Vol 3	A guideline that is the following: • An overview of the cybersecurity strategy used by the CSWG to develop the high-level cybersecurity smart grid requirements; • A tool for organizations that are researching, designing, developing, implementing, and integrating smart grid technologies—established and emerging; • An evaluative framework for assessing risks to smart grid components and systems during design, implementation, operation, and maintenance; and	A guideline published by NIST in 2010. It was developed through a participatory public process that, starting in March 2009, included several workshops as well as weekly teleconferences, all of which were open to all interested parties. There were two public reviews of drafts of the report, both announced through notices in the *Federal Register*. The guidelines are not prescriptive, nor mandatory. Rather they are advisory, intended to facilitate each organization's efforts to develop a cybersecurity strategy effectively focused on prevention, detection, response, and recovery.	Y	Cybersecurity

120

#	Standard	Application	Comments	Included in SGIP Catalog of Standards?[111]	SG Conceptual Architecture Domains
	http://csrc.nist.gov/publications/nistir7628/nistir-7628_vol3.pdf This is the reference document for the CSWG reviews	• A guide to assist organizations as they craft a smart grid cybersecurity strategy that includes requirements to mitigate risks and privacy issues pertaining to smart grid customers and uses of their data.			

4.4. Process for Future Smart Grid Standards Identification

In all, hundreds of standards, including the many parts in the families of standards, will likely be required to build a safe and secure smart grid that is interoperable, end to end. Useful, widely accepted criteria and guidelines will aid identification and selection of standards. Clearly, any set of guidelines and processes for evaluating candidate standards will have to evolve as the smart grid is developed, new needs and priorities are identified, and new technologies emerge.

The future NIST smart grid standard identification process will be carried out through work with various SGIP committees, working groups, and PAPs, as well as with Interoperability Testing and Certification Authorities. The SGIP will serve as the forum to further develop and improve the standard identification process for smart grid standards. From its inception, the SGIP has incorporated the cybersecurity and architectural reviews into the standard-assessment and PAP-activity-assessment processes. Moving forward, standard conformance and interoperability testing results will also provide feedback to the standard identification process.

All existing and new standards identified as supporting smart grid interoperability are required to undergo a thorough cybersecurity review as part of the current and future standard identification process. Results of future reviews will be available to SGIP members on their SGCC website. As described in Section 3.5, the SGIP has established the process for adopting and adding standards to the SGIP CoS. As standards are reviewed and added to the CoS, NIST will consider adding these standards to Table 4-1. New candidate standards that emerge through the ongoing work of the SGIP and its various working groups, and others, will be considered for addition to this Table after NIST has applied an additional analysis based on the guiding principles given in Section 4.1.

5.   Architectural Framework

5.1.   Introduction

The smart grid is a complex system of systems, serving the diverse needs of many stakeholders. It must support:

- Devices and systems developed independently by many different solution providers
- Many different utilities
- Millions of industrial, business, and residential customers
- Different regulatory environments

Moreover, these systems that must work together are not just across smart grid's technical domains but across stakeholder communities in enterprises not part of the existing utility industry. Achieving interoperability in such a massively scaled, distributed system requires architectural guidance, which is provided by the smart grid architectural model (SGAM) described in this chapter.

The power industry, like other industries that increasingly depend on automation to function, developed different architectural and system engineering approaches to translate stakeholders' business goals into implementations that performed as desired, mitigating risk and minimizing cost overruns. These efforts lead to a consensus that an architectural process employing the concept of discrete levels of abstraction layers and stakeholder viewpoints provides the flexibility needed to address smart grid's new demands while keeping the existing infrastructure running undisturbed.

The SGAM is a template for architects to follow while building aspects of a smart grid architecture, regardless of an architect's specialty (such as in areas of transmission, distribution, IT, back office, communications, asset management, and grid planning).

The SGAM utilizes an enterprise-wide, service-oriented approach to describe a smart grid architecture. This enterprise architecture approach mitigates stranded costs typically experienced in "one-off" siloed solutions. Those siloed solutions are usually developed and implemented without regard to cross-business unit impact or enterprise-wide long-term goals. A service-oriented approach, on the other hand, minimizes the expense, configuration, and management complexity that built-to-purpose applications often experience.

The architectural framework provided by SGAM will be used for several important purposes:

- To provide stakeholders a common understanding of the elements that make up the smart grid and their relationships
- To provide key stakeholder communities traceability between the functions and the goals of the smart grid

- To provide a series of high-level and strategic views of the envisioned business and technical services, supporting systems, and procedures

- To provide a technical pathway to the integration of systems across domains, companies, and businesses

- To guide the various implementation architectures, systems, organizational structures and supporting standards that make up the smart grid

The architectural framework described in this chapter includes the following:

- Architectural goals for the smart grid (Section 5.2)

- Conceptual Architecture, which comprises the conceptual domain models used to define smart grid viewpoints (Section 5.3.1)

- Smart grid architecture methodology (Section 5.3.2)

- Legacy system logical model, which illustrates where existing utility systems fit in the smart grid conceptual domain model (Section 5.3.2)

- Smart grid information networks (Section 5.3.3)

- Conceptual Business Services (Section 5.5.1)

Other important, architecture-related topics discussed in this chapter include the following:

- Use cases (Section 5.4)

- Standards review by the Smart Grid Architecture Committee (SGAC) (Section 5.5.3)

- Legacy integration and legacy migration (Section 5.3.3)

- Common understanding of information (Section 5.5.3)

5.2. Architectural Goals for the Smart Grid

Fundamental architectural goals for the smart grid include:

- **Options** – Architectures should support a broad range of technology options—both legacy and new. Architectures should be flexible enough to incorporate evolving technologies as well as to work with legacy applications and devices in a standard way, avoiding as much additional capital investment and/or customization as possible.

- **Interoperability** – Architectures should support standard interfaces with other systems and manual processes if a standard exists. This includes interoperability among third-party products and management and cybersecurity infrastructures.

- **Maintainability** – Architectures should support the ability of systems to be safely, securely, and reliably maintained throughout their life cycle.

- **Upgradeability** – Architectures should support the ability of systems to be enhanced without difficulty and to remain operational during periods of partial system upgrades.

- **Innovation** – Architectures should enable and foster innovation. This includes the ability to accommodate innovation in regulations and policies; business processes and procedures; information processing; technical communications; and integration of new and innovative energy systems.

- **Scalability** – Architectures should include architectural elements that are appropriate for the applications that reside within them. The architectures must support development of massively scaled, well-managed, and secure systems with life spans appropriate for the type of system, which range from 5 to 30 years.

- **Legacy** – Architectures should support legacy system integration and migration.

- **Security** – Architectures should support the capability to resist un-vetted/unauthorized intrusion, access, or use of physical and cyber assets. This support must satisfy all security requirements of the system components. (This is covered in more detail in Chapter 6.)

- **Flexibility** – Architectures should allow an implementer to choose the type and order of implementation. Flexibility also allows parts of an implementation to deviate from the original plan without incurring a penalty.

- **Governance** – Architectures should promote a well-managed system of systems that will be enabled through consistent policies over its continuing design and operation for its entire life cycle.

- **Affordability** – Architectures should fundamentally enable capital savings as well as life cycle savings through standards-based operations and maintenance. They must enable multi-vendor procurement of interoperable smart grid equipment through the development of mature national and international markets.

5.3. Smart Grid Architecture Model

5.3.1. Overview – Conceptual Domain Model

The conceptual domain model presented in this chapter supports planning, requirements development, documentation, and organization of the diverse, expanding collection of interconnected networks and equipment that will compose the smart grid. For this purpose, NIST adopted the approach of dividing the smart grid into seven domains, as described in Table 5-1 and shown graphically in Figure 5-1.

Each domain—and its sub-domains—encompass smart grid conceptual *roles* and *services.* They include types of services, interactions, and stakeholders that make decisions and exchange information necessary for performing identified goals, such as: customer management, distributed generation aggregation, and outage management. Services are performed by one or more roles within a domain. For example, corresponding services may include home automation, distributed energy resource (DER) and customer demand response, load control and near real-time wide-area situation awareness (WASA).

The *roles*, *services*, and *requirements* that enable the functionality of the smart grid are described in various architectural artifacts and at lower levels of architecture by standardized *business* and *use cases,* which detail specific envisioned smart grid requirements.

Appendix B (Specific Domain Diagrams) describes the seven smart grid domains in more detail. It contains domain-specific diagrams intended to illustrate the type and scope of interactions within and across domains.

Table 5-1. Domains and Roles/Services in the Smart Grid Conceptual Model

	Domain	Roles/Services in the Domain
1	Customer	The end users of electricity. May also generate, store, and manage the use of energy. Traditionally, three customer types are discussed, each with its own domain: residential, commercial, and industrial.
2	Markets	The operators and participants in electricity markets.
3	Service Provider	The organizations providing services to electrical customers and to utilities.
4	Operations	The managers of the movement of electricity.
5	Generation	The generators of electricity. May also store energy for later distribution. This domain includes traditional generation sources (traditionally referred to as generation) and distributed energy resources (DER). At a logical level, "generation" includes coal, nuclear, and large-scale hydro generation usually attached to transmission. DER (at a logical level) is associated with customer- and distribution-domain-provided generation and storage, and with service-provider-aggregated energy resources.
6	Transmission	The carriers of bulk electricity over long distances. May also store and generate electricity.
7	Distribution	The distributors of electricity to and from customers. May also store and generate electricity.

In general, roles in the same domain have similar objectives. However, communications within the same domain may have different characteristics and may have to meet different requirements to achieve interoperability.

To enable smart grid functionality, the roles in a particular domain often interact with roles in other domains, as shown in Figure 5.1. Moreover, particular domains may also contain components of other domains. For example, the Independent System Operators (ISOs) and Regional Transmission Organizations (RTOs) in North America have roles in both the markets and operations domains. Similarly, a distribution utility is not entirely contained within the distribution domain—it is likely to contain roles in the operations domain, such as a distribution management, and in the customer domain, such as monitoring. On the other hand, a vertically integrated utility may have roles in many domains.

Underlying the Conceptual Model is a legal and regulatory framework that enables the implementation and management of consistent policies and requirements that apply to various actors and applications and to their interactions. Regulations, adopted by the Federal Energy Regulatory Commission (FERC) at the federal level and by public utility commissions at the state and local levels, govern many aspects, including policy implementations of the smart grid. Such regulations are intended to ensure that electric rates are fair and reasonable and that security, reliability, safety, privacy, and other public policy requirements are met.[113]

The transition to the smart grid introduces new regulatory considerations, which may transcend jurisdictional boundaries and require increased coordination among federal, state, and local lawmakers and regulators. The conceptual model is intended to be a useful tool for regulators at all levels to assess how best to achieve public policy goals that, along with business objectives, motivate investments in modernizing the nation's electric power infrastructure and building a clean energy economy. Therefore, the conceptual model must be consistent with the legal and regulatory framework and support its evolution over time. Similarly, the standards and protocols identified in the framework must align with existing and emerging regulatory objectives and responsibilities.

---

[113] See, for example, the mission statements of the National Association of Regulatory Utility Commissioners (NARUC, http://www.naruc.org/about.cfm) and FERC (http://www.ferc.gov/about/about.asp)

Conceptual Model

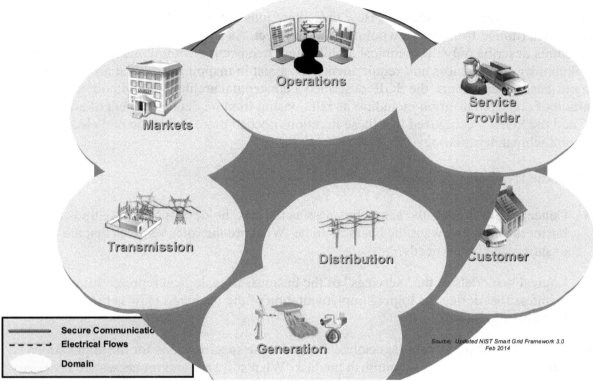

Figure 5-1. Interaction of Roles in Different Smart Grid Domains through Secure Communication

5.3.2. Description of Smart Grid Architecture Model (SGAM)

The SGAM utilizes several information and communications technology (ICT) architecture standards. Any mention of commercial products within this NIST document is for information only; it does not imply recommendation or endorsement by NIST. References to specific standards are given to provide additional documentation.

The SGAM is an evolving framework, and NIST is working through the SGIP's Smart Grid Architecture Committee (SGAC) to align this effort with the European Union Smart Grid-Coordination Group (SG-CG), the International Electrotechnical Commission (IEC) TC57 WG19 (IEC 62357), and IEC TC8 WG5 and 6 (Use cases).

128

5.3.3. Architecture Process - Evolution of the Conceptual Architecture to SGAM

SGAM iterations

Architecture is an iterative endeavor. How these iterations are accomplished, however, is generally determined from the viewpoint of the architect. As a result, many smart grid architectures describe only the technical architectural perspective without mapping them back to the stakeholder and business unit requirements. To assist in mapping technical architectures to those business requirements, the SGIP described a conceptual architecture without a crisp definition of conceptualization including its relationship to more detailed layers of architecture. NIST and the SGAC recognized that these iterations needed more definition and elected to leverage Zachman terminology.[114]

Briefly, these levels are:

- Conceptual -- models the actual business as the stakeholder conceptually thinks the business is, or may want the business to be. What are the roles/services that are required to satisfy the future needs?

- Logical -- models of the "services" of the business uses, logical representations of the business that define the logical implementation of the business. How is the architecture (ideally) structured?

- Physical -- where systems specialize. They are the specifications for the applications and personnel necessary to accomplish the task. What software and processes are necessary?

- Implementation -- software product, personnel, and discrete procedures selected to perform the actual work.

As of this publication, TC57 WG19's IEC 62357 and EU SC-CG methodology groups' smart grid architectures are aligning on the use of this approach.

SGAM Layers

The SGAC decomposed the conceptual domain model in Figure 5-1 into layers of increasing technical focus to understand how various smart grid requirements are satisfied within each interaction of architecture. Originally, the concept of layers as defined by the GridWise Architecture Council (GWAC) interoperability stack (see Figure 2-2) was cited and used by the EU M490 reference architecture. As part of the SGAC's alignment activities, The Open Group's Architecture Framework (TOGAF)[115] was adopted for guidance to re-align these layers to a broader architecture standard. This doesn't mean that the original GWAC stack or EU M490

---

[114] Zachman International: <u>Conceptual Logical Physical: It is Simple</u>
(see http://www.zachman.com/ea-articles-reference/58-conceptual-logical-physical-it-is-simple-by-john-a-zachman)

[115] The Open Group Architecture Framework – Architecture Development Methodology:
http://pubs.opengroup.org/architecture/togaf9-doc/arch/

layers aren't addressed, but rather they are redefined as sub-layers that are already part of the broader architecture framework shown in Figure 5-2.

GWAC & SGAM Alignment with TOGAF

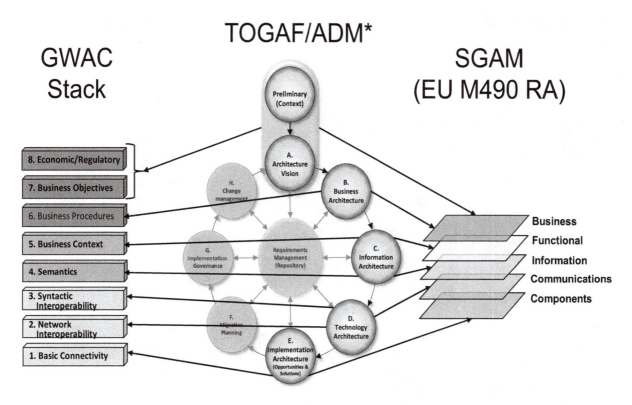

* The Open Group Architecture Framework – Architecture Development Methodology (TOGAF/ADM)

Figure 5-2. SGAC and SGAM Alignment with TOGAF ADM

Alignment of the GWAC stack and EU M490 RA (reference architecture) efforts with more mainstream enterprise architecture standards (TOGAF) helps to connect different work efforts and to embed smart grid requirements within existing frameworks.

Architecture matrix

Combining the practice of iterations and architectural focus, an architect can understand the relationship and impact of a decision in one segment upon another. The matrix in Figure 5-3 describes what decisions are made each step of the way and illustrates where decisions at one step may impact an adjacent decision. This process is started by defining the stakeholders' requirements and goals; this is the context from which all subsequent architecture decisions are made. Context is not set by technology, although technology may have an influence on stakeholders' goals. Context identifies those organizations most affected and which receive the most value from the work. Context also allows other organizations to see where change may affect their capacity and work. Each block in the architecture matrix briefly describes the goals of that block and its subsequent step, and it suggests interaction and iteration across layers and levels based upon decisions that were made at a higher level.

Architecture layers and iteration levels

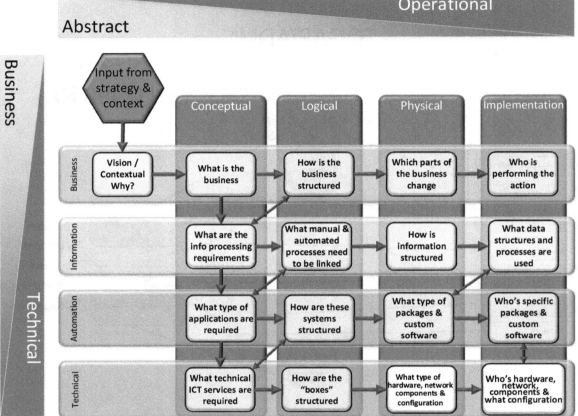

Fig 5-3. Architecture Layers and Iteration Levels

SGAM Plane

Each level of architecture (conceptual, logical, physical, and implementation) can be represented as a plane (Figure 5-4) in which the original smart grid domain model is decomposed into domains and zones. "Zones" is a new concept introduced in this document; zones illustrate the physical and management aspects of the grid. The notion of zones is derived from IEC62264[116] manufacturing process interfaces. Zones describe the process hierarchy from the power system through the various entities that participate in the production, transmission, and consumption of electricity. The domains roughly correspond to NIST Conceptual Domains. The details for domains and zones for each component layer depend on the level of architecture.

---

[116] Enterprise control system integration "Purdue Reference Architecture CIM for manufacturing": https://webstore.iec.ch/webstore/webstore.nsf/mysearchajax?Openform&key=iec%2062264&sorting=&start=1&onglet=1

electricity. The domains roughly correspond to NIST Conceptual Domains. The details for domains and zones for each component layer depend on the level of architecture.

Details for each plane are still under discussion and development. However, Figure 5-4 depicts the proposed detail for each plane. In this diagram, for each plane, "domains" is the horizontal axis and "zones" is the vertical axis.

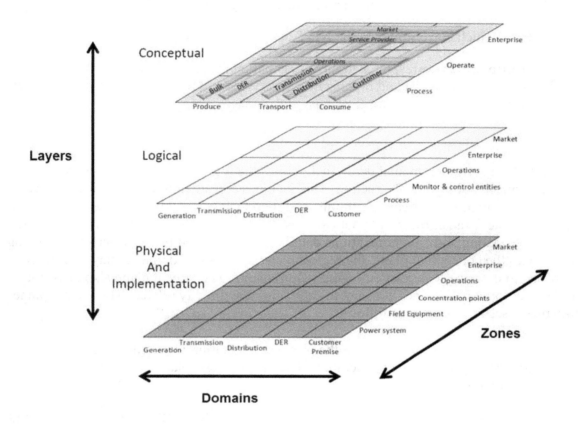

Figure 5-4. Architecture Layers and Iteration Levels

Conceptual Plane

The conceptual plane aligns with the seven domains in the NIST conceptual domain model. At this level of abstraction, emphasis is focused on broad issues, and these broad issues are addressed with organizational entities, roles, and services performed. Additionally, while blocks within a plane can be decomposed further into the power industry's traditional business units, it does not prescribe that domains or zones adjacent to each other are directly related. The conceptual plane's electrical grid domain processes are grouped as follows:

- Produce, which today decomposes into bulk generation and distributed energy resources (DER)

- Transport, which today decomposes into NIST conceptual transmission and distribution domains

132

The conceptual plane is also grouped by a hierarchy called zones. Each zone describes the increased specialization of purpose. These zones are as follows:

- Process is an abstraction of physical grid, which includes the physical, chemical, or spatial transformation of energy. This zone is a new entity in order to represent the physical domain of the power infrastructure through its entire chain.

- Operate, which corresponds to the NIST operations domain

- Enterprise, which corresponds to the NIST market and service provider domains. These include the commercial and organizational services and roles needed to manage any support service necessary for the smart grid environment.

Logical Plane

The logical plane adds incremental detail that defines the logical services and actors necessary to support the conceptual layer's abstraction. This includes considerations for business processes, organizational structure, physical constraints, and monitoring/control. At this layer, roles and services begin their transformation to actors. This encompasses the 2012 EU M.490 SGAM[117] layers for information and communications detail, which are considered sub-layers of the logical plane. As with the conceptual plane, the logical plane's zones and domains may be further decomposed to describe legacy or emerging requirements. The logical plane also does not prescribe that domains or zones adjacent to each other are directly related. The logical plane's domain processes are grouped as follows:

- Generation, which translates into the physical generation requirements unique to transmission-grid-attached generation. They are closely related to generation facilities that create power in bulk quantities.

- Transmission, which represents the physical and locational attributes involved in high-voltage transmission. They are closely related to transporting electricity at high voltages over long distances.

- Distribution, which represents the local grid that directly servers customers. Currently, this is directly related to the low-voltage distribution.

- DER, which is an emerging domain (i.e., the types, use, and deployment of distributed energy resources are evolving). These DER may be directly controlled by the customer (e.g., in situations where they elect to participate or opt-out of DER signals); by operations for safety and contracted dispatch; or by service providers (via the market). This domain is also necessary to understand microgrids.

- Customer, which is the end user of the electrical process. End users may consume and produce electricity for premise use or resale. As an electricity producer, they are also

---

[117] EU Commission Mandate M.490:
http://ec.europa.eu/energy/gas_electricity/smartgrids/doc/xpert_group1_reference_architecture.pdf

members of the DER domain when the electricity produced is sold. Customers include residential, commercial, and industrial facilities.

The logical management zones decompose into logical abstractions of the conceptual roles and services. These are not product-level descriptions but rather logical representations of the services, roles, and actors necessary to support the conceptual stakeholder view of roles and services. These are categorized into the following:

- Process is a logical abstraction of physical grid. This includes the physical, chemical or spatial transformation of energy.

- Monitor and control entities are generic logical descriptions of the type of devices needed to monitor and control the electrical process.

- Operations are the logical representations of the conceptual processes and services necessary to coordinate the electrical process from generation through customer.

- Enterprise provides logical abstractions of the conceptual support services (non-operations).

- Market is the market necessary to purchase and sell adequate energy-related services to support cost-effective, necessary operations of the grid

Physical Plane

The physical plane completes the transition from services to actors. This plane describes specific descriptions of human, automated (i.e., devices, systems, communications networks, ICT), and locational attributes necessary to perform the desired requirements inherited from the logical plane level. The physical plane provides sufficient detail to select solution-provider products or custom development and to organize a specific business unit's resources.

The physical plane repeats most of the logical plane, but it further decomposes two operations and monitor & control actors into three more detailed locational zones: operations, field equipment, and concentration points. ("Concentration points" roughly corresponds to "substation" in the EU M490 RA, but "substation" was determined to be too prescriptive and did not allow for future options.)

Implementation Plane

The implementation plane documents the applications and equipment purchased, the topography employed, and the personnel assigned to the tasks. In short, it is the physical instantiation of the goals originally described by the business and regulatory stakeholders.

Because the implementation plane is unique to each enterprise, the SGAM does not delve into its details. At this point, other industry practices take over; they include the subsequent phases covering the rest of the architecture's lifecycle. Combining iterations and planes, the entire cycle flows are shown in Figure 5-5.

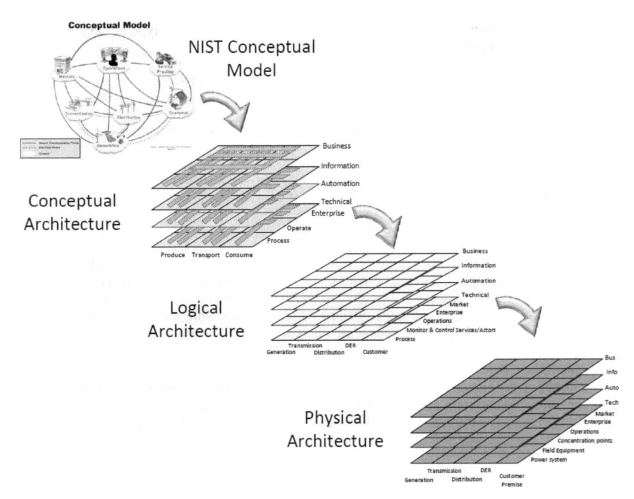

Figure 5-5. SGAM Iterations, Layers, and Planes

NIST Conceptual Architecture

The intent of the NIST conceptual architecture is to provide grid participants with sufficient foundational architecture building blocks to accelerate and support development of their own internal architectures.

Generally, a conceptual architecture defines abstract roles and services necessary to support smart grid requirements without delving into application details or interface specifications. It identifies key constructs, their relationships, and architectural mechanisms. Architectural mechanisms are designed to address cross-cutting concerns, such as those not localized within a single role. The resulting conceptual architecture can be used as a vehicle to communicate to technical and non-technical audiences a role's decomposition in terms of its domain-level responsibilities. The required inputs necessary to define a conceptual architecture are the organization's goals and requirements.

This NIST conceptual architecture further decomposed the conceptual domain model in to the architecture matrix. It was developed through a process of face-to-face and webinar workshops attended by industry experts and conducted by the SGAC starting in spring 2010. The final artifact was completed in fall 2012.[118] This work is continuing in the Architecture Development Working Party (ADWP), which is incorporating and refining the definition of these artifacts into the SGAM process.

The process used to define the conceptual architecture was based on five key tasks:

- Develop a list of smart grid architecture goals from national energy goals and national policy documents

- Develop a formalized list of requirements relating and mapping to each of the accepted grid architecture goals

- Develop a list of business services based on the list of accepted requirements

- Develop a list of corresponding automation services required to support the business services

- Develop archetypical interaction diagrams defining the type of messages and roles/services required for the automation services to function

Additionally, a list of use-case actors was built using input from numerous standards organizations. The SGAC expanded this actors list to include actors from the EU SG-CG Methodology effort. This list was then refined using the SGAM and service-oriented ontology. The resulting list identifies if the contributed actor is an actor, role, or service. Additionally, it identifies the SGAC-identified architecture block for which this entity exists (i.e., conceptual,

---

[118] The NIST conceptual architecture is now documented in the continuing work of the Architecture Development Working Party (ADWP): http://collaborate.nist.gov/twiki-sggrid/bin/view/SmartGrid/SGIPConceptualArchitectureDevelopmentSGAC

logical, physical) and for which plane. Using the architecture matrix, Figure 5-6 depicts the areas of the smart grid for which the conceptual architecture artifacts were created.

NIST Conceptual Architecture mapping to Matrix

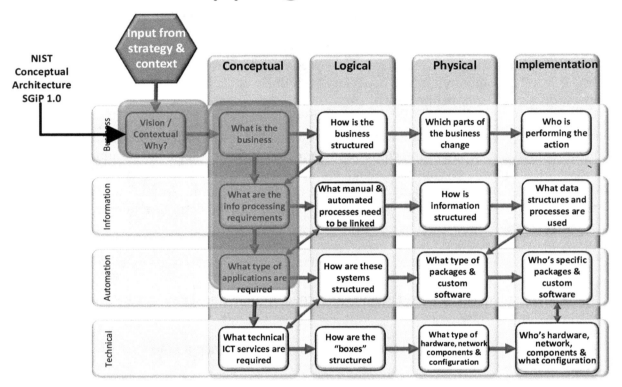

Figure 5-6. NIST Conceptual Architecture Mapped onto the Architecture Matrix Service Orientation and Ontology

One of the largest challenges in architecture is to clarify terminology and constructs used to describe the smart grid. There exist vast and numerous repositories of knowledge, defining siloed perspectives, but unfortunately none of them have been submitted to the exercise of ontological definition as regards architectural and industry alignment.

One of the core tenants of contemporary architecture design is service orientation. Service orientation is specifically intended to modularize work into atomic services that model the interoperation of different parts of a business. By applying this approach, it is possible to limit the impact of changes as they occur and to understand in advance the likely chain of impacts a change brings to the organization.

To a limited extent, this service-oriented approach is embraced in current use-case practice and documented in IEC PAS 62559 IntelliGrid Methodology, in which actors are described as black boxes. In early 2013, the SGAC's Semantic Development Working Party (SDWP) agreed to defer work until these core issues are identified. It was agreed that bridging or even accurately mapping canonical domain models proved to be a difficult task, because the underlying ontological models were not defined.

To solve this problem, the SGAC's Architecture Development Working Party (ADWP) elected to embrace a service-oriented ontology[119] as defined by The Open Group.[120] Thus far, the SGAC has examined ontology itself, and a few areas were found to be misleading. The group has strived to minimize changes from the standard's specification while also embracing a few terms missing from the reference standard. The ADWP work started with the conceptual architecture actors list gleaned from several sources. It has grown to include lists from other standard bodies, as well as the architecture concepts discussed earlier in this document. The full ontology can be found in Appendix C.

5.3.4. Description of Legacy Logical Application Types within the Context of the Conceptual Domains

The viewpoint described here provides a high-level, overarching logical architecture representation of a few major relationships that existing applications have to smart grid domains. This diagram is also a useful tool in identifying which existing applications may be a good candidate for a smart grid role, it also suggests what their possible communications paths could be in a smart grid. It is also a useful way to identify potential intra- and inter-domain interactions between existing and new applications, along with capabilities enabled by these interactions. The model represented in Figure 5-7 is intended to aid in analysis by providing a view of the types of interactions that existing applications may play while providing core smart grid services; it is ***not*** a design diagram or recommended reference architecture that defines a solution and its implementation. Architecture documentation goes much deeper than what is illustrated here and is covered by the SGAM. It does not specify application selection or implementation detail. In other words, this model is descriptive and not prescriptive. It is meant to foster understanding of smart grid operational intricacies within the context of existing applications commonly used in the power industry today.

---

[119] The Open Group service-oriented architecture ontology: http://www.opengroup.org/soa/source-book/ontology/

[120] Any mention of commercial products within NIST documents is for information only; it does not imply recommendation or endorsement by NIST. The use of a specific standard is only to provide referenceability and consistency within this document.

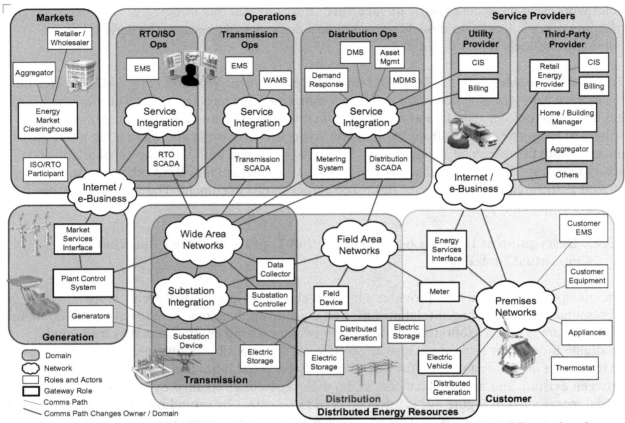

Figure 5-7. Logical Model of Legacy Systems Mapped onto Conceptual Domains for Smart Grid Information Networks

Domain: Each of the seven smart grid conceptual domains (Figure 5-1 and Table 5-1) is a high-level grouping of physical organizations, buildings, individuals, systems, devices, or other actors that have similar objectives and that rely on—or participate in—similar types of services. Communications among roles and services in the same domain may have similar characteristics and requirements. Domains contain sub-domains. Moreover, domains have many overlapping functionalities, as in the case of the Transmission and Distribution domains. Because transmission and distribution often share networks, they are represented as overlapping domains.

Actor: Actors exist primarily in the physical and implementation architectures. They include devices, computer systems, software applications, or the individuals within an organization that participates in the smart grid. Actors perform roles to make decisions and to exchange information with other roles. Organizations may have roles and use services and ultimately actors in more than one domain. The actors illustrated here are representative examples of existing logical services, application, and device types but are by no means an inclusive smart grid list.

Information Network: An information network is a collection, or aggregation, of interconnected computers, communication devices, and other information and communication technologies that exchange information and share resources. The smart grid consists of many different types of networks, not all of which are shown in the diagram. The networks include: a Service Integration capability that connects applications within a domain and to other domains with which it shares information; Wide Area Networks that connect geographically distant sites; Field Area Networks that connect devices, such as intelligent electronic devices (IEDs) that control circuit breakers and transformers; and Premises Networks that include customer networks, as well as utility networks within the customer domain. These networks may be implemented using a combination of public (e.g., the Internet) and nonpublic networks. Both public and nonpublic networks will require implementation and maintenance of appropriate security and access control to support the smart grid. Examples of where communications may go through the public networks include: customers to third-party providers; generation to grid operators; markets to grid operators; and third-party providers to utilities.

Communications Path: The communications path shows the logical exchange of data between actors, services, and roles or between them and networks. Secure communications are not explicitly shown in the figure and are addressed in more detail in Chapter 6.

5.4. Use Cases

Use cases are an accepted methodology that can be used to understand how new capabilities may be delivered and are an important part of the architectural process. Many of them are proprietary to a commercial enterprise or limited to members of standards organizations. The largest collection of publicly available use cases are found in the Smart Grid Information Center's (SGIC) National Repository. [121]

Smart grid use cases are typically developed for two audiences—engineering/ICT stakeholders or business stakeholders.

- Although use cases exist at all levels of architecture in the power industry, most use cases that have an engineering perspective are often "fine toothed," because they were developed to understand—at a physical or implementation layer—how a narrowly defined requirement can be accomplished.

- Use cases that represent the business perspective are usually referred to as business cases. Business cases have a similar structure, but the viewpoint deals with broader issues regarding organizational structure, economic impact, stakeholder goals, and regulatory requirements.

There are far fewer publicly available business cases, compared to the number of engineering/ICT use cases, because most business cases are specific to the core mission of a commercial entity.

In both engineering/ICT use cases and business cases, current practice does not include the concept of architectural levels of abstraction. As a result, terms quite often take on different meanings depending on the perspective of the use-case developer. This can lead to

---

[121] Smart Grid Information Clearinghouse: see http://www.sgiclearinghouse.org/

misinterpretation when another group reuses a specific term without understanding the original intent of the term. Architecturally, from a conceptual and logical layer perspective, use cases describe the interaction between a smart grid role or service where the role uses one or more services to accomplish a specified goal. At the logical, physical, and implementation layers, services map increasingly to actors that perform the tasks requested. This is a shift from an actor-centric approach that applies the concept of levels of architecture and uses service orientation to maximize architecture flexibility.

A use case describes the interactions between entities. Use cases are usually classified as "black box" or "white box." In a service-oriented model, black-box services describe the functional requirements, including services interaction, process, and the quality attributes (also commonly referred to as non-functional) requirements to achieve the goal, but they leave the details of the inner workings of the system to the implementer. Black-box services are "descriptive." The conceptual reference model provides a useful tool for constructing these sorts of use cases. In contrast, white-box use-case services exist at the physical and implementation level of architecture. They describe the internal details of a process, application, or component, in addition to the interaction and associated requirements. White-box services are "prescriptive," because they do not allow the implementer to change the internal system design. They are useful in specifying solution specifications.

For this interoperability standards framework and roadmap, the focus is on the black-box services and their associated use cases that describe how abstracted systems within the smart grid interact. Because white-box component specifications, which describe the individual components of a particular solution, are prescriptive, they are not covered by the framework. The focus on black-box service descriptions allows maximum innovation and flexibility in specific smart grid use cases, ensuring their ready deployment and interoperability within the smart grid as it evolves.

Individually and collectively, use cases are helpful for scoping out interoperability requirements at lower levels of architectural focus for specific areas of functionality—such as on-premises energy management or predictive maintenance for grid equipment. When viewed from a variety of stakeholder perspectives and application domains, combining the roles and interactions from multiple use cases using existing roles permits the smart grid to be rendered as a collection of transactional relationships that allow possible re-use of legacy applications, within and across domains, as illustrated in Figure 5-2.

Many requirement-specific smart grid intra- and inter-domain use cases exist, and the number is growing substantially. The scope of the body of existing use cases also includes cross-cutting requirements, including cybersecurity, network management, data management, and application integration, as described in the *GridWise Architecture Council Interoperability Context-Setting Framework* (GWAC Stack).[122] See Section 2.5 for further discussion of the layers of interoperability and "GWAC stack" discussed in this document. See Section 5.3 above for discussion of the integration of the GWAC Stack into the SGAM.

---

[122] The GridWise Architecture Council. (2008, March). GridWise™ Interoperability Context-Setting Framework http://www.gridwiseac.org/pdfs/interopframework_v1_1.pdf

Workshops have begun by the IEC Task Group 8 Working Parties 5 and 6[123] to formalize the use case methodology using the IntelliGrid framework and SGAM as a basis. The goal is to provide stakeholders with a normalized use case repository of architecturally significant use cases and assist in the development of evolving standards' requirements.

Detailed use cases can be found on the NIST Smart Grid Collaboration Site.[124] The use cases include the SGCC's use cases in priority and supplemental areas.

5.5. Ongoing Work of the Smart Grid Architecture Committee (SGAC)

The preceding sections of this chapter, Sections 5.2 – 5.4, provide updated versions of architecture-related material included in Framework 1.0 and Framework 2.0. Since the publication of those earlier documents, the SGAC has identified additional issues requiring attention. For the newly identified issues, SGAC subgroups, called Working Parties, have been established; some deliverables have been published; and much work is in process. The subsections below—and the collaborative web pages listed here as references—provide a snapshot of the current status of SGAC activities as of October 2013.

5.5.1. Conceptual Business Services

The SGAC created a set of conceptual business services for the smart grid. The Open Group, an organization that promotes the development of open, vendor-neutral standards and certification,[125] defines a "business service" as a unit of business capability supported by a combination of people, process, and technology.[126] The SGAC used The Open Group's Architecture Framework (TOGAF) as a methodology for its work.
The output of the activity includes:

- An analysis of U.S. legislation and regulations pertaining to improving the grid

- An analysis of goals, called goal decomposition, relating the high-level goals into lower business-level goals

- A review of the use cases and requirements created by the smart grid community

- A set of conceptual services, or building blocks, that support these requirements.

---

[123] IEC TC8 Working Group 6, system aspects for electric energy supply: http://www.iec.ch/dyn/www/f?p=103:14:0::::FSP_ORG_ID,FSP_LANG_ID:9555,25

[124] NIST Smart Grid Collaboration Site. IKB Use Cases http://collaborate.nist.gov/twiki-sggrid/bin/view/SmartGrid/IKBUseCases

[125] See http://www3.opengroup.org/

[126] See http://pubs.opengroup.org/architecture/togaf9-doc/arch/chap22.html

The following bullets describe the building blocks that will be used by the SGIP:

- Map SDOs' standards efforts to the overall smart grid "ecosystem." This mapping will help determine the location of gaps in the standards under development and also help determine where there are gaps in existing standards.

- Use the business services within the DEWGs to create prototype models by combining several business services. The Business and Policy Group is using them, for example, to develop a "prices to devices" white paper that will allow prices to be directly sent from wholesale markets to end devices.

- Compare the coverage of one smart grid architecture to the SGIP architecture framework and to the coverage of other smart grid architectures.

The Conceptual Architecture Development Working Party has been established to lead the SGAC's work in this area, and the outputs are published on its collaborative web page.[127]

5.5.2. Architecture Development Working Party

This sub-group's current work efforts are focused on clearly defining the architecture process by defining the types of architecture and their relationship to one another; providing ontological clarity to terms used to define new smart grid requirements; mapping these terms to the appropriate use in the SGAM; identifying the mapping between layers of architecture; and working with the EU SC-CG, IE TC 57 WG19, and TC8 WG 5 and 6 for as much alignment and mapping of concepts as possible.

To accomplish this, the sub-group is focused first on the definition of architecture. The portions of that work for which there is a consensus are discussed earlier in this chapter. The portions that are still under discussion are in this section.

The sub-group's second focus has been to work on the ontology to be used for the NIST conceptual architecture actor list. This list is critical because it contains the terms and concepts used to define smart grid functionality. The group defined only as much of the ontology as was necessary to clearly identify the actor. The ontology defined, and traceability to the reference ontology, are described in more detail in Appendix C.

The sub-group's third focus is to begin applying the ontology to the actors list. The actor list is changing as new insights and needs are identified by the ADWP team and by the EU SC-CG team. The original list was composed basically of the actor name, domain in which it resides, description, and information source. The working party changed "actor" to "entity" to reflect the ontological definitions that applied to each actor. By applying its ontological definitions, the team discovered that many of the actors were not only actors but also services, service collections and zones. The actors list may expand as the group continues its work. Additional attributes added at this time are the following:

---

[127] See http://collaborate.nist.gov/twiki-sggrid/bin/view/SmartGrid/SGIPConceptualArchitectureDevelopmentSGAC

- The level of architecture of each entity, specifically, conceptual, logical, physical or implementation

- The domain of each entity ("cross-cutting" was added because several names were required across all domains)

- The zone to identify the hierarchy within the physical domain

- The related role/service/actor, providing mapping across architecture boundaries.

Since the ADWP began this work, the team added the conceptual architectures service definitions and the EU SC-CG team contributed its actors lists. Additionally, discussions have been started with the IEC TC8 WG 5 and 6 to align their charters and to standardize use cases and artifacts necessary to support them. The ADWP plans to incorporate security quality entities and service contract constraints to this list once the entity list review is completed, along with a further analysis of service contract artifacts requirements.

It is expected that when the team begins defining the necessary logical architecture artifacts, that the semantic development working party will re-start their efforts using the ontology to incorporate their canonical domain model efforts.

5.5.3. The SGAC Smart Grid Semantic Framework

When the ADWP's efforts begin identifying what artifacts and process are required for a logical architecture, the need to identify how to integrate semantics to more abstract interaction messages becomes a critical part of the architecture. The previous efforts of the semantic development working party (SDWP) identified the need to define canonical data models but had not addressed the necessary framework or tools to enable it.

There is substantial benefit to promoting coordination and consistency of relevant semantic models within and across domains. The SDWP was established to provide guidance, and to undertake the initial engagement of relevant stakeholders and SDOs in this effort. Planned deliverables, including the following, will be posted to the working party's collaborative web page[128] as they are produced:

- Definitions of semantic concepts and methodologies to support SGAM processes

- Requirements to guide SDOs in the development and coordination of canonical data models (CDMs)

- A "map" showing the overall relationships among domain industry-standard CDMs, and showing which standard exchanges belong to which domains

- Documentation describing where exchanges go across domain boundaries and how harmonization between the domains is established

---

[128] See http://collaborate.nist.gov/twiki-sggrid/bin/view/SmartGrid/SGIPSemanticModelSGAC

144

- Identification of semantic methodologies, procedures, and design principles, along with identified toolsets

- A library of common semantic building blocks

- Semantic alignment scenarios for use by smart grid standards development groups. These scenarios will spell out how the framework can be used to integrate (in the general sense) two or more standards. The group began exploring the use of select standards to further a CDM in Figure 5.8; this activity was tabled until the entity list and SGAM details are defined.

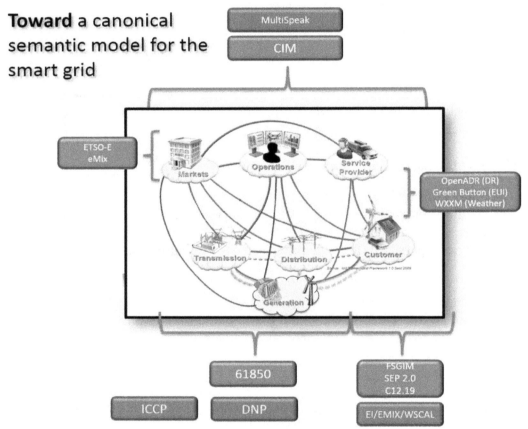

Figure 5-8.   Proposal to Use Select Models for Canonical Data Model

5.5.4. Standards Review by the SGAC

As part of the overall NIST effort to identify standards and protocols that ensure smart grid interoperability, it is important to evaluate and review the architectural elements of each proposed standard. The SGIP's formal process for evaluating standards and adding them to the Catalog of Standards (see Section 4.2 for more details) includes a review by the SGAC. The SGAC continues to review standards based upon the priority assigned by the CoS review queue and tracking tool. To improve the evaluation process, the SGAC developed a standards review checklist.[129] Where needed, the SGAC review teams supplement their reviews with outside subject-matter experts to ensure a standard's architectural nuances are adequately understood and addressed.

---

[129] See http://collaborate.nist.gov/twiki-sggrid/pub/SmartGrid/SGIPDocumentsAndReferencesSGAC/SGAC_PAP_Closeout_Check_list_0v1.doc

6. Cybersecurity Strategy

6.1. Cybersecurity in the Smart Grid

Major elements of the smart grid, in addition to the infrastructure that produces and carries electric power, are the Information Technology (IT), the Industrial Control Systems (ICS), and the communications infrastructure used to send command information across the grid. These elements are also used to exchange usage and billing information between utilities and their customers. It is critical that cybersecurity is designed into the new systems that support the smart grid, and if possible, added into existing systems without impacting operations. The electric grid is fundamental to the economic and physical well-being of the nation, and emerging cyber threats targeting electricity systems highlight the need to integrate advanced security to protect critical assets.

Traditionally, cybersecurity for IT focuses on the protection of information and information systems from unauthorized access, use, disclosure, disruption, modification, or destruction in order to provide confidentiality, integrity, and availability. Cybersecurity for the smart grid requires an expansion of this focus to address the combined IT, ICS, and communication systems, and their integration with physical equipment and resources in order to maintain the reliability and the security of the smart grid and to protect the privacy of consumers. Smart grid cybersecurity must include a balance of both electricity- and cyber-system technologies and processes in IT and in ICS operations and governance. When practices from one sector, such as the IT or communications sector, are applied directly to the electricity sector, care must be taken because such practices may degrade reliability and increase risk. This is because the requirements for the electricity sector, for timing of communications, for example, may be different from the IT and communications sectors. In the electricity sector, the historical focus has been on implementation of equipment that could improve electricity system reliability. Communications and IT equipment were formerly viewed as just supporting electricity system reliability. However, both the communications and IT sectors are becoming more critical to the reliability of the electricity system.

Each of these sectors have existing cybersecurity standards to address vulnerabilities and assessment programs to identify known vulnerabilities in their systems, but these vulnerabilities also need to be assessed in the context of the smart grid infrastructure. Additionally, the smart grid will have additional vulnerabilities not only because of its complexity, but also because of its large number of stakeholders and highly time-sensitive operational requirements. These standards are often developed over a time period of many months, with review cycles averaging every five years to determine if any updates are necessary. As a result, there are many standards that do not include cybersecurity, nor have up-to-date normative references to cybersecurity standards. Through the ongoing efforts of the SGIP Smart Grid Cybersecurity Committee (SGCC), smart grid-relevant standards are being reviewed for cybersecurity, and recommendations are made for how to include cybersecurity in future revisions and how to include cybersecurity in implementations of the standards.

A collaborative effort across all smart grid stakeholders in this space has resulted in tailored guidance, analysis, and tools to advance cybersecurity. Such efforts include collaboration with the Department of Energy to develop the Electricity Subsector Cybersecurity Capability Maturity Model (ES-C2M2) and the Electricity Subsector Cybersecurity Risk Management Process (RMP). Additionally, analysis of existing cybersecurity regulations relevant to electricity subsector stakeholders and NIST security guidance was completed by the SGCC in response to the Federal Energy Regulatory Commission Notice of Public Rulemaking (NOPR) for the North American Electric Reliability Corporation's Version 5 of the Critical Infrastructure Protection Reliability Standards (CIP v5).[130] The analysis intends to identify the relationship, similarities, and differences between requirements and controls in NISTIR 7628, NIST Special Publication (SP) 800-53 and NERC CIP v5, with the understanding that each document has a unique scope and purpose. The work accomplished within the NIST smart grid program can be used as an example of a successful public-private partnership collaborating on facilitating the development and revision of secure, interoperable standards that encompass IT, ICS, and the communications infrastructure.

In addition to the efforts focused on smart grid and electricity subsector cybersecurity, there has also been additional attention to the cybersecurity of all the critical infrastructure sectors. Recognizing that the national and economic security of the United States depends on the reliable functioning of critical infrastructure, the president under the Executive Order "Improving Critical Infrastructure Cybersecurity"[131] has directed NIST to work with stakeholders to develop a voluntary framework for reducing cyber risks to critical infrastructure. The Cybersecurity Framework (CSF)[132], created through collaboration between government and the private sector, uses a common language to address and manage cybersecurity risk in a cost-effective way based on business needs without placing additional regulatory requirements on businesses. The CSF focuses on using business drivers to guide cybersecurity activities and considering cybersecurity risks as part of the organization's risk management processes. The CSF enables organizations – regardless of size, degree of cybersecurity risk, or cybersecurity sophistication – to apply the principles and best practices of risk management to improving the security and resilience of critical infrastructure. Ultimately, it provides organization and structure to today's multiple approaches to cybersecurity by assembling standards, guidelines, and practices that are working effectively in industry today. The prioritized, flexible, repeatable, and cost-effective approach of the CSF can help owners and operators of critical infrastructure to manage cybersecurity-related risk while protecting business confidentiality, individual privacy, and civil liberties. The CSF, published in February 2014, serves as a national-level framework that is flexible enough to apply across multiple sectors. Because the CSF was developed based on stakeholder input, it is intended to help ensure that existing work within the sectors, including the energy sector, can be utilized within the Framework. The existing voluntary smart grid cybersecurity standards, guidelines, and practices can be leveraged to address the CSF functions in the context of an organization's risk management program.

---

[130] See http://collaborate.nist.gov/twiki-sggrid/pub/SmartGrid/CSCTGHighLevelRequirements/NERC_CIPv5_Mapping_v2.xlsx

[131] See http://www.gpo.gov/fdsys/pkg/FR-2013-02-19/pdf/2013-03915.pdf

[132] See http://www.nist.gov/cyberframework/upload/cybersecurity-framework-021214.pdf

6.2. NIST's Role in Smart Grid Cybersecurity

To address the cross-cutting issue of cybersecurity, NIST established the Cybersecurity Coordination Task Group (CSCTG) in early 2009. This group was integrated into the Smart Grid Interoperability Panel (SGIP) as a standing working group and was renamed the SGIP Cybersecurity Working Group (CSWG). In January 2013, the SGIP became a membership-supported non-profit organization and the CSWG was renamed the Smart Grid Cybersecurity Committee (SGCC).

The SGCC has designated liaisons within the SGIP Smart Grid Architecture Committee (SGAC), the Smart Grid Testing and Certification Committee (SGTCC), and the Priority Action Plans (PAPs). Some members of the SGCC are also active participants in the SGAC, the SGTCC, the PAPs, and the DEWGs in the SGIP. Currently, a NIST representative chairs the SGCC. The SGCC management team also includes three vice chairs and a secretariat, volunteers from the membership who are able to commit a portion of their time to participate in SGCC activities.

The SGCC creates and disbands subgroups as needed to meet present demands. Since NISTIR 7628, *Guidelines for Smart Grid Cybersecurity* was published in 2010, some of the SGCC subgroups were merged, while others regrouped as new tasks emerged. Since its inception in 2009, the SGCC has had 13 different subgroups; Table 6-1 provides a description of the subgroups and their activities. Subgroups that are currently active at the time of publication are noted with an *, while subgroups that are not marked have been disbanded upon completion of their deliverables.

The SGCC has national and international members from smart grid stakeholder categories including utilities, vendors, service providers, academia, regulatory organizations, state and local government, and federal agencies. Members of the SGCC assist in defining the activities and tasks of the SGCC, and participate in the development and review of the SGCC subgroups' projects and deliverables. A biweekly conference call is held by the SGCC chair to update the membership on the subgroups' activities, SGIP activities, and other related information. Subgroups hold regular conference calls while actively working on a project. Information on the SGCC, subgroups, and associated documents can be found on the SGIP web site at: www.sgip.org. Historical information can be found on the NIST Smart Grid Collaboration Site.[133]

Table 6-1. SGCC Subgroups

SGCC Subgroup	Subgroup Description
Architecture Subgroup*	The Architecture subgroup has initiated the development of a conceptual smart grid cybersecurity architecture based on the high-level requirements, standards analysis, overall smart grid architecture, and other cybersecurity information

---

[133] See http://collaborate.nist.gov/twiki-sggrid/bin/view/SmartGrid/CyberSecurityCTG.

SGCC Subgroup	Subgroup Description
	from NISTIR 7628. The subgroup continues to refine the conceptual architecture as new smart grid architectures emerge.
Bottom-Up Analysis Subgroup	The Bottom-Up Analysis subgroup identified a number of specific cybersecurity problems in the smart grid for further work by the smart grid community.
Cloud Computing Subgroup	The Cloud Computing subgroup is researching the unique issues of using the cloud in smart grid applications. The subgroup will develop a white paper that provides a short introduction to cloud computing, introduces considerations and risks, and then offers a framework for use in evaluating and implementing specific cloud computing applications in the smart grid.
Cryptography Subgroup	The Cryptography subgroup was founded on the basis of identifying technical cryptographic and key management issues across the scope of systems and devices found in the smart grid along with possible solutions. The identified solutions may be existing standards, methods, or technologies, and their optimal adaptations for the smart grid.
Design Principles Subgroup	The Design Principles subgroup was founded to continue the work of bottom-up problems and design considerations developed by the Bottom-Up and Cryptography subgroups.
High-Level Security Requirements Subgroup*	The High-Level Requirements subgroup developed an initial set of security requirements applicable to the smart grid, published in NISTIR 7628. The subgroup continues to review security requirement documents to ensure harmonization with other organizations' smart grid requirements.
NISTIR 7628 User's Guide Subgroup	The NISTIR 7628 User's Guide subgroup developed an easy-to-understand guide that utilities and other entities involved in implementing smart grid-based systems can use to navigate NISTIR 7628 to identify and select the security requirements needed to help protect those systems.[134]
Privacy Subgroup*	The Privacy subgroup identifies and describes privacy risks and concerns within developed or

---

[134] Available for download at: http://sgip.org/NISTIR-7628-User-s-Guide---Smart-Grid-Cyber-Security-Implementation-Guidelines

SGCC Subgroup	Subgroup Description
	emerging interoperability standards for the smart grid.
Research and Development (R&D) Subgroup	The R&D subgroup was founded on the basis of identifying advanced research and development themes for cybersecurity across the scope of systems and devices found in the smart grid.
Risk Management Process (RMP) Case Study Subgroup	The RMP Case Study subgroup refined narrative story that documents a hypothetical "real world" implementation of the RMP. The goal of the group is to help readers understand the opportunities and challenges of transitioning theoretical ideas of the RMP into a factious utility using casual, conversational storytelling. This case study will cover the major activities of the RMP, reference existing, related bodies of work, provide example inputs and outputs, and leverage the subgroup's own lessons learned.
Standards Subgroup*	The Standards subgroup assesses standards and other documents with respect to the cybersecurity and privacy requirements from NISTIR 7628. These assessments are performed on the standards contained in the Framework or when PAPs are finalizing their recommendations.
Testing and Certification	The purpose of the Testing & Certification subgroup was to establish guidance and methodologies for cybersecurity testing of smart grid systems, subsystems, and components.
Vulnerabilities Subgroup	The Vulnerabilities subgroup identified classes of potential vulnerabilities for the smart grid and provided example vulnerabilities relevant to the smart grid, identified by category.

6.3. Progress to Date

Since early 2009, NIST has been actively addressing the cybersecurity needs of the smart grid whether through the work of the SGCC or through collaborative activities with other organizations. This section describes major work efforts that NIST has completed.

6.3.1. Release of National Institute of Standards and Technology Interagency Report (NISTIR) 7628 and Companion Documents

NISTIR 7628, Revision 1 is to be released in September 2014 and includes updates to the document for such areas as security architecture and privacy.[135] The draft of Revision 1 was

---

[135] See http://csrc.nist.gov/publications/PubsNISTIRs.html#NIST-IR-7628r1

released for public comment in October 2013.[136] The intent of the revision is to keep the majority of the document unchanged, while only modifying those areas that have moved forward technologically since its initial publication in August 2010.

An introduction to NISTIR 7628,[137] released in September 2010, provides a high-level summary of the three-volume report, and serves as an introduction and background to the technical report. This document was written for an audience that is not familiar with cybersecurity.

The initial version of NISTIR 7628[138] addressed documented comments submitted on the second draft and included chapter updates, detailed below. The new content contained basic information on security architecture and a section on cryptography and key management. The responses to the comments received on the second draft of the NISTIR were also posted on the NIST SGIP Collaboration web site.[139]

Prior to the initial release, a second draft of NISTIR 7628 was released in February 2010 and contained sections on the overall security strategy for the smart grid, updated logical interface diagrams, privacy, bottom-up analysis, and vulnerability class analysis sections. New chapters on research and development themes, the standards assessment process, and a functional logical smart grid architecture were also included. The first draft of NISTIR 7628 was released in September 2009. The preliminary report distilled use cases collected to date, requirements and vulnerability classes identified in other relevant cybersecurity assessments and scoping documents, as well as other information necessary for specifying and tailoring security requirements to provide adequate protection for the smart grid.

Additionally, two companion documents to the NISTIR have also been developed. The SGIP document, "Guide for Assessing the High-Level Security Requirements in NISTIR 7628, Guidelines for Smart Grid Cyber Security" (Assessment Guide) provides a set of guidelines for building effective security assessment plans and a baseline set of procedures for assessing the effectiveness of security requirements employed in smart grid information systems.[140] The Assessment Guide is written to provide a foundation to facilitate a security assessment of the high-level security requirements. It includes descriptions of the basic concepts needed when assessing the high-level security requirements in smart grid information systems, the Security Assessment process (including specific activities carried out in each phase of the assessment), the assessment method definitions, the Assessment Procedures Catalog, and a Sample Security Assessment Report outline. Additionally, the Assessment Procedures Catalog has been placed in a companion spreadsheet tool for assessors that can be used to record the findings of an assessment and used as the basis for the development of a final assessment report.

---

[136] See http://csrc.nist.gov/publications/PubsDrafts.html#NIST-IR-7628r1

[137] See http://csrc.nist.gov/publications/nistir/ir7628/introduction-to-nistir-7628.pdf

[138] See http://csrc.nist.gov/publications/PubsNISTIRs.html#NIST-IR-7628

[139] See http://collaborate.nist.gov/twiki-sggrid/bin/view/SmartGrid/NISTIR7628Feb2010

[140] See https://collaborate.nist.gov/twiki-sggrid/pub/SmartGrid/CSCTGTesting/NISTIR_7628_Assessment_Guide-v1p0-24Aug2012.pdf

The other companion document is the draft SGIP document, "NISTIR 7628 User's Guide"[141] which is intended to provide an easy-to-understand approach to navigate the NISTIR 7628. While NISTIR 7628 covers many significant cybersecurity topics, this User's Guide is primarily focused on the application of NISTIR 7628 Volume 1 (Smart Grid Cybersecurity Strategy, Architecture, and High-Level Requirements) in the context of an organization's risk management practices. Although NISTIR 7628 Volume 1 references NIST Special Publication (SP) 800-39, "Managing Information Security Risk: Organization, Mission, and Information System View,"[142] the electricity subsector has tailored SP 800-39 to meet its unique attributes. This tailored approach is now presented in the Department of Energy's "Electricity Subsector Cybersecurity Risk Management Process" (RMP)[143]; which provides the risk management framework and organizational structure needed before system-specific controls identified in NISTIR 7628 can be applied.

The intent of the User's Guide is to provide an end-to-end implementation guide for smart grid cybersecurity activities. This approach begins with the RMP and walks through an approach for identifying an organization's most important smart grid organizational business functions, processes, and the systems (and the associated assets) that support them. Then it helps the user identify and select the security requirements needed to protect those smart grid systems as part of a repeatable risk management process.

Additional white papers addressing cybersecurity areas such as defense-in-depth-and-breadth, cloud computing and the smart grid, and a case study on risk management, have been developed by the SGCC subgroups and are pending publication through the SGIP.[144]

6.3.2. Standards Reviews

Cybersecurity must be viewed as a stack of different security technologies, solutions, and procedures, woven together to meet the requirements of policy, procedural, and technical standards. The cybersecurity of each component of the stack is important, but must also be considered in the context of an organization's implementation. The SGCC Standards subgroup assesses standards and related documents with respect to the high-level security requirements and privacy recommendations from NISTIR 7628. These assessments are performed on the standards contained in the Framework or on PAP documents. During these assessments, the subgroup determines if the standard or PAP document does or should contain privacy or cybersecurity requirements, correlates those requirements with the cybersecurity requirements found in NISTIR 7628, and identifies any gaps. Finally, recommendations are made to the PAPs or the standards bodies on further work needed to mitigate any gaps.

---

[141] See http://www.sgip.org/NISTIR-7628-User-s-Guide---Smart-Grid-Cyber-Security-Implementation-Guidelines

[142] See http://csrc.nist.gov/publications/nistpubs/800-39/SP800-39-final.pdf

[143] See http://energy.gov/oe/downloads/cybersecurity-risk-management-process-rmp-guideline-final-may-2012

[144] See http://www.sgip.org/Publications

As stated earlier, the SGCC review and SGAC review are required for inclusion into the SGIP Catalog of Standards. While gaps identified during the review do not prevent it from being added to the Catalog of Standards, SGCC recommendations for mitigating the cybersecurity gaps should be considered when an organization implements the standard. The SGCC cybersecurity review reports conducted prior to January 2013 are available on the NIST smart grid collaboration wiki web site.[145] Reviews conducted after January 2013 are available on the SGIP site.[146]

In the past three years, the SGCC has conducted over 70 cybersecurity reviews. Most of the reviews have resulted in cybersecurity recommendations. In many cases, the standards bodies or the PAPs have taken the results of the reviews and modified the standards or PAP documents to address our recommendations. The Standards subgroup has worked closely with some of the standards bodies or PAPs to ensure that the recommendations are interpreted correctly and the mitigation strategies selected meet the intent of the high-level security requirements. The result is that cybersecurity is getting "baked-in" to the standards as they are developed rather than "bolted-on" after being implemented.

6.3.3. Risk Management Framework

The SGCC and NIST partnered with DOE's Office of Electricity Delivery and Energy Reliability and NERC to develop a harmonized energy sector enterprise-wide risk management process, based on organization missions, investments, and stakeholder priorities. The DOE Guide, "Electricity Subsector Cybersecurity Risk Management Process"[147] (RMP) provides guidance for an integrated organization-wide approach to managing cybersecurity risks for operations, assets, data, personnel, and organizations across the United States electric grid and the interconnections with Canada and Mexico.

The primary goal of this guideline is to describe a risk management process that is tuned to the specific needs of electricity sector organizations. The NIST SP 800-39, "Managing Information Security Risk,"[148] provides the foundational methodology for this document. NISTIR 7628 and NERC critical infrastructure cybersecurity standards further refine the definition and application of effective cybersecurity for all organizations in the electricity sector. This guideline is being used as a positive example of how a public-private partnership can tailor a Government publication to fit the needs of a critical infrastructure sector.

6.3.4. Cyber-Physical System Research

Cyber-Physical Systems (CPS) are hybrid networked cyber and engineered physical elements co-designed to create adaptive and predictive systems for enhanced performance. These smart

---

[145] See http://collaborate.nist.gov/twiki-sggrid/bin/view/SmartGrid/CSCTGStandards

[146] See http://www.sgip.org/Member-Dashboard

[147] See http://energy.gov/sites/prod/files/Cybersecurity%20Risk%20Management%20Process%20Guideline%20-%20Final%20-%20May%202012.pdf

[148] See http://csrc.nist.gov/publications/nistpubs/800-39/SP800-39-final.pdf

systems present a key opportunity to create a competitive advantage for U.S. industrial innovation and to improve the performance and reliability of new and existing systems. From smart manufacturing and smart grid to smart structures and smart transportation systems, CPS will pervasively impact the economy and society.

Cybersecurity is a critical cross-cutting discipline that provides confidence that cyber-physical systems, their information, and supporting communications and information infrastructures are adequately safeguarded. CPS are increasingly being utilized in critical infrastructures and other settings. However, CPS have many unique characteristics, including the need for real-time response and extremely high availability, predictability, and reliability, which impact cyber-security decisions, including in the distributed energy resource (DER) environment.[149]

As described in NISTIR 7628 and in the Government Accountability Office (GAO) Report,[150] the smart grid is vulnerable to coordinated cyber-physical attacks. NIST hosted a workshop in April 2012 and a follow up workshop in April 2013 to explore CPS cybersecurity needs, with a focus on research results and real-world deployment experiences. The workshops concluded that assessing the impact of coordinated cyber-physical attacks to the smart grid requires expertise in cybersecurity, physical security, and the electric infrastructure. NIST recognizes that collaboration is critical to the effective identification of cyber and physical vulnerabilities and threats. The NIST Cyber-Physical Systems Program is a collaborative effort of NIST's Engineering Laboratory (EL), Information Technology Laboratory (ITL), Physical Measurement Laboratory (PML), and others.

6.3.5. Advanced Meter Upgradeability Test Guidance

As electric utilities turn to Advanced Metering Infrastructures (AMIs) to promote the development and deployment of the smart grid, one aspect that can benefit from standardization is the upgradeability of smart meters. While many elements of smart grid installations are found on the utility side of the smart grid system, the deployment of smart meters is often what customers associate with smart grid. With the expected lifetime for a smart meter to span 10-15 years, it is critical that these devices, which will one day replace all electric meters, have the ability to upgrade the firmware and software that allows critical services and data to be exchanged between the utility and customer. The National Electrical Manufacturers Association (NEMA) standard SG-AMI 1-2009, "Requirements for Smart Meter Upgradeability," describes functional and security requirements for the secure upgrade—both local and remote—of smart meters.

In July 2012, NIST developed the draft NISTIR 7823, "Advanced Metering Infrastructure Smart Meter Upgradeability Test Framework,"[151] which describes conformance test requirements that

---

[149] *Cybersecurity for DER Systems*, Ver. 1.0, Electric Power Research Institute, July 2013.

[150] GAO Report 11-117, *"Electricity Grid Modernization: Progress Being Made on Cybersecurity Guidelines, but Key Challenges Remain to Be Addressed"* defines cyber-physical attack as using both cyber and physical means to attack a target. Available at: http://www.gao.gov/products/GAO-11-117

[151] See http://csrc.nist.gov/publications/drafts/nistir-7823/draft_nistir-7823.pdf

may be used voluntarily by testers and/or test laboratories to determine whether smart meters and upgrade management systems conform to the requirements of NEMA SG-AMI 1-2009. For each relevant requirement in NEMA SG-AMI 1-2009, the document identifies the information to be provided by the vendor to facilitate testing, and the high-level test procedures to be conducted by the tester/laboratory to determine conformance.

In August 2012, NIST, DOE, and the Oak Ridge National Laboratory (ORNL) collaborated to provide a government-controlled test environment to validate the test criteria contained in NISTIR 7823. The test environment at ORNL contains the key components of an AMI network—meters, an aggregator, and back-end network management system. The results of the comprehensive tests will be used to update draft NISTIR 7823 and to provide input into the revision of the NEMA SG-AMI standard.

6.4.   Future Activities

NIST will continue to provide a technical leadership role in the SGCC while pursuing related research that will enable the development of industry standards and guidance in order to successfully implement secure smart grid technologies. Below is a list of planned future activities:

- Technical leadership of the SGCC: Providing cybersecurity expertise, technical leadership, and oversight required to manage the SGCC.

- Review identified standards and smart grid interoperability requirements against the high-level security requirements in NISTIR 7628 Revision 1, "Guidelines for Smart Grid Cyber Security" to identify any cybersecurity gaps and provide recommendations for further work to mitigate gaps.

- Cybersecurity Smart Grid Test Lab: Develop a Cybersecurity Smart Grid Test Lab as part of the NIST Smart Grid Testbed Facility now under construction. Conduct cybersecurity analyses in relation to the IEEE 1588, Precision Time Protocol, standard on time synchronization.

- Participate in the National Cybersecurity Center of Excellence Energy Sector use cases.[152]

---

[152] See http://nccoe.nist.gov/?q=content/energy

7. Smart Grid Testing and Certification Framework

7.1. NIST Role in Smart Grid Testing and Certification

The National Institute of Standards and Technology recognizes the importance of ensuring the development and implementation of an interoperability testing and certification framework for smart grid standards. In order to support interoperability of smart grid systems and products, smart grid products should undergo a rigorous testing process.

Within NIST's plan to expedite the acceleration of interoperable smart grid standards an important component is developing and implementing a framework for smart grid interoperability testing and certification. While standards do promote interoperability, test programs are needed to ensure products are developed with compliant implementation of standards to further promote interoperability. Because of this, when NIST created the SGIP in November 2009, it included the establishment of a permanent Smart Grid Testing and Certification Committee (SGTCC) within the Smart Grid Interoperability Panel. The SGTCC continues to support NIST in its EISA 2007 responsibilities.

As part of the SGIP's relationship with NIST, the SGTCC has assumed the responsibility for constructing an operational framework, as well as developing documentation and associated artifacts supporting testing and certification programs that enables smart grid interoperability. Recognizing that some efforts exist today to test products and services based on certain smart grid standards, and others are under way, NIST is working with stakeholders through the SGIP to develop and implement an operational framework for interoperability testing and certification that supports, augments, and leverages existing programs wherever practical.

The SGIP/SGTCC has made significant progress in developing its testing and certification framework during the past several years, since inception of the SGIP. During 2012, NIST and the SGTCC began transitioning their focus to implementation of the framework and acceleration of new test program creation.

This section reviews the key components and deliverables from the testing and certification framework development activities. The emerging implementation phase projects and activities are then discussed, as well as views on the longer term implementation needs and challenges in maintaining a robust testing and certification ecosystem for interoperable smart grid systems and devices.

7.2. NIST-Initiated Efforts Supporting the Framework Development

NIST launched its support for the accelerated development of an operational framework for smart grid testing and certification in 2010, initiating and completing the following two major efforts: 1) delivering a high-level guidance document for the development of a testing and certification framework, and 2) performing an assessment of existing smart grid standards testing programs (this assessment was also updated in late 2012 as described below in Section 7.2.2 detailing this work). Utilizing input from NIST, the SGTCC developed a roadmap for developing and implementing an operational framework and related action plans, and has launched a number of focused efforts to develop various documents, tools, and components for the framework. Further development and implementation of the operational framework by the SGTCC is an ongoing process.

An important aspect of the testing and certification framework is the feedback loop between standards-setting organizations (SSOs) and the testing and certification programs supporting those standards. This information exchange facilitates continuous improvement over the lifecycle of both standards and test programs. Errors, clarifications, and enhancements to existing standards are typically identified throughout the normal interoperability testing and certification process. In order to improve the interoperability of the smart grid, an overall process is critical to ensure that changes and enhancements are incorporated continuously, and this process has been included as a part of the framework.

NIST will continue to work closely with the SGTCC in its efforts. The SGTCC provides a forum for continuing visibility for smart grid interoperability testing and certification efforts and programs. The SGTCC engages all stakeholders to recommend improvements and means to fill gaps, and will work with current standards bodies and user groups to develop and implement new test programs to fill voids in smart grid interoperability testing and certification.

7.2.1. Testing and Certification Framework Development Guide

A development guide[153] was produced by NIST to accelerate the development of a comprehensive operational framework. The guide defined and discussed the scope, the rationale, and the need for developing a comprehensive framework and action plan for smart grid interoperability testing and certification. The document also described various entities that have a primary role in ensuring that interoperability is achieved, and it presented high-level workflow and framework artifacts for guiding the framework development.

Goals of the Framework

As stated in the guide, "the primary goal of creating a testing and certification framework is to have a comprehensive approach to close the gaps uncovered in the NIST-initiated study and to accelerate the development and implementation of industry programs that enable smart grid interoperability." The development guide defines goals of the framework, which are to:

- Help ensure a consistent level of testing for products based on the same smart grid standards, as well as ensure consistency in the implementation of test programs among different standards

---

[153]See https://collaborate.nist.gov/twiki-sggrid/pub/SmartGrid/SGIPDocumentsAndReferencesSGTCC/TandCFrameworkDevelopmentGuide__FINAL-083010.pdf

- Address test implementation and execution issues, including qualification criteria for test laboratories and accrediting organizations, and recommend best practices to ensure that test results achieve their desired intent and are used in an appropriate and consistent manner

- Take into consideration the evolutionary progression of the smart grid, and be structured to allow maturation of existing technologies and introduction of emerging technologies

In order for smart grid testing and certification programs to be successful and broadly adopted, these programs must be financially viable. Two key factors for successful new testing and certification programs are:

- The cost of testing must be reasonable relative to other product costs and volume of deployment.

- The cost of testing must be reasonable relative to the risk of product failure in the field. Product failures in the field create cost because they may require technical remedies to be performed in the field, equipment to be replaced, service interruptions, and reduced customer satisfaction. Testing may identify these problems before the product is deployed. However, testing costs should be justified by the risk of the potential costs associated with the failed product after deployment to ensure that overall cost is minimized.

7.2.2. Assessment of Existing Smart Grid Standards Testing Programs

NIST initiated and completed an in-depth study in early 2010 to assess the existing testing and certification programs associated with the priority smart grid standards identified by NIST. That study was updated and released in late 2012 to align with revisions to the smart grid standards cited in NIST's 2012 version of its *Framework and Roadmap for Smart Grid Interoperability Standards, Release 2.0*, as well as to update progress made by testing organizations over that time. The results of the study are summarized in a report titled "Existing Conformity Assessment Program Landscape."[154] In this report, the testing and conformity assessment programs relevant to the smart grid standards identified in the NIST Framework were evaluated in detail.

The results of these reports provided NIST and the SGIP's SGTCC with the current status of existing testing programs for ensuring interoperability, cybersecurity, and other relevant characteristics. The assessment included all elements of a conformity assessment system, including accreditation bodies, certification bodies, testing and calibration laboratories, inspection bodies, personnel certification programs, and quality registrars. The reports also helped to uncover present gaps and deficiencies in the evaluated programs.

---

[154] "Existing Conformity Assessment Program Landscape" by EnerNex for NIST,http://collaborate.nist.gov/twiki-sggrid/bin/view/SmartGrid/SGIPDocumentsAndReferencesSGTCC. (See https://collaborate.nist.gov/twiki-sggrid/pub/SmartGrid/SGIPDocumentsAndReferencesSGTCC/Smart_Grid_TC_Landscape_2012_-_Final.doc)

Assessment Results

The initial 2010 report resulted in several findings of major gaps in existing test programs. This report was updated in 2012 and key findings are summarized below:

- There are currently 13 test programs that have been developed or are in the process of being developed. This remains a low percentage of the overall identified smart grid standards in Chapter 4.

- Of these test programs, nearly half of them have begun to implement the SGTCC Interoperability Reference Manual (IPRM) recommendations. (See Section 7.3.1 for details about the IPRM.)

- Standards supported by users groups are more likely to have successful test programs.

- Most test programs are based on conformance but there are growing trends to put increased efforts into interoperability aspects as their programs evolve.

- More programs are introducing cybersecurity aspects as part of their testing regiments.

The gaps uncovered in this study show the urgent and important need for developing and implementing an interoperability testing and certification framework to provide a comprehensive approach to close these gaps and to accelerate the development and implementation of industry programs that enable smart grid interoperability. NIST and the SGTCC have used the insights resulting from the study to direct subsequent interoperability testing and certification framework development efforts. In particular, a key 2013 deliverable on prioritizing the development of needed testing programs uses these testing landscape reports as a key source to support decision making. The prioritization deliverable and follow-on activities are described below in Section 7.5.

As implementation of the testing and certification framework moves forward, NIST and the SGTCC will review and revise the program landscape document to assess industry progress in program development and use those findings to further guide priority issues for the SGTCC to address.

7.3. SGTCC Framework Development Activities

The SGTCC was launched in February 2010 with an inaugural meeting hosted by NIST. It is composed of a diverse set of technical experts specializing in testing and certification activities. The SGTCC has representation from utilities, manufacturers, test laboratories, test program operators, standards specifying organizations, accreditors, and certifiers. The SGTCC is charged with the development of the operational framework and action plan for smart grid interoperability testing and certification. Since its establishment, SGTCC has undertaken a number of activities in the framework development process. The action plan of the SGTCC is included in a "Testing & Certification Roadmap"[155] document, which describes the plans and

---

[155] See http://collaborate.nist.gov/twiki-sggrid/bin/view/SmartGrid/SGTCCRoadMap

deliverables to be developed through the SGTCC. It is a living document that evolves through close collaboration with NIST and other industry stakeholders to ensure that identified issues and needs in framework development and implementation are addressed.

The SGTCC's mission is "to coordinate creation of documentation and organizational frameworks relating to compliance testing and certification to smart grid interoperability and cybersecurity standards."[156] Its objectives include "the development of an action plan, with the support of relevant parties, to establish a standardized framework (e.g., tools, materials, components, and examples) that can be used by those performing testing for and certification of compliance with interoperability and cybersecurity standards."[157]

Using the NIST-contributed reports cited earlier (i.e., the framework development guide and the existing program assessment report), the SGTCC initial deliverables focused on two foundational projects. The first was an analysis of industry best practices related to testing that led to the creation of the Interoperability Process Reference Manual (IPRM).[158] The second was an Interoperability Maturity Assessment Model[159] that built upon the program assessment report to assess the maturity of standards-setting activities relative to the achievement of interoperable products. Each of these deliverables is described in greater detail below.

7.3.1. Interoperability Process Reference Manual (IPRM)

The interoperability testing and certification framework centers on the concept of an Interoperability Testing and Certification Authority (ITCA) that supports one or more key smart grid standards. An ITCA will be "the organization whose function is to promote and facilitate the introduction of interoperable products based on standards into the marketplace."[160] NIST had observed that "standards [that] moved from release to market adoptions very frequently had this type of organization defined. Those that moved slowly from standards release to market did not."[161] SGTCC believes that "the formation and maintenance of these organizations, ad hoc or formal, is key to increasing the velocity of the adoptions of interoperable standards in the marketplace."[162]

Recognizing this, the Interoperability Process Reference Manual (IPRM) was developed for use by ITCAs. The IPRM can be used as a "how to" guide to set up an ITCA. The IPRM outlines the

---

[156] Ibid.

[157] Ibid.

[158] See https://collaborate.nist.gov/twiki-sggrid/pub/SmartGrid/SmartGridTestingAndCertificationCommittee/IPRM_final_-_011612.pdf

[159] SGTCC Working Group 3 internal documents: "SGIP TCC Interoperability Maturity Assessment, V0.92" and "SGIP TCC Interop Assessment Questionnaire, V0.52"

[160] Ibid.

[161] Ibid.

[162] Ibid.

roles and requirements of an ITCA and specifies the mandatory testing and certification processes associated with achieving interoperability for a specific standard. The IPRM also includes the recommended best practices for interoperability test constructs.

The IPRM is intended to be used by any ITCA that is responsible for coordinating testing and certification based on a smart grid technology standard and driving adoption of the technology within the industry. The SGTCC has concluded that those organizations that incorporate the IPRM guidelines into their testing programs will have a greater opportunity to ensure the products' interoperability. As stated in the IPRM, once an ITCA is in place, "The ITCA shall provide governance and coordination for the maintenance and administration of Interoperability Testing Laboratories and Certification Bodies in cooperation with the relevant SSOs and user groups."[163] The roles and requirements of an ITCA, and the best practices described in the IPRM, are summarized below.

During the second half of 2011, the SGTCC assessed lessons learned in early efforts by Interoperability Testing and Certification Authorities (ITCAs) in implementation of the IPRM version 1.0 and used those findings to update the IPRM version 2.0, releasing the new version in January 2012. The new issue of the IPRM transitioned the first version of the document from an informational focus to an operational focus, providing greater clarity to ITCAs to guide their implementation of the IPRM recommendations. It incorporates internationally recognized quality and performance standards for certification bodies and test laboratories to provide confidence to end purchasers (e.g., utilities) and requirements for testing procedures to assure that testing is comprehensive and rigorous as required to meet deployment expectations.

Summary of Roles and Requirements of an ITCA

The role of an ITCA is to provide governance and coordination for the maintenance and administration of Interoperability Testing Laboratories and Certification Bodies in cooperation with the relevant SSOs and user groups. It manages the end-to-end processes associated with interoperability testing and certification with appropriate infrastructure in place to support this function.

The requirements for an ITCA as specified in the IPRM are divided into the following five categories:

- **Governance** defines the structures, policies, rules, and regulations associated with the ITCA certification program. For example, a governance process would require the ITCA to establish and maintain an independent and vendor-neutral testing and certification oversight authority.

- **Lab Qualification** defines the requirements that shall be applied by ITCAs when recognizing testing laboratories. It should be noted that additional requirements are further detailed in International Organization for Standardization (ISO) 17025.

---

[163] Ibid.

- **Technical Design for Interoperability and Conformance Program** defines the requirements needed to effectively manage the procedures and processes associated with interoperability and conformance testing.

- **Improvements** cover the continuing improvement controls that are required to support the interoperability testing processes.

- **Cybersecurity** covers the requirements that shall be used by the ITCA to validate the security-related components of the interoperability testing program.

Adoption of these requirements by an ITCA is essential for implementing a successful interoperability testing and certification program.

Leveraging of Industry Best Practices

In addition to meeting the governance, lab qualification, technical design, improvements, and cybersecurity requirements, ITCAs should also leverage industry's best practices in their implementations. The IPRM has included a list of recommended best practices and guidelines for ITCAs in their development and operation of interoperability and conformance testing programs. The recommendations provided in the IPRM were generated based on input from experienced testing organizations that have evolved interoperability and conformance programs through lessons learned in executing tests for both software and hardware applications.

The recommendations may not apply directly to all testing applications; however, NIST and the SGTCC recommend that ITCAs consider them for interoperability and conformance test programs, as these practices have proven to be valuable in executing a broad cross-section of program types. Each ITCA should evaluate how these recommendations, observations, and practices apply to their specific programs and should incorporate the recommendations into their programs where applicable.

The recommended best practices in interoperability test constructs in the IPRM address three main areas:

- General test policies—includes policies related to information that product vendors need to know relative to a specific testing and certification program

- Test suite specification (TSS) — includes the need to establish a common TSS for use by multiple test labs; a TSS that is test-tool agnostic; and revision control of TSS

- Attributes of a test profile in lieu of complete test suite specification

7.3.2 Interoperability Maturity Assessment Model

The SGTCC developed and refined the assessment metrics used in the "landscape" document into a more rigorous Interoperability Maturity Assessment Model (IMAM).[164] The IMAM

---

[164] SGTCC Working Group 3 internal documents: "SGIP TCC Interoperability Maturity Assessment, V0.92" and "SGIP TCC Interop Assessment Questionnaire, V0.52"

provides a unique set of tools for assessing the maturity of a smart grid testing and certification program for products conforming to a standard. The IMAM includes associated metrics and tools for quick and high-level maturity assessment of a standard's testing and certification program. The IMAM is an extension and refinement of the process used in the NIST study report. It includes "filtering" metrics for evaluating critical characteristics of a successful test program, and "assessment" metrics for deeper evaluation of specific strengths and weaknesses of a test program. These metrics can be evaluated through a spreadsheet questionnaire developed by the SGTCC, which includes more detailed questions for each metric.

The IMAM was originally envisioned for use by the SGIP, standards bodies, and ITCAs in their analyses of standards and associated test programs. Over time, the SGTCC recognized that the content developed for the IMAM could be put to good use in two of its initiatives: Catalog of Standards reviews and ITCA Assessments of IPRM implementation. These initiatives, which launched in 2012, are described more fully later in Section 7.4.

7.4. SGTCC Progress since Framework 2.0

7.4.1. IPRM Version 2

The IPRM was updated to version 2 to enhance the utility of the document to support implementation of the criteria and recommendations by an ITCA and to structure it in a way to better facilitate assessments of ITCA implementation for both internal assessments within the ITCA and for external independent assessments. The changes in structure and clarity are major. The changes in content are minor.

Fundamentally, version 2 has an operational focus, while version 1 provided an informational focus. Most of the key informative material from version 1 has been retained in version 2. The main body of the IPRM emphasizes the operational aspects, while the informational material is provided in a series of separate informational annexes to the document.

Significant changes in IPRM version 2 as compared to the prior version include:
- Greater emphasis on the importance of independent accreditation and adherence to internationally recognized standards for testing labs and certification bodies

- Restructuring the document sections to align with the interests of key stakeholder groups—ITCAs, cybersecurity testing organizations, certification bodies, and test laboratories (i.e., the revised sections are targeted at the interests and responsibilities of specific stakeholders)

- An expanded section on cybersecurity providing much more detailed coverage in this new release, and the ITCA role in cybersecurity testing and certification is clarified further

- The requirements tables were condensed to eliminate redundancy and non-measurable criteria. The tables were also relocated in the document to align with the applicable sections (removes the need to jump back and forth between sections of interest). The requirements in IPRM version 2 are intended to be more easily implementable for third-party accreditation and other assessment operations.

7.4.2. Engagement with ITCAs, Labs, Certifiers, and Accreditors

Among the key enablers of testing programs for smart grid standards are the emergence of new Interoperability Testing and Certification Authorities (ITCAs) and the engagement of laboratories and certification bodies that will support these ITCAs. Further, industry accreditation organizations must also be engaged as there is the need to establish services that provide for the independent assessment and accreditation of labs and certifiers as recommended in the IPRM. Engagement with these organizations will be an ongoing activity, and the SGTCC has placed a strong focus on establishing these relationships within its work program. Engagement with ITCAs, labs, and certifiers has been through the SGTCC's Working Group for IPRM Implementation. This working group has several key responsibilities:

- Development and management of processes for use by industry third-party assessment organizations to help them evaluate ITCAs for IPRM implementation

- Maintenance of an informational tool that identifies available smart grid test programs, including links to their industry third-party accreditations and certifications that meet IPRM recommendations

- Liaison relationships with ITCAs initially to monitor their IPRM implementation status and long term to capture lessons learned that may be used for future revisions of SGTCC documents and processes

The SGTCC has successfully collaborated with ITCAs and third-party industry assessment and accreditation providers to implement the IPRM recommendations. To date, seven ITCAs announced plans to implement the IPRM recommendations within their programs (NEMA, UCAIug 61850, UCAIug Green Button, OpenADR, MultiSpeak, SEP2 Consortia, and USnap Alliance). OpenADR and USnap were the first to provide SGTCC with information on their IPRM implementation for inclusion in its informational tool.

In January 2012, five organizations that provide independent accreditation of test labs and certification bodies announced their intent to begin offering services in 2012 in support of the SGIP testing recommendations. These included the American National Standards Institute (ANSI), American Association for Laboratory Accreditation (A2LA), Laboratory Accreditation Bureau (L-A-B), ACLASS, and Perry Johnson Lab Accreditation. A first joint meeting between ITCAs and accreditors, which took place at the SGIP spring meeting in 2012, facilitated accreditors plans for the necessary services to assess an ITCA's labs and certification bodies for operation of their testing and certification programs.

Accrediting bodies are a key enabler of IPRM implementation as the IPRM specifies that labs and certifiers be accredited in accordance with ISO standards. The SGTCC success in gaining commitments by these accreditors to develop and provide these services will help to accelerate the availability of IPRM-conforming test and certification programs.

Emerging ITCA Support

The SGTCC has been engaging directly with newly emerging ITCAs by providing guidance as those organizations form and develop their processes with an aim towards IPRM implementation. The Green Button ITCA initiative has progressed farthest thus far with the support of the SGTCC. SGTCC volunteers have participated in planning activities and meetings hosted by UCAIug (the program operator) providing input on necessary steps in the process and review of documents soliciting the engagement of labs, certifiers, and accreditors. Lessons learned from this support have also been fed back to the SGTCC working groups to clarify processes and other materials to better help future ITCA developers.

In addition to the Green Button activity, SGTCC volunteers have participated in a task force hosted by NASPI investigating opportunities for ITCA programs for synchrophasors. The work of UCAIug on their Green Button program has the added benefit of being leveraged to also support IPRM implementation in their IEC 61850 test programs. Additionally, other organizations, such as DNP3, have requested presentations and dialogue with the SGTCC to evaluate how they may integrate the SGTCC recommendations into existing or emerging programs.

IPRM - ITCA Development Guide

It is envisioned that, over time, many of the standards included in the SGIP Catalog of Standards (CoS) will have associated testing and/or certification services overseen by an ITCA. New ITCAs are just beginning to emerge, and during 2012, it became apparent that there was a need to provide guidance to these organizations to help them develop and implement programs that align with the expectations cited in the IPRM.

In setting up and operating an ITCA, there are a series of activities and responsibilities that are addressed specifically or implied in the IPRM, most of them enumerated in a separate section. A guidance document[165] has been developed and released to support these emergent ITCAs. It is intended to organize the IPRM's explicit and implicit requirements and suggested best practices for an ITCA into a roadmap to follow in launching its program.

7.4.3. SGTCC Input for SGIP CoS Review

The SGTCC launched a working group in 2012 to perform analyses of standards proposed for inclusion in the SGIP CoS. Previously, standards reviews had been performed by the SGIP Architecture and Cybersecurity committees relative to a standard's alignment with SGIP recommendations in those topic areas. The addition of reviews from a testing perspective provides an additional viewpoint that will be valuable to users of the standards listed in the CoS.

SGTCC standards reviews provide product purchasers with the information they need to understand the state of a standard with respect to test readiness and help industry accelerate the

---

[165] See https://collaborate.nist.gov/twiki-sggrid/pub/SmartGrid/SGIPDocumentsAndReferencesSGTCC/ITCA_Development_Guide_-_Version_1.0_-_FINAL.pdf

development of programs to address identified gaps in test program availability. Initially, the SGTCC prepared a review process and set of filtering metrics by which to evaluate standards as a part of the overall CoS review process. Actual reviews of a number of standards already cited in the CoS began in late 2012, with the first ten completed by spring of 2013.

The filtering metrics measure the testing-related attributes of a standard with respect to the following five areas:

- A series of considerations to assess whether the standard is implementable in products

- Status of ITCA availability and maturity to support testing and certification for the standard

- The quality of the standard itself relative to clear definition for assessing conformance;

- Considerations that explore whether the standard addresses interoperability as well as conformance

- Customer expectations relative to test programs for the standard and whether those expectations are being satisfied

The SGTCC CoS reviews are documented and submitted to the SGIP for inclusion in the CoS documentation. The SGTCC reviews are intended as an informational resource. They are not intended as a required approval or rejection for inclusion in the CoS. The intent of the reviews is to complement the perspectives submitted from other SGIP groups to provide users of standards with as comprehensive a perspective as possible to support their understanding of the standard.

7.5.   Current Smart Grid Testing Initiatives

This section discusses testing and certification initiatives that have launched since the beginning of 2013.

7.5.1. Prioritization of Test Programs – Gaps/Opportunities

NIST developed and issued a white paper[166] in early 2013 discussing the need for accelerated availability of testing programs, and a proposed process for industry to identify those programs that should be prioritized to best focus available resources on these needs. Currently, only a small percentage of smart grid standards are supported by associated test programs. The *NIST Framework and Roadmap for Smart Grid Interoperability Standards, Release 2.0,* in its Tables 4-1 and 4-2, cites over one hundred key smart grid standards. Ideally, Interoperability Testing and Certification Authorities (ITCAs) and test programs should be in place to address each of these standards, with programs adopting the recommendations and best practices developed by the SGTCC in its Interoperability Process Reference Manual (IPRM) to assure rigorous and high quality programs.

---

[166] See https://collaborate.nist.gov/twiki-sggrid/pub/SmartGrid/SmartGridTestingAndCertificationCommittee/Testing_Prioritization_White_Paper_-_Final.pdf

As noted earlier, the availability of test programs in support of smart grid standards is in its early stages. A challenge in addressing the availability of test programs across the many standards cited in this Framework is the sheer level of effort required relative to available resources. A methodology for prioritization across these standards is essential to solving the problem. Without a prioritization, efforts will lack focus, and resources will be diluted across multiple efforts, some lacking industry demand.

Effective implementation of a prioritization requires a well-thought-out methodology that considers a broad range of issues, both technical and business driven. The NIST white paper on prioritization was provided as a contribution to the SGIP. The white paper is intended to provide a roadmap and guidance to assist the SGIP in developing strategies to effectively identify critical testing needs for the smart grid, and help in the future to develop strategies to effectively focus the resources necessary to incubate and accelerate new test programs that address the gaps in test program availability. Accelerating the availability of test programs in support of smart grid standards is a significant objective for NIST and the SGIP.

Prioritization Initiative

The SGTCC has launched a working group, based upon the NIST white paper recommendations, to implement the proposed process for identifying and acting upon industry priority testing needs. While the SGTCC, in collaboration with NIST, is driving this initiative, it is engaging with other groups within the SGIP that are stakeholders within this effort, notably the Implementation Methods Committee. An initial output of this working group has been the development of an information-gathering effort intended to gather industry input on testing needs and priorities. The initial phase of this information gathering focused on utility stakeholders to better understand the testing programs that would provide benefit in their product evaluation and selection process. The initial phase has a goal of developing a list of 10 to 20 priority testing needs that will then be socialized with a broader stakeholder community. The priority list will be augmented as necessary based upon this additional stakeholder input. The "action" phase will follow the socialization phase.

The NIST white paper proposes the eventual creation of an SGIP PAP proposal for each of the top testing priorities identified for recommendation to the SGIP Board for approval. These action plans will be used to define the requirements to work with industry to develop a smart grid test program. This action will drive additional industry attention to the need and buy in for new smart grid test program development. Collaboration will take place with defined industry groups to establish test programs based on the vetted smart grid test program priorities as agreed to by industry.

7.5.2. Outreach

Several issues have been identified that have driven the need to develop a proactive outreach initiative for smart grid testing and certification.

- The need to engage key stakeholders and product decision makers in advocating the value of smart grid test programs

- The need to better align end-user technology priorities with the areas where SGTCC can focus its efforts in accelerating the creation of new test programs

- The need to build broader awareness of testing programs, processes, and resources across the smart grid community

- Testing and certification programs require demand drivers for their success. Demand drivers lead to widespread adoption of testing programs. Demand may be market driven or via regulatory mandate (e.g., product safety, FCC radio frequency). Market-driven programs are those where end users (e.g., utilities) require suppliers to provide testing data, certification, etc. as a condition within their product evaluation and selection process. Another market-driven example is one where suppliers voluntarily complete selected test programs as a de facto part of their product verification processes (i.e., a peer-pressure-driven activity where suppliers execute the testing to remain on equal competitive footing) but most often this occurs as a result of end-customer demand.

Demand drivers are a result of key stakeholders identifying specific issues where product testing provides a clear value and benefit—public safety, critical infrastructure concerns, resiliency, and reliability are example issues that drive testing to assess product characteristics and attributes relevant to the subject issue. The most successful testing and certification programs in any industry are those that are perceived as contributing high value to assure they satisfy end user and end customer concerns.

The SGTCC plans to launch an Education and Outreach effort to drive industry demand for test programs and to build awareness of the value of testing and certification programs, as well as awareness of the SGIP and NIST efforts and accomplishments in advancing smart grid interoperability via support for testing and certification programs. The SGIP, with support from NIST, will work to drive further industry interest and demand for existing programs, and accelerate the development and adoption of new testing programs and activities. Activities in this area may include such approaches as white papers highlighting key issues on smart grid test programs, as well as targeted direct engagements with individual stakeholders and at industry venues with broader audiences. A focus will be driving demand for test programs and building towards a critical mass of adoption that result in broad-based implementation of test programs.

7.6. Future Directions

Developing and implementing a framework for testing and certification of smart grid interoperability standards is a long-term process. NIST plans to continue working with SGIP and its Board of Directors, the SGTCC, and industry stakeholders in accelerating the launch and availability of testing and certification programs in support of smart grid standards. In addition, NIST will continue to engage with these stakeholders in refining the testing and certification framework and providing necessary support for its implementation. This section describes anticipated and proposed future initiatives to facilitate the proliferation of smart grid testing programs and achieve their widespread adoption.

7.6.1. Incubation of New Testing Initiatives via Priority Action Plans

The migration of the testing prioritization initiative towards priority action plans to address identified needs will be an ongoing and long-term activity. Currently, launch of an initial testing related PAP is in its early stages. With many needs anticipated for potential PAPs, and limited SGIP volunteer resources available, there is a need to develop a long-range plan for PAP development and execution that aligns with the priority needs. NIST will continue to interact with utilities and other stakeholders within the smart grid ecosystem to assure congruence with evolving needs and priorities.

7.6.2. Catalog of Test Programs

NIST plans to engage with the SGIP on a proposed concept being referred to as a Catalog of Test Programs (CoTP). The concept is similar to the SGIP Catalog of Standards (CoS) approach. The parallel is that, where the CoS provides a directory of standards that help to enable smart grid interoperability, the CoTP will provide a directory of industry test programs that support assessments against those standards.

As noted previously, the SGTCC has already embarked on an informational tool initiative that provides information on ITCA programs including references and links to help users of the tool to easily locate accreditation, certifications and other information associated with IPRM implementation via public third-party accreditor records. While full implementation of the IPRM recommendations might be considered the highest level of achievement that a test program can strive for, it will take time for programs to complete their implementations. There are a number of industry test programs that are beneficial to smart grid systems and devices. These additional programs have varying levels of industry adoption and some may in the future expand their scopes, necessitating IPRM implementation. The CoTP is anticipated to build upon the informational tool initiative and provide a resource to industry to better understand the test programs that can help in achieving smart grid interoperability. The intention is to raise industry awareness of test programs to the same level of visibility as smart grid standards in the CoS.

A comprehensive directory of available test programs such as that provided by the CoTP, will provide value to smart grid stakeholders for several reasons. The first is to provide a one-stop source to support utilities and vendors to identify resources available to them for system and device testing. An added advantage is that this initiative would foster collaboration between many test programs and labs, with NIST and the SGIP, thereby expanding engagement across the testing and certification community. The directory may also serve as a platform to distinguish progress on IPRM implementation, and may encourage new entrant test programs to aspire towards more comprehensive implementation of the IPRM recommendations.

7.6.3. IPRM Version 3

Activity initiated in mid-2014 to revisit the IPRM with respect to the successes and challenges that ITCAs have experienced in building their programs using the recommendations. A third version of the IPRM is anticipated to address these lessons learned with refinements made to the document to better align with ITCA experiences. Additionally, several complementary efforts to the IPRM have taken place since its last issue. These include the IPRM implementation guidance document developed by the SGTCC, a NEMA-sponsored document[167] that addresses roles and responsibilities for each of the main participants in the interoperability testing scheme in order to create the necessary level of checks and balances for the overall testing process, and a policies/procedures document prepared by the Green Button ITCA development team with support from SGTCC members that provides further insights on certification marks and their management. Ideally, all of this newly developed information should be incorporated into a single source, and as each of these new efforts were designed as extensions to the IPRM, inclusion in an IPRM Version 3 would be beneficial to the smart grid ecosystem to provide a definitive collection of pertinent information that supports ITCA development and operations.

7.6.4. International Engagement

NIST is actively engaged with international smart grid organizations that provide similar technical and coordination initiatives that mirror the SGIP. Testing and certification activities by those international organizations are in an early, but growing phase. Examples include an introductory collaboration meeting including testing with a Korean smart grid delegation, as well as coordination with European Union testing participants within the Smart Grid Coordination Group. The SGIP, along with the SGTCC, has become a model for other international organizations supporting smart grid implementation. As these worldwide organizations progress their own initiatives, there will be a mutual benefit to aligning activities. Active collaboration on testing and certification issues and initiatives are anticipated going forward to assure smart grid interoperability is not impeded by geographic boundaries.

---

[167] See http://www.nema.org/News/Pages/NEMA-Smart-Grid-Interoperability-Standard-Receives-ANSI-Approval.aspx

8.   Cross-Cutting and Future Issues

8.1.   Introduction

NIST continues to engage with smart grid interoperability in a number of ways. The execution of the Priority Action Plans (PAPs) presently under way will continue until their objectives to fill identified gaps in the standards portfolio have been accomplished. As new gaps and requirements are identified, the SGIP will continue to initiate PAPs to address them. NIST and the SGIP will work with SSOs and other stakeholders to fill the gaps and improve the standards that form the foundation of the smart grid.

Work on the SGIP CoS will continue to fully populate the Catalog and ensure robust architectural and cybersecurity reviews of the standards. Efforts will continue to partner with the private sector as it establishes testing and certification programs consistent with the SGIP testing and certification framework. Work will continue to coordinate with related international smart grid standards efforts to promote alignment and harmonization and to support U.S. manufacturer access to international markets.

Many of the Department of Energy (DOE) Smart Grid Investment Grants are coming to fruition. Principal investigators were required to include in their proposals a description of how the projects would support the NIST Framework. As the experiences with new smart grid technologies are gained from these projects, NIST will use these "lessons learned" to further identify the gaps and shortcomings of applicable standards.

NIST will continue to support the needs of regulators as they address standardization matters in the regulatory arena. Under EISA, the Federal Energy Regulatory Commission (FERC) is charged with instituting rulemaking proceedings to adopt the standards and protocols as may be necessary to ensure smart grid functionality and interoperability once, in FERC's judgment, the NIST-coordinated process has led to sufficient consensus.[168] FERC obtained public input through two Technical Conferences on Smart Grid Interoperability Standards in November 2010 and January 2011,[169] and through a supplemental notice requesting comments in February 2011.[170] As a result, FERC issued an order in July 2011[171] stating that while there was insufficient consensus for it to institute a rulemaking at that time, FERC "encourages stakeholders to actively participate in the NIST interoperability framework process to work on the development of interoperability standards and to refer to that process for guidance on smart grid standards." The Commission's order further stated that the NIST Framework is comprehensive and represents the best vehicle for developing standards for the smart grid.

---

[168] Energy Independence and Security Act of 2007 [Public Law No: 110-140], Sec. 1305.

[169] See
http://ferc.gov/EventCalendar/EventDetails.aspx?ID=5571&CalType=%20&CalendarID=116&Date=01/31/2011&View=Listview

[170] See http://ferc.gov/EventCalendar/Files/20110228084004-supplemental-notice.pdf

[171] See http://www.ferc.gov/EventCalendar/Files/20110719143912-RM11-2-000.pdf

NIST supported the Commission's order, which notes that "In its comments, NIST suggests that the Commission could send appropriate signals to the marketplace by recommending use of the NIST Framework without mandating compliance with particular standards. NIST adds that it would be impractical and unnecessary for the Commission to adopt individual interoperability standards."[172]

State and local regulators play important roles in establishing the regulatory framework for the electrical industry. Broad engagement of smart grid stakeholders at the state and local levels is essential to ensure the consistent voluntary application of the standards being developed, and both NIST and SGIP leaders have met frequently with this stakeholder group. The National Association of Regulatory Utility Commissioners (NARUC) has indicated its support for the SGIP process, stating that "When evaluating smart grid investments, State commissions should consider how certified smart grid interoperability standards may reduce the cost and improve the performance of smart grid projects and encourage participation in the Smart Grid Interoperability Panel, a public-private partnership that is coordinating and accelerating the development of interoperability standards for the smart grid."[173]

Currently, many states and their utility commissions are pursuing smart grid-related projects. Ultimately, state and local projects will converge into fully functioning elements of the smart grid "system of systems." Therefore, the interoperability and cybersecurity standards developed under the NIST framework and roadmap must support the role of the states in modernizing the nation's electric grid. The NIST framework can provide a valuable input to regulators as they consider the prudency of investments proposed by utilities.

A key objective of the NIST work is to create a self-sustaining, ongoing standards process that supports continuous innovation as grid modernization continues in the decades to come.[174] NIST envisions that the processes being put in place by the SGIP, as they mature, will provide the mechanism to evolve the smart grid standards framework as new requirements and technologies emerge. The SGIP processes will also evolve and improve as experience is gained. Additionally, NIST has and will continue to provide technical contributions aligned with NIST's core measurements and standards missions that advance development of the smart grid. NIST leadership on these committees and working groups, as well as its technical contributions, provide strong support for the acceleration of the standards necessary for the safe, secure, and reliable smart grid.

The following sections review several key cross-cutting issues that are receiving NIST attention now and in the near future.

---

[172] See http://www.ferc.gov/EventCalendar/Files/20110719143912-RM11-2-000.pdf, p. 6

[173] See http://www.naruc.org/Resolutions/Resolution%20on%20Smart%20Grid%20Principles.pdf

[174] As part of this process, the SGIP will help to prioritize and coordinate smart grid-related standards. See Chapter 5 for further discussion.

8.2. Electromagnetic Disturbances and Interference

The foundation for the new smart grid is built on increasingly sophisticated electronic sensing, control, and communications systems. The expected rise in the use of distributed renewable energy sources, plug-in electric vehicles and smart appliances in the home, wired and wireless communications, and other "smart" systems throughout the grid, along with the increasing electromagnetic sources in the general environment, will result in unprecedented exposure to possible electromagnetic disturbances and interference. These "smart" systems are being deployed throughout the power grid in locations ranging from single-family homes to complex industrial facilities and will require a broad array of measures to protect the grid and other electronic systems from interference and possible failures. Because the smart grid components are so diverse, there is not a one-size-fits-all solution. Therefore, a range of standards or recommendations specific to particular environments or devices is anticipated. The criteria for smart appliances in the home will be quite different from systems located in substations or industrial facilities. Fortunately, many of the applicable electromagnetic compatibility (EMC) specifications and requirements already exist in various standards.

The term "electromagnetic compatibility" describes the ability to function properly in a given environment without causing or suffering from electromagnetic interference. EMC within the smart grid systems and in the external environment, along with immunity to serious natural and man-made threats, should be systematically and holistically addressed for reliable operation of the smart grid. This means that EMC includes controlling emissions and disturbances, designing for an adequate level of immunity and/or protection, and following appropriate installation guidelines. Also, EMC, coexistence with other devices, and fault tolerance should be considered early in the design of smart grid systems to avoid costly remedies and redesigns after the systems are widely deployed.

The original SGIP Governing Board recognized this situation and chartered a DEWG (which has continued under the new, industry-led SGIP) to investigate enhancing the immunity of smart grid devices and systems to the detrimental effects of natural and man-made electromagnetic interference, both radiated and conducted. The focus is to address these EMC issues and to review the application of standards and testing criteria to help ensure EMC for the smart grid, with a particular focus on issues directly related to interoperability of smart grid devices and systems, including impacts, avoidance, generation, and mitigation of and immunity to electromagnetic interference (original Electromagnetic Interoperability Issues Working Group (EMII WG) Charter). This working group has enjoyed the input of experts from a variety of stakeholder categories including electric utilities, manufacturers, trade associations, EMC consultants, utility commissions, and government.

The December 2012 EMII WG white paper [175] presents a compilation of important smart grid EMC issues, identified gaps in standards, and recommendations for specifying appropriate EMC tests and standards for smart grid devices. The working group identified specific electromagnetic environments at strategic locations throughout the power grid where new smart grid devices are likely to play an important role. Then the EMII WG examined possible electromagnetic

---

[175] Electromagnetic Compatibility and Smart Grid Interoperability Issues, SGIP 2012-005, December 2012

disturbances (i.e., sources of interference) and appropriate EMC test standards to address these disturbances for each of the specific locations. These disturbances originate from a range of narrowband and broadband sources and generate both conducted and radiated interference. This exercise identified existing IEEE-, IEC-, and ANSI-sponsored EMC standards such that, if devices are designed and tested to these standards, it could reduce potential equipment failures resulting from these interference sources.

The electromagnetic disturbances that impact the reliability of the smart grid include typical events such as switching transients and other power line disturbances, electrostatic discharge, lightning bursts, and radio frequency interference, as well as infrequent, but potentially catastrophic, high-power electromagnetic (HPEM) events such as severe geomagnetic storms, intentional electromagnetic interference (IEMI), and high-altitude electromagnetic pulse (HEMP).

The Congressional Electromagnetic Pulse (EMP) Commission has documented some of the more severe electromagnetic-disturbance-based risks and threats to critical U.S. national infrastructures, including the electric power grid upon which other infrastructures depend.[176] These threats and their potential impacts provide impetus to evaluate, prioritize, and protect/harden the new smart grid. The EMII WG white paper also has a summary of the HPEM events (Appendix B) and the various standards and SDOs that address these disturbances. An important observation in the white paper is that "the first level of protection against HPEM disturbances is a solid EMC program and robust smart grid immunity to the typical electromagnetic interference events. The application of protective measures for high power events then builds on the immunity at the equipment level."

The standards for immunity to electromagnetic disturbances that have been reviewed and found relevant by the EMII WG for Smart Grid devices are listed in the following table:

Table 8.1. Standards for Immunity to Electromagnetic Interference

Standard	Title
IEC 61000-2-5 Ed. 2.0 (2011-05)	Electromagnetic compatibility (EMC) - Part 2-5: Environment – Description and classification of electromagnetic environments Note: This document gives guidance to product committees to determine which basic EMC tests to perform and how to select the test levels.

[176] http://www.empcommission.org

Standard	Title
IEC 61000-4-2 Ed. 2.0 (2008-12)	Electromagnetic compatibility (EMC) - Part 4-2: Testing and measurement techniques - Electrostatic discharge immunity test
IEC 61000-4-3 Ed. 3.2 (2010-04)	Electromagnetic compatibility (EMC) - Part 4-3: Testing and measurement techniques - Radiated, radio-frequency, electromagnetic field immunity test
IEC 61000-4-4 Ed. 3.0 (2012-04)	Electromagnetic compatibility (EMC) - Part 4-4: Testing and measurement techniques - Electrical fast transient/burst immunity test
IEC 61000-4-5 Ed. 3.0 (2014-05)	Electromagnetic compatibility (EMC) - Part 4-5: Testing and measurement techniques - Surge immunity test
IEC 61000-4-6 Ed. 4.0 (2013-10)	Electromagnetic compatibility (EMC) - Part 4-6: Testing and measurement techniques - Immunity to conducted disturbances, induced by radio-frequency fields
IEC 61000-4-8 Ed. 2.0 (2009-09)	Electromagnetic compatibility (EMC) - Part 4-8: Testing and measurement techniques - Power frequency magnetic field immunity test
IEC 61000-4-11 Ed. 2.0 (2004-03)	Electromagnetic compatibility (EMC) - Part 4-11: Testing and measurement techniques - Voltage dips, short interruptions and voltage variations immunity tests
IEC 61000-4-12 Ed. 2.0 (2006-09)	Electromagnetic compatibility (EMC) - Part 4-12: Testing and measurement techniques – Ring wave immunity test
IEC 61000-4-16 Ed. 1.0 (2001-07)	Electromagnetic compatibility (EMC) - Part 4-16: Testing and measurement techniques – Test for immunity to conducted, common mode disturbances in the frequency range 0 Hz to 150 kHz
IEC 61000-4-18 Ed. 1.1 (2011-03)	Electromagnetic compatibility (EMC) - Part 4-18: Testing and measurement techniques - Damped oscillatory wave immunity test
IEC 61000-4-19 Approved FDIS	Electromagnetic compatibility (EMC) - Part 4-19: Testing and measurement techniques - Test for immunity to

Standard	Title
	conducted, differential mode disturbances and signaling in the frequency range from 2 kHz to 150 kHz, at a.c. power ports Note: The standard will be published in several months
IEC 61000-4-23 Ed. 1 (2000-10)	Electromagnetic compatibility (EMC) - Part 4-23: Testing and measurement techniques - Test methods for protective devices for HEMP and other radiated disturbances
IEC 61000-4-24 Ed. 1.0 (1997-02)	Electromagnetic compatibility (EMC) - Part 4-24: Testing and measurement techniques - Test methods for protective devices for HEMP conducted disturbances
IEC 61000-4-25 Ed. 1.1 (2012-05)	Electromagnetic compatibility (EMC) - Part 4-25: Testing and measurement techniques – HEMP immunity test methods for equipment and systems
IEC 61000-4-33 Ed. 1.0 (2005-09)	Electromagnetic compatibility (EMC) - Part 4-33: Testing and measurement techniques – Measurement methods for high-power transient parameters
IEC/TS 61000-6-5 Ed. 1.0 (2001-07)	Electromagnetic compatibility (EMC) – Part 6-5: Generic standards – Immunity for power station and substation environments
IEC 61000-6-6 Ed. 1.0 (2003-04)	Electromagnetic compatibility (EMC) – Part 6-6: Generic standards – HEMP immunity for indoor equipment
IEC 60255-26 Ed. 3.0 (2013-05)	Measuring relays and protection equipment - Part 26: Electromagnetic compatibility requirements
IEC 60870-2-1 Ed. 2.0 (1995-12)	Telecontrol equipment and systems - Part 2: Operating conditions - Section 1: Power supply and electromagnetic compatibility
IEC 61850-3 Ed. 2.0 (2013-12)	Communication networks and systems for power utility automation - Part 3: General requirements Note: EMC aspects are found in clause 6.7

Standard	Title
IEEE P1642	IEEE Draft Recommended Practice for Protecting Public Accessible Computer Systems from Intentional EMI Note: To be published in 2014
IEEE Std 1613.1-2013	Standard Environmental and Testing Requirements for Communications Networking Devices Installed in Transmission and Distribution Facilities
IEEE Std C37.90.3-2001	IEEE Standard Electrostatic Discharge Tests for Protective Relays
IEEE Std C37.90.2-2004	IEEE Standard for Withstand Capability of Relay Systems to Radiated Electromagnetic Interference from Transceivers
IEEE Std C37.90.1-2012	IEEE Standard for Surge Withstand Capability (SWC) Tests for Relays and Relay Systems Associated with Electric Power Apparatus
IEEE Std C37.90-2005	IEEE Standard for Relays and Relay Systems Associated with Electric Power Apparatus

The EMC standards in the above table include basic immunity test methods (e.g., IEC 61000-4 series) along with a number of product or device specific standards that typically refer to the basic test methods. EMC for smart grid devices also includes test standards related to control of electromagnetic emissions that may interfere with other devices or adversely affect licensed radio services. These emissions tests and standards are not included here because the emissions from most devices are limited by rules from various regulatory agencies. (These regulations typically rely on standard test methods.) However, there is ongoing activity within the EMC standards bodies (IEC, CISPR, and IEEE in particular) related to both the immunity and emissions test methods and standards directed toward specific product families. This reflects the need for EMC requirements to keep pace with evolving technology and product development. Thus, the above list of EMC standards will also need to be revised, expanded, and updated as more standards are identified or developed for the smart grid.

8.3. Implementability, Safety, Reliability and Resiliency

8.3.1. Implementability and Safety

Implementability covers a number of key issues, such as the following:

- Whether each proposed interoperability standard would enhance functionality of the development of smart grid technologies

- What the impacts on consumers are

- What the potential impacts on the electric industry are

- Whether the standard/protocol pertains to interoperability and functionality of the implementations of these standards and protocols

- Whether the standard is ready to be implemented by utilities

In addition, implementability addresses impacts on consumers, as well as potential impacts upon the electric industry associated with implementing smart grid standards and protocols.

At a Federal Energy Regulatory Commission (FERC) Technical Conference on Smart Grid Interoperability Standards held in January 2011[177] and in subsequent filings, concerns were expressed by presenters at the meeting and in comments submitted to FERC regarding how new standards and technologies will impact the reliability and security of the national power grid. Additionally, concerns about the maturity of implementations and maturity of the underlying technologies used in a particular standard were also raised, including legacy issues. The standards information forms and posted narratives described in Chapter 4 contain some of the information regarding maturity of the standards and implementations, as well as the FERC-approved North American Energy Reliability Corporation (NERC) reliability standards that may be impacted by adoption of the standards, but formal reviews related to the reliability and implementability issues were not part of the original NIST or SGIP CoS processes. During the evolution of the legacy grid to the smart grid, the introduction of new standards and technologies may pose implementation and transition challenges and may affect the reliability, resiliency, and safety of the grid.

Safety should be a key attribute of smart grid technology as it is integrated into the electrical infrastructure. Electric utility and communications installations have used the National Electrical Safety Code® (ANSI C2) as the rules for the practical safeguarding of persons for utility and communications installation since 1913. The code was originally sponsored by the National Bureau of Standards (the name by which NIST was known from 1905 to 1988[178]). Since 1973,

---

[177] See
http://ferc.gov/EventCalendar/EventDetails.aspx?ID=5571&CalType=%20&CalendarID=116&Date=01/31/2011&View=Listview

[178] See http://www.100.nist.gov/directors.htm

the Institute of Electrical and Electronics Engineers (IEEE) has been the administrative secretariat. New editions are published every five years.

In the customer domain, electrical installations are governed by the National Electrical Code® (NEC®) (ANSI/NFPA70). First published in 1897, the National Electrical Code® is adopted at the state or local level in all 50 states and in many other countries. The code is intended to protect persons and property from hazards arising from the use of electricity. The installation requirements of the code are enforced by government or private electrical inspectors or building officials. A companion standard, Electrical Safety in the Workplace (ANSI/NFPA70E), provides requirements for workers who may be exposed to electrical hazards. Both the NEC and NFPA 70E have three-year revision cycles.

Because the NEC is an important element in the safe implementation of smart grid technology in new as well as existing installations, NIST funded a research project through the Fire Protection Research Foundation to study the impact of smart grid on the electrical infrastructure in the customer domain. Researchers from California Polytechnic State University studied customer domain requirements along with the impacts of energy management and emerging alternative energy technologies. Their findings are covered by a report of the research entitled "Smart Grid and NFPA Electrical Safety Codes and Standards"[179]. This report is being used as a basis for smart grid-related changes for the 2014 edition of the NEC.

8.3.2. Reliability and Resiliency

The U.S. Department of Energy (DOE) has used definitions for reliability and resiliency in some of its publications. One publication defines "reliability" as the ability of power system components to deliver electricity to all points of consumption, in the quantity and with the quality demanded by the customer.[180] Another DOE publication defines "resiliency" as the ability of an energy facility to recover quickly from damage to any of its components or to any of the external systems on which it depends.[181] Resiliency measures do not prevent damage; rather they enable energy systems to continue operating despite damage and/or promote a rapid return to normal operations when damage/outages do occur. Other definitions are also available. The North American Electric Reliability Corporation (NERC) defines "operating reliability"[182] as the ability of the electric system to withstand sudden disturbances such as electric short circuits or unanticipated loss of system components. The National Infrastructure Advisory Council (NIAC)

---

[179] See http://www.nfpa.org/itemDetail.asp?categoryID=1878&itemID=35445&URL=Research/Fire%20Protection%20Research%20Foundation/Reports%20and%20proceedings/Electrical%20safety

[180] See *Reliability of the U.S. Electricity System: Recent Trends and Current Issues*, p. 2, Aug 2001, at http://emp.lbl.gov/sites/all/files/REPORT%20lbnl%20-%2047043.pdf

[181] See *Hardening and Resiliency—U.S. Energy Industry Response to Recent Hurricane Seasons*, p. 9, Aug 2010, at http://www.oe.netl.doe.gov/docs/HR-Report-final-081710.pdf

[182] NERC document, *Definition of "Adequate Reliability"*, December 2007. See http://www.nerc.com/docs/pc/Definition-of-ALR-approved-at-Dec-07-OC-PC-mtgs.pdf

defines "infrastructure resilience"[183] as the ability to reduce the magnitude or duration of disruptive events.

Recent events such as Hurricane Sandy in 2012 and the Southwest Blackout of September 2011 have raised the public visibility and concern about reliability and resiliency. A DOE report, "U.S. Energy Sector Vulnerabilities to Climate Change and Extreme Weather (July 2013)"[184] found that "the pace, scale, and scope of combined public and private efforts to improve the climate preparedness and resilience of the energy sector will need to increase, given the challenges identified. Greater resilience will require improved technologies, polices, information, and stakeholder engagement."

A White House report, "Economic Benefits of Increasing Electric Grid Resilience to Weather Outages (August 2013),"[185] found that weather-related outages in the period from 2003 to 2012 are estimated to have cost the U.S. economy an inflation-adjusted annual average of $18 billion to $33 billion. The report concluded, "Continued investment in grid modernization and resilience will mitigate these costs over time—saving the economy billions of dollars and reducing the hardship experienced by millions of Americans when extreme weather strikes."

There is an increased awareness of the impact of power grid disruptions from weather related events as a consequence of Hurricane Sandy. Reliability and resilience of the power delivery system has become a top priority for utilities, regulators, and the DOE. Potential threats to the grid from cyber- and/or physical-attacks compound the importance of considering solutions to strengthen the power system in light of these threats and low probability, high impact events (e.g. geo-magnetic storms). Smart grid technologies in different configurations in the distribution system offer answers to these threats and the disruption that they bring to the normal functioning of the social and economic environment.

Microgrids offer an ideal solution for such disruptions by bringing smart grid technologies and communications together to maintain the supply of power to critical loads and non-critical loads alike to assure continuity of power delivery to critical systems and facilities, while also providing a more adaptive and reliable power system during normal operating conditions. The SGIP has recently added a group focused on information exchange and standards for microgrids, and the NIST smart grid laboratory programs include a focus on advanced technologies and interoperability for microgrid scenarios.

---

[183] NIAC document, *A Framework for Establishing Critical Infrastructure Resilience Goals—Final Report and Recommendations by the Council*, October 19, 2010. See http://www.dhs.gov/xlibrary/assets/niac/niac-a-framework-for-establishing-critical-infrastructure-resilience-goals-2010-10-19.pdf

[184] See http://energy.gov/sites/prod/files/2013/07/f2/20130716-Energy%20Sector%20Vulnerabilities%20Report.pdf

[185] See http://energy.gov/sites/prod/files/2013/08/f2/Grid%20Resiliency%20Report_FINAL.pdf

8.3.3. SGIP action

The SGIP is now considering the addition of reviews for implementability, safety, reliability, and resilience considerations to the CoS process described in Sections 3.6 and 4.5. New working groups that would conduct these reviews would analyze candidate standards for:

- Potential for unintended consequences for existing protection and control schemes, and other market or grid operational systems

- Potential impacts of complexities introduced into the electric system and market management complexities

- Possible reliability and resiliency enhancements by utilizing the capabilities of the candidate standard

- Impacts of the candidate standard on the safety of the electrical grid

In addition, depending on the existing legacy technologies and processes, there are various implementation and migration challenges present in adopting new standards and integrating their implementations with legacy technologies. Regulatory commissions, utilities, and others will consider implementation factors, such as sufficient maturity of a standard as demonstrated in standards-compliant commercially available products, effective technology transition plans to maintain reliable operations, and cost-effective deployment.

To address some of these issues, the SGIP created the Implementation Methods Committee (IMC), whose mission is to identify, develop, and support mechanisms and tools for objective standards impact assessment, transition management, and technology transfer in order to assist in deployment of standards-based smart grid devices, systems and infrastructure.

Presently the SGIP provides a means of addressing such issues, upon identification by an industry participant, by assigning resolution to an existing working group or forming a new PAP to scope out the resolution. An example of this is PAP18, which was formed to address the issue of Smart Energy Profile (SEP) 1.x migration to SEP 2.0.

The SGIP is now considering alternatives to this approach, such as creating a new review process within the CoS process to assess implementation considerations and prepare guidance for each new standard proposed or included in the CoS. This review would analyze the issues involved in implementation of new standards, potentially including:

- Technology transition risks and any potential stranded equipment implications

- Business process changes required

- Relative implementation maturity of the standard and related implementation consideration

- Cost drivers that facilitate evaluation of relative cost-effectiveness of alternate solutions

- Applicable federal and state policy considerations related to standards implementation.

This additional implementation review would be included in the SGIP CoS process.

8.4. The Smart Grid Community Effort to Further Define R&D Needs

Although the focus of this Framework document is on standards and protocols to ensure interoperability, it is important to note that standards and protocols are not enough. There is also a clear need for R&D—to take advantage of new data, innovations, technologies, and functionalities. R&D will lead to new and innovative methods for advancing the grid. There is also a clear need for R&D to address new problems, constraints, and challenges as they arise.

To help identify the major technical and societal issues impeding advanced development of the smart grid, and determine a set of recommended actions to address these issues, the NIST Smart Grid and Cyber-Physical Systems Program Office, in collaboration with the Renewable and Sustainable Energy Institute (RASEI), hosted an invitational workshop at the University of Colorado in Boulder, Colorado, on August 13-14, 2012. The workshop was attended by approximately 95 topical experts from industry, academia, and government laboratories, and sought consensus in four main areas of smart grid technology and measurement science that had been initially discussed during preparatory teleconferences during the previous several months.

The workshop was oriented toward the industrial community, and was consensus-driven, as opposed to tutorial in nature. The primary output of the workshop was a high-level Strategic R&D Opportunities document, now in the public domain.[186] This document outlines a set of strategic R&D opportunities that must be addressed to enable the smart grid to reach its potential and deliver broad societal and economic benefits to the nation. The document indicates opportunities in:

- Optimizing smart grid capabilities for system planning and operations
- Developing smart tools and technologies to optimize demand-response, load control, and energy efficiency
- Expanding and upgrading infrastructure to improve communications and interconnectivity
- Developing infrastructure to assure security and resilience
- Creating models to foster smart grid investment and inform regulatory frameworks

It is particularly useful for technology managers and industrial decision makers as they develop new programs in the smart grid arena. In addition, it will be useful to senior managers at NIST as they guide the development of the NIST smart grid measurement science effort.

---

[186] *Strategic R&D Opportunities for the Smart Grid*, Report of the Steering Committee for Innovation in Smart Grid Measurement Science and Standards, March 2013; see http://www.nist.gov/smartgrid/upload/Final-Version-22-Mar-2013-Strategic-R-D-Opportunities-for-the-Smart-Grid.pdf

8.5. Framework Updates

As the SGIP progresses in its work to identify and address additional standards gaps and provide ongoing coordination to accelerate the development of smart grid standards, NIST will continue to publish Interoperability Framework updates as needed. There are continued opportunities for participation by new smart grid community members in the overall NIST process, including within the SGIP and its committees and working groups. Details about future meetings, workshops, and public comment opportunities will appear on the NIST smart grid web site[187] and smart grid collaboration site.[188]

---

[187] See http://www.nist.gov/smartgrid/

[188] NIST Smart Grid Collaboration Site. See http://collaborate.nist.gov/twiki-sggrid/bin/view/SmartGrid/WebHome

Appendix A: List of Acronyms and Abbreviations

ADWP	SGAC's Architecture Development Working Party
AEIC	Association of Edison Illuminating Companies
AMI	Advanced Metering Infrastructure
AMI-SEC	Advanced Metering Infrastructure Security
ANSI	American National Standards Institute
ARRA	American Recovery and Reinvestment Act
AS	Australian Standard
ASHRAE	American Society of Heating, Refrigerating and Air Conditioning Engineers
BAS	Building Automation System
CEA	Consumer Electronics Association
CIM	Common Information Model
CIP	Critical Infrastructure Protection
CISPR	International Special Committee on Radio Interference
CoS	Catalog of Standards
COSEM	Companion Specific for Energy Metering
CSCTG	Smart Grid Cyber Security Coordination Task Group
CSRC	Computer Security Resource Center
CSWG	Cybersecurity Working Group
DA	Distribution Automation
DER	Distributed Energy Resources
DEWG	Domain Expert Working Group
DG	Distributed Generation
DGM	Distribution Grid Management
DHS	Department of Homeland Security
DMS	Distribution Management System
DNP	Distributed Network Protocol
DOE	Department of Energy
DR	Demand Response
DRGS	Distributed Renewable Generation and Storage
EISA	Energy Independence and Security Act of 2007
EMIX	Energy Market Information Exchange

EMS	Energy Management System
ENTSO-E	European Network of Transmission System Operators for Electricity
EPRI	Electric Power Research Institute
ESI	Energy Services Interface
ESP	Energy Service Provider
EU SG-CG	European Commission Smart Grid Coordination Group
EV	Electric Vehicle
EVSE	Electric Vehicle Supply Equipment
F2F	Face to Face
FCC	Federal Communications Commission
FERC	Federal Energy Regulatory Commission
GML	Geography Markup Language
GOOSE	Generic Object-Oriented Substation Event
GWAC	GridWise Architecture Council
HAN	Home Area Network
HEMP	High-Altitude Electromagnetic Pulse
HPEM	High Power Electromagnetic
HTTP	Hypertext Transfer Protocol
ICCP	Inter-Control Centre Communications Protocol
ICS	Industrial Control Systems
ICT	Information and Communications Technology
IEC	International Electrotechnical Commission
IED	Intelligent Electronic Device
IEEE	Institute of Electrical and Electronic Engineers
IETF	Internet Engineering Task Force
IKB	Interoperability Knowledge Base
IMAM	Interoperability Maturity Assessment Model
IP	Internet Protocol
IPRM	Interoperability Process Reference Manual
ISO	International Organization for Standardization
ISO	Independent Systems Operator
IT	Information Technology
ITCA	Interoperability Testing and Certification Authority

ITU	International Telecommunication Union
LAN	Local Area Network
MAC	Medium Access Control
MDMS	Meter Data Management System
MMS	Manufacturing Messaging Specification
NAESB	North American Energy Standards Board
NARUC	National Association of Regulatory Utility Commissioners
NASPI	North American Synchrophasor Initiative
NEMA	National Electrical Manufacturers Association
NERC	North American Electric Reliability Corporation
NIST	National Institute of Standards and Technology
NISTIR	NIST Interagency Report
NSTC	National Science and Technology Council
OASIS	Organization for the Advancement of Structured Information Standards
OGC	Open Geospatial Consortium
OMB	Office of Management and Budget
OMG	Object Management Group
OSI	Open Systems Interconnection
PAP	Priority Action Plan
PEV	Plug-in Electric Vehicles
PDC	Phasor Data Concentrator
PHEV	Plug-in Hybrid Electric Vehicle
PHY	Physical Layer
PLC	Power Line Carrier
PMO	Program Management Office
PMU	Phasor Measurement Unit
PSRC	Power System Relaying Committee
PUC	Public Utility Commission
QOS	Quality of Service
RFC	Request for Comments, Remote Feedback Controller
RTO	Regional Transmission Operator
RTU	Remote Terminal Unit
SAE	Society of Automotive Engineers

SCADA	Supervisory Control and Data Acquisition
SDO	Standards Development Organization, Standards Developing Organization
SGAC	Smart Grid Architecture Committee
SGIP	Smart Grid Interoperability Panel
SGIP-CSWG	Smart Grid Interoperability Panel - Cybersecurity Working Group
SGIPGB	Smart Grid Interoperability Panel Governing Board
SGTCC	Smart Grid Testing and Certification Committee
SOA	Service-Oriented Architecture
SSO	Standards-Setting Organization
TASE	Telecontrol Application Service Element
TCP	Transport Control Protocol
TDL	Table Definition Language
TOGAF	The Open Group Architecture Framework
UCAIug	UCA International Users Group
UDP	User Datagram Protocol
UML	Unified Modeling Language
VAR	Volt-Ampere Reactive
WASA	Wide-Area Situational Awareness
WG	Working Group
XML	eXtensible Markup Language

Appendix B: Specific Domain Diagrams

Introduction

The conceptual model consists of several *domains*, each of which contains many *applications* and *roles* that are connected by *associations*, through *interfaces.*

- **Actor** is considered to be a person, organization, or system that has at least one role that initiates or interacts with activities. Actors may be internal or external to an organization Actors may be devices, computer systems, or software programs and/or the organizations that own them. Actors have the capability to make decisions and exchange information with other actors through interfaces.

- **Role** is the usual or expected function, capability of, or service played by an actor, or the part somebody or something plays in a particular action or event. An actor may play a number of roles.

- **Applications** are automated processes that perform services at the request of or by roles within the domains. Some applications are performed by a single role, others by several actors /roles working together.

- **Domains** group roles together to discover the commonalities that define the interfaces. In general, roles in the same domain have similar objectives. Communications within the same domain may have similar characteristics and requirements. Domains may contain other domains or sub-domains.

- **Associations** are logical connections between roles that establish bilateral relationships. Roles interact with associated roles through interfaces. In Fig. 5-1, the electrical associations between domains are shown as dashed lines, and the communications associations are shown as solid lines.

- **Interfaces** represent the point of access between domains. Communication interfaces are at each end of the communication associations and represent the access point for information to enter and exit a domain (interfaces are logical). Communication interfaces define roles that connect actors to enable applications. Interfaces show either electrical connections or communications connections. Each of these interfaces may be bidirectional. Communications interfaces represent an information exchange between two domains and the actors within; they do not represent physical connections. They represent logical connections in the smart grid information network interconnecting various domains (as shown in Figure 5-3).

There are seven domains represented within the smart grid system, as shown in Table B-1 and in Figure B-1. These diagrams represent logical domains based on the present and near-term view of the grid. In the future, some of the domains may combine, such as Transmission and Distribution. Some of the domain names may evolve, such as Bulk Generation now becoming simply Generation as distributed energy resources (DER) and renewable resources play an increasingly important role.

NOTE TO READER: The tables, figures, and discussion in this chapter are essentially the same as the tables, figures, and discussion in Release 1.0, Chapter 9. A few grammatical and other editorial changes have been made, but the basic content has not been changed, except for the addition of "Storage" to the customer domain application categories in (Table B-2), and of "DER" to the distribution domain application categories (Table B-8).

Table B-1. Domains in the Smart Grid Conceptual Model

Domain	Description
Customer	The end users of electricity. May also generate, store, and manage the use of energy. Traditionally, three customer types are discussed, each with its own sub-domain: home, commercial/building, and industrial.
Markets	The operators and participants in electricity markets.
Service Provider	The organizations providing services to electrical customers and to utilities.
Operations	The managers of the movement of electricity.
Generation	The generators of electricity. May also store energy for later distribution.
Transmission	The carriers of bulk electricity over long distances. May also store and generate electricity.
Distribution	The distributors of electricity to and from customers. May also store and generate electricity.

It is important to note that domains are *not* organizations. For instance, an Independent Systems Operator (ISO) or Regional Transmission Operator (RTO) may have actors in both the Markets and Operations domains. Similarly, a distribution utility is not entirely contained within the Distribution domain—it is likely to also contain actors in the Operations domain, such as a distribution management system (DMS), and in the Customer domain, such as meters.

Conceptual Model

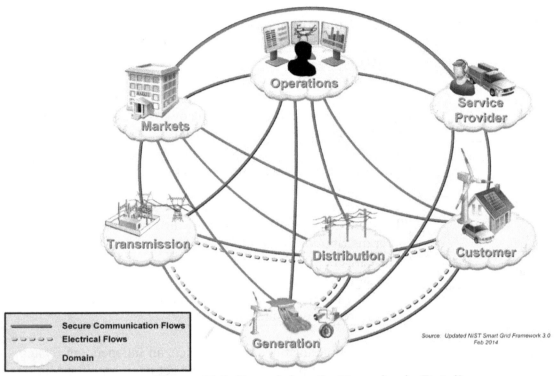

Secure Communication Flows
Electrical Flows
Domain

Source: *Updated NIST Smart Grid Framework 3.0*
Feb 2014

Figure B-1. Examining the Domains in Detail

The purpose of the domain diagram is to provide a framework for discussing both the existing power system and the evolving smart grid. While Chapter 5 shows domain interactions and overall scope, the following sections describe the details of the specific domains. Note that the domain diagrams, as presented, are not intended to be comprehensive in identifying all actors and all paths possible in the smart grid. This achievement will only be possible after additional elaboration and consolidation of use cases are achieved by stakeholder activities that are ongoing.

It is important to note that the domain diagram (or the conceptual model) of the smart grid is not limited to a single domain, single application, or single use case. For example, the use of "smart grid" in some discussions has been applied to only distribution automation or in other discussions to only advanced metering or demand response. The conceptual model assumes that smart grid includes a wide variety of use cases and applications, especially (but not limited to) functional priorities and cross-cutting requirements identified by the Federal Energy Regulatory Commission (FERC). The scope also includes other cross-cutting requirements including data management and application integration, as described in the GridWise Architecture Council *Interoperability Context-Setting Framework.*[189]

---

[189] See http://www.gridwiseac.org/pdfs/interopframework_v1_1.pdf

Customer Domain

The customer is ultimately the stakeholder that the entire grid was created to support. This is the domain where electricity is consumed (see Fig. B-2). Actors in the Customer Domain enable customers to manage their energy usage and generation. Some actors also provide control and information flow between the Customer domain and the other domains. The boundaries of the Customer domain are typically considered to be the utility meter and the energy services interface (ESI). The ESI provides a secure interface for utility-to-customer interactions. The ESI in turn can act as a bridge to facility-based systems, such as a building automation system (BAS) or a customer's premise management system. (For further discussion of the utility meter and the ESI, see Section 3.6 in Framework 2.0.[190])

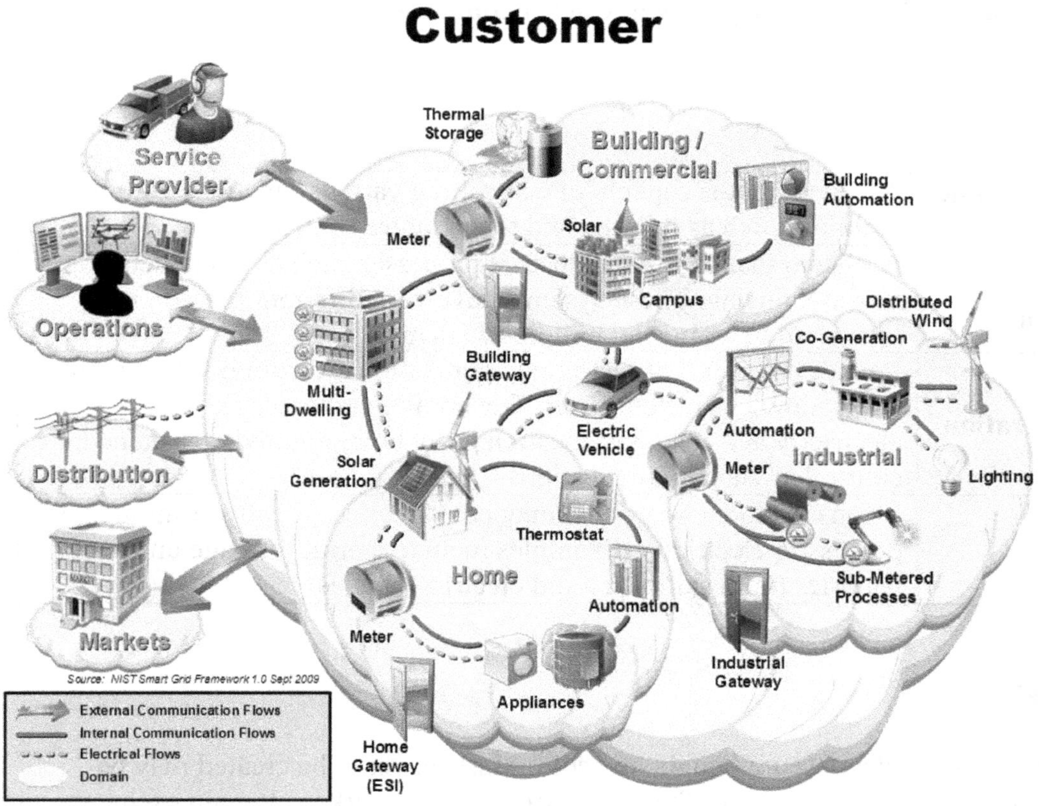

Figure B-2. Overview of the Customer Domain

The Customer domain is usually segmented into sub-domains for home, commercial/building, and industrial. The energy needs of these sub-domains are typically set at less than 20 kW of demand for a residence, 20-200 kW for commercial buildings, and over 200kW for industrial. Each sub-domain has multiple actors and applications, which may also be present in the other sub-domains. Each sub-domain has a meter actor and an ESI, which may reside in the meter, in a premise-management system, or outside the premises, or at an end-device. The ESI is the primary service interface to the Customer domain. The ESI may communicate with other

---

[190] See http://nist.gov/smartgrid/upload/NIST_Framework_Release_2-0_corr.pdf

domains via the advanced metering infrastructure (AMI) or another means, such as the internet. The ESI provides the interface to devices and systems within the customer premises, either directly or via a home area network (HAN), other local area network (LAN) or some other mechanism in the future.

There may be more than one communications path per customer. Entry points may support applications such as remote load control, monitoring and control of distributed generation, in-home display of customer usage, reading of non-energy meters, and integration with building management systems and the enterprise. They may provide auditing/logging for cybersecurity purposes. The Customer domain is electrically connected to the Distribution domain. It communicates with the Distribution, Operations, Market, and Service Provider domains.

Table B-2. Typical Application Categories in the Customer Domain

Example Application Category	Description
Building or Home Automation	A system that is capable of controlling various functions within a building, such as lighting and temperature control.
Industrial Automation	A system that controls industrial processes such as manufacturing or warehousing. These systems have very different requirements compared to home and building systems.
Micro-generation	Includes all types of distributed generation including: solar, wind, and hydroelectric generators. Generation harnesses energy for electricity at a customer location. May be monitored, dispatched, or controlled via communications.
Storage	Means to store energy that may be converted directly or through a process to electricity. Examples include thermal storage units, and batteries (both stationary and electric vehicles)

Markets Domain

The markets are where grid assets are bought and sold. Markets yet to be created may be instrumental in defining the smart grid of the future. Roles in the markets domain exchange price and balance supply and demand within the power system (see Fig. B-3). The boundaries of the Markets domain include the edge of the Operations domain where control happens, the domains supplying assets (e.g., Generation, Transmission, etc.), and the Customer domain.

Markets

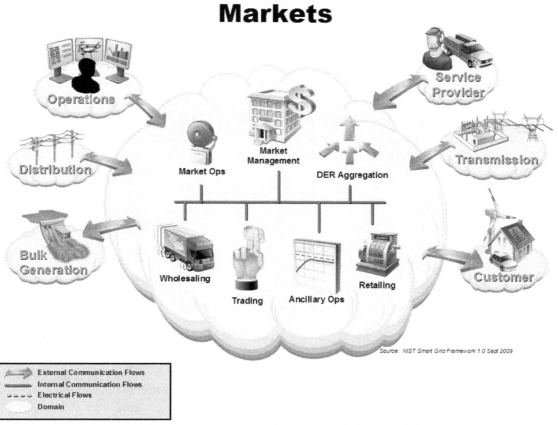

Source: NIST Smart Grid Framework 1.0 Sept 2009

- → External Communication Flows
- — Internal Communication Flows
- - - Electrical Flows
- ⬭ Domain

Figure B-3. Overview of the Markets Domain

Communication flows between the Markets domain and the domains supplying energy are critical because efficient matching of production with consumption is dependent on markets. Energy supply domains include the Generation domain. The North American Electric Reliability Corporation (NERC) Critical Infrastructure Protections (CIP) standards consider suppliers of more than 300 megawatts to be bulk generation; most DER is smaller and is typically served through aggregators. DER participates in markets to some extent today, and will participate to a greater extent as the smart grid becomes more interactive.

Communications for Markets domain interactions must be reliable, traceable, and auditable. Also, these communications must support e-commerce standards for integrity and non-repudiation. As the percentage of energy supplied by small DER increases, the allowed latency in communications with these resources must be reduced.

The high-priority challenges in the Markets domain are: extending price and DER signals to each of the Customer sub-domains; simplifying market rules; expanding the capabilities of aggregators; ensuring interoperability across all providers and consumers of market information; managing the growth (and regulation) of retailing and wholesaling of energy; and evolving communication mechanisms for prices and energy characteristics between and throughout the Markets and Customer domains.

Table B-3. Typical Applications in the Markets Domain

Example Application	Description
Market Management	Market managers include ISOs for wholesale markets or New York Mercantile Exchange (NYMEX)/ Chicago Mercantile Exchange (CME) for forward markets in many ISO/RTO regions. There are transmission, services, and demand response markets as well. Some DER Curtailment resources are treated today as dispatchable generation.
Retailing	Retailers sell power to end-customers and may in the future aggregate or broker DER between customers or into the market. Most are connected to a trading organization to allow participation in the wholesale market.
DER Aggregation	Aggregators combine smaller participants (as providers, customers, or curtailment) to enable distributed resources to play in the larger markets.
Trading	Traders are participants in markets, which include aggregators for provision, consumption, curtailment, and other qualified entities. There are a number of companies whose primary business is the buying and selling of energy.
Market Operations	Market operations make a particular market function smoothly. Functions include financial and goods-sold clearing, price quotation streams, audit, balancing, and more.
Ancillary Operations	Ancillary operations provide a market to provide frequency support, voltage support, spinning reserve, and other ancillary services as defined by FERC, NERC, and the various ISOs. These markets normally function on a regional or ISO basis.

Service Provider Domain

Actors in the Service Provider domain perform services to support the business processes of power system producers, distributors, and customers (see Fig. B-4). These business processes range from traditional utility services, such as billing and customer account management, to enhanced customer services, such as management of energy use and home energy generation.

Service Provider

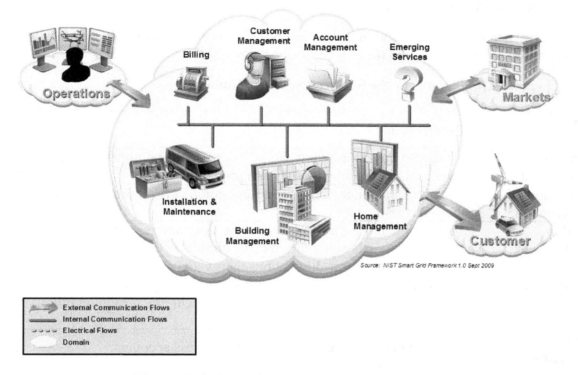

Source: NIST Smart Grid Framework 1.0 Sept 2009

External Communication Flows
Internal Communication Flows
Electrical Flows
Domain

Figure B-4. Overview of the Service Provider Domain

The Service Provider domain shares interfaces with the Markets, Operations, and Customer domains. Communications with the Operations domain are critical for system control and situational awareness; communications with the Markets and Customer domains are critical for enabling economic growth through the development of "smart" services. For example, the Service Provider domain may provide the interface enabling the customer to interact with the market.

Service providers create new and innovative services and products to meet the requirements and opportunities presented by the evolving smart grid. Services may be performed by the electric service provider, by existing third parties, or by new participants drawn by new business models. Emerging services represent an area of significant new economic growth.
The priority challenge in the Service Provider domain is to develop key interfaces and standards that will enable a dynamic market-driven ecosystem while protecting the critical power infrastructure. These interfaces must be able to operate over a variety of networking technologies while maintaining consistent messaging semantics. The service provider must not compromise the cybersecurity, reliability, stability, integrity, or safety of the electrical power network when delivering existing or emerging services.

Some benefits to the service provider domain from the deployment of the smart grid include:

- The development of a growing market for non-utility providers to provide value-added services and products to customers, utilities, and other stakeholders at competitive costs;

- The decrease in cost of business services for other smart grid domains; and

- A decrease in power consumption and an increase in power generation as customers become active participants in the power supply chain.

Table B-4. Typical Applications in the Service Provider Domain

Example Application	Description
Customer Management	Managing customer relationships by providing point-of-contact and resolution for customer issues and problems.
Installation & Maintenance	Installing and maintaining premises equipment that interacts with the smart grid.
Building Management	Monitoring and controlling building energy and responding to smart grid signals while minimizing impact on building occupants.
Home Management	Monitoring and controlling home energy and responding to smart grid signals while minimizing impact on home occupants.
Billing	Managing customer billing information, including providing billing statements and payment processing.
Account Management	Managing the supplier and customer business accounts.

Operations Domain

Actors in the Operations domain are responsible for the smooth operation of the power system. Today, the majority of these functions are the responsibility of a regulated utility (see Fig. B-5). The smart grid will enable more of these functions to be provided by service providers. No matter how the Service Provider and Markets domains evolve, there will still be functions needed for planning and operating the service delivery points of a regulated "wires" company.

Operations

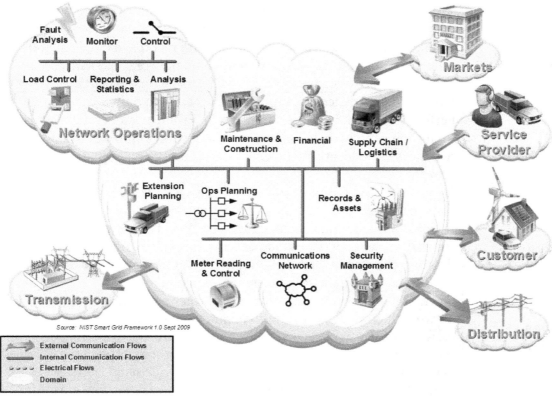

Source: NIST Smart Grid Framework 1.0 Sept 2009

External Communication Flows
Internal Communication Flows
Electrical Flows
Domain

Figure B-5. Overview of the Operations Domain

Currently, at the physical level, various energy management systems are used to analyze and operate the power system reliably and efficiently.

Representative applications within the Operations domain are described in Table B-5. These applications are derived from the International Electrotechnical Commission (IEC) 61968-1 Interface Reference Model (IRM) for this domain.

Table B-5. Typical Applications in the Operations Domain

Example Application	Description
Monitoring	Network operation monitoring roles supervise network topology, connectivity, and loading conditions, including breaker and switch states, as well as control equipment status. They locate customer telephone complaints and field crews.
Control	Network control is coordinated by roles in this domain. They may only supervise wide area, substation, and local automatic or manual control.
Fault Management	Fault management roles enhance the speed at which faults can be located, identified, and sectionalized, and the speed at which

Example Application	Description
	service can be restored. They provide information for customers, coordinate workforce dispatch, and compile information statistics.
Analysis	Operation feedback analysis roles compare records taken from real-time operation related with information on network incidents, connectivity, and loading to optimize periodic maintenance.
Reporting and Statistics	Operational statistics and reporting roles archive online data and perform feedback analysis about system efficiency and reliability.
Network Calculations	Real-time network calculations roles (not shown) provide system operators with the ability to assess the reliability and security of the power system.
Training	Dispatcher training roles (not shown) provide facilities for dispatchers that simulate the actual system they will be using.
Records and Assets	Records and asset management roles track and report on the substation and network equipment inventory, provide geospatial data and geographic displays, maintain records on non-electrical assets, and perform asset-investment planning.
Operation Planning	Operational planning and optimization roles perform simulation of network operations, schedule switching actions, dispatch repair crews, inform affected customers, and schedule the importing of power. They keep the cost of imported power low through peak generation, switching, load shedding, DER or demand response.
Maintenance and Construction	Maintenance and construction roles coordinate inspection, cleaning, and adjustment of equipment; organize construction and design; dispatch and schedule maintenance and construction work; and capture records gathered by field technicians to view necessary information to perform their tasks.
Extension Planning	Network extension planning roles develop long-term plans for power system reliability; monitor the cost, performance, and schedule of construction; and define projects to extend the network, such as new lines, feeders, or switchgear.
Customer Support	Customer support roles help customers to purchase, provision, install, and troubleshoot power system services. They also relay and record customer trouble reports.

Generation Domain

Applications in the Generation domain are the first processes in the delivery of electricity to customers (see Fig. B-6). Electricity generation is the process of creating electricity from other forms of energy, which may include a wide variety of sources, using chemical combustion, nuclear fission, flowing water, wind, solar radiation, and geothermal heat. The boundary of the Generation domain is either the Transmission or Distribution or Customer domain. The Generation domain is electrically connected to the Transmission or Distribution or Customer domain and shares interfaces with the Operations, Markets, Transmission and Distribution domains.

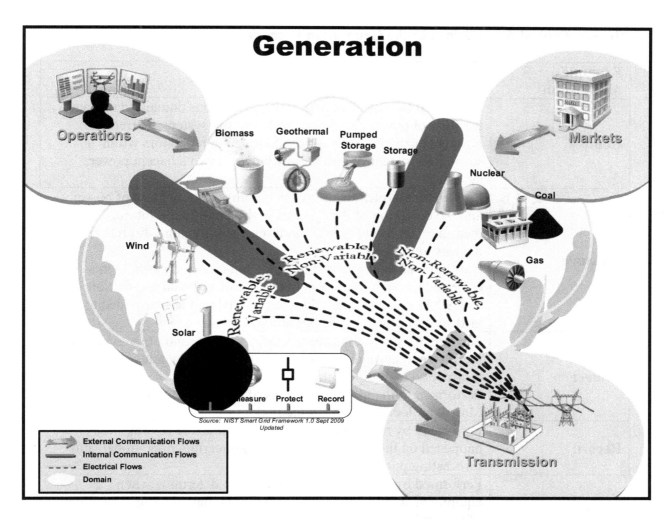

Figure B-6. Overview of the Generation Domain

Communications with the Transmission and Distribution domains are critical, because without a delivery mechanism, customers cannot be served. The Generation domain should communicate key performance and quality of service issues such as scarcity (especially for wind and solar, which are variable sources) and generator failure. These communications may cause the routing of electricity from other sources. A lack of sufficient supply is addressed directly (via operations) or indirectly (via markets).

New requirements for the Generation domain may include controls for greenhouse gas emissions, increases in renewable energy sources, and provision of storage to manage the variability of renewable generation. Roles in the Generation domain may include various physical actors, such as protection relays, remote terminal units, equipment monitors, fault recorders, user interfaces, and programmable logic controllers.

Table B-6. Typical Applications in the Generation Domain

Example Application	Description
Control	Performed by roles that permit the Operations domain to manage the flow of power and the reliability of the system. Currently a physical example is the use of phase-angle regulators within a substation to control power flow between two adjacent power systems.
Measure	Performed by roles that provide visibility into the flow of power and the condition of the systems in the field. In the future, measurement might be built into increasingly more discrete field devices in the grid. Currently, an example is the digital and analog measurements collected through the supervisory control and data acquisition (SCADA) system from a remote terminal unit and provided to a grid control center in the Operations domain.
Protect	Performed by roles that react rapidly to faults and other events in the system that might cause power outages, brownouts, or the destruction of equipment. Performed to maintain high levels of reliability and power quality. May work locally or on a wide scale.
Record	Performed by roles that permit other domains to review what happened on the grid for financial, engineering, operational, and forecasting purposes.
Asset Management	Performed by roles that work together to determine when equipment should have maintenance, calculate the life expectancy of the device, and record its history of operations and maintenance so it can be reviewed in the future for operational and engineering decisions.

Transmission Domain

Transmission is the bulk transfer of electrical power from generation sources to distribution through multiple substations (see Fig. B-7). A transmission network is typically operated by a transmission-owning utility, Regional Transmission Operator or Independent System Operator (RTO, ISO respectfully), whose primary responsibility is to maintain stability on the electric grid by balancing generation (supply) with load (demand) across the transmission network. Examples of physical actors in the Transmission domain include remote terminal units, substation meters, protection relays, power quality monitors, phasor measurement units, sag monitors, fault recorders, and substation user interfaces.

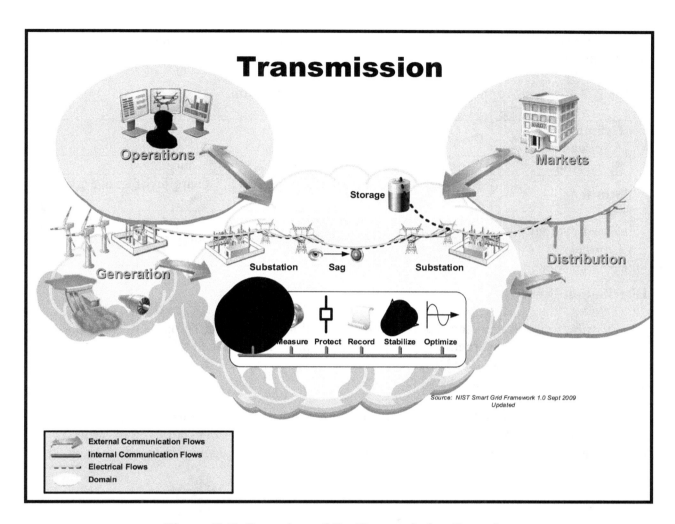

Figure B-7. Overview of the Transmission Domain

Roles in the Transmission domain typically perform the applications shown in the diagram (Fig. B-7) and described in the table (Table B-7). The Transmission domain *may* contain DER, such as electrical storage or peaking generation units.

Energy and supporting ancillary services (capacity that can be dispatched when needed) are procured through the Markets domain; scheduled and operated from the Operations domain; and finally delivered through the Transmission domain to the Distribution domain and ultimately to the Customer domain.

A transmission electrical substation uses transformers to step up or step down voltage across the electric supply chain. Substations also contain switching, protection, and control equipment. Figure B-7 depicts both step-up and step down substations connecting generation (including peaking units) and storage with distribution. Substations may also connect two or more transmission lines.

Transmission towers, power lines, and field telemetry (such as the line sag detector shown) make up the balance of the transmission network infrastructure. The transmission network is typically monitored and controlled through a SCADA system that uses a communication network, field monitoring devices, and control devices.

Table B-7. Typical Applications in the Transmission Domain

Example Application	Description
Substation	The control and monitoring systems within a substation.
Storage	A system that controls the charging and discharging of an energy storage unit.
Measurement & Control	Includes all types of measurement and control systems to measure, record, and control, with the intent of protecting and optimizing grid operation.

Distribution Domain

The Distribution domain is the electrical interconnection between the Transmission domain, the customer domain, and the metering points for consumption, distributed storage, and distributed generation (see Fig. B-8). The Distribution domain may contain DER, such as electrical storage or peaking generation units.

The electrical distribution system may be arranged in a variety of structures, including radial, looped, or meshed. The reliability of the distribution system varies depending on its structure, the types of actors that are implemented, and the degree to which they communicate with each other and with roles in other domains.

Distribution

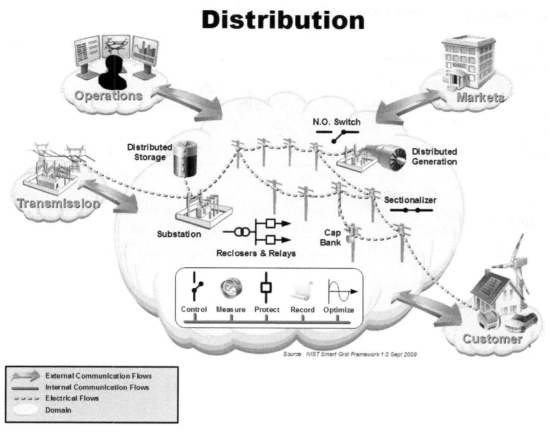

Source: NIST Smart Grid Framework 1.0 Sept 2009

Figure B-8. Overview of the Distribution Domain

Historically, distribution systems have been radial configurations, with little telemetry, and almost all communications within the domain was performed by humans. The primary installed sensor base in this domain is the customer with a telephone, whose call initiates the dispatch of a field crew to restore power. Many communications interfaces within this domain have been hierarchical and unidirectional, although they now generally can be considered to work in both directions, even as the electrical connections are just beginning to support bidirectional flow. Distribution actors may have local inter-device (peer-to-peer) communication or a more centralized communication methodology.

In the smart grid, the Distribution domain will communicate in a more granular fashion with the Operations domain in real-time to manage the power flows associated with a more dynamic Markets domain and other environmental and security-based factors. The Markets domain will communicate with the Distribution domain in ways that will affect localized consumption and generation. In turn, these behavioral changes due to market forces may have electrical and structural impacts on the Distribution domain and the larger grid. Under some models, service providers may communicate with the Customer domain using the infrastructure of the Distribution domain, which would change the communications infrastructure selected for use within the domain.

Table B-8. Typical Applications within the Distribution Domain

Example Application	Description
Substation	The control and monitoring systems within a substation.
Storage	A system that controls the charging and discharging of an energy storage unit.
Distributed Generation	A power source located on the distribution side of the grid.
DER	Energy resources that are typically located at a customer or owned by the distribution grid operator
Measurement & Control	Includes all types of measurement and control systems to measure, record, and control, with the intent of protecting and optimizing grid operation.

Appendix C: Smart Grid Service Orientation and Ontology

C.1 Overview

Like all other industries the utility / smart grid sector has a rich legacy of terms which often have contradictory understanding descriptions. Too often, there is no reference standard for them. Recognizing this, the SGIP's SGAC elected to expand on the previous conceptual architecture work and in conjunction with the EU M490 and IEC 6257 decided to apply The Open Group's service-oriented architecture and service-oriented ontology to existing and evolving smart grid terms.

C.2 Service Orientation

Service-oriented architecture (SOA) is an often-misunderstood term, so this document simply refers to it as service orientation. By definition:
"Service orientation" is a way of thinking in terms of services and service-based development and the outcomes of services.

A "service"[191]:

- Is a logical representation of a repeatable business activity that has a specified outcome (e.g., check customer credit, provide weather data, and consolidate drilling reports)

- Is self-contained

- *May be* composed of other services

- Is a "black box" to consumers of the service

Services are independent of any underlying technical implementation. The genesis of service orientation began with loosely-coupled design efforts in the 1970s to support distributed computing followed quickly with the client-server models. However, SOA is usually misunderstood to mean a specific sort of ICT technology such as XML, web services, or HTTP. These are all technologies that lend themselves to service orientation, but they do not guarantee service-oriented architectures. This misinformation is widely communicated through ICT vendors' sales and marketing efforts to sell their products. It is not consistent with the original architectural philosophy of the modularity, openness, flexibility, scalability, and lower ongoing operations cost.

C.3 Service-Oriented Ontology

"Ontology" is simply the definition of concepts within a domain and their relationships to each other. The word's background came from philosophy, where "ontology" is the study of being. It was adopted by information scientists to assist in artificial intelligence definitions and became part of object-oriented architecture in the late 1990s.

---

[191] The Open Group SOA ontology: see http://www.opengroup.org/soa/source-book/soa/soa.htm#soa_definition

As part of the conceptual architecture work, an actors list was created including every actor name and definition that a standard body was willing to contribute. During the exercise to identify where the actor participated in architecture, the two following questions were asked: Is it a conceptual-, logical-, physical-, or implementation-level thing? Is it used to describe business, information, automation or technical things? It was discovered that many of the actors were also referred to as roles or services. It was decided to apply an ontology to crisply define these things. The Open Group's service-oriented ontology was used for alignment. The SGAC's Architecture Development Working Party discovered that there is a one to one relationship between roles and service collections. The ADWP team then began creating an ontology that aligned with, but was not identical to, the SOA ontology. To date, the ADWP has worked through only enough of the ontology to identify the proper description of things in the actors list. At this time, the ADWP decided that a better name for the actors are entities. Therefore, for convenience, the group agreed to continue using the original list in order to allow traceability to its origin.

The Open Group's ontology is described in English and with World Wide Web Consortium (W3C) Web Ontological Language (OWL) definitions. Figure C.3.1 shows the ontology with circles around the terms that the team agreed made sense in light of this industry's requirements. Corrections were made in the case of a few areas where technology was not crisp enough or overly prescriptive.

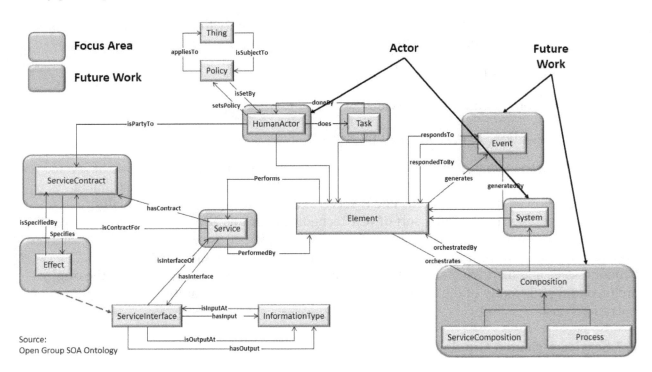

Figure C.3.1. SOA Ontology Mapping

The subsequent descriptions outline the ontology of each of these terms:

Core classes and Properties

❑ Service collections are a re-usable collection of business, IT, or architectural services that can be combined with other service collections to deliver architectures and solutions. Service collections exist at various levels of architecture, depending on what stage of architecture development has been reached.

Only service collections exist in conceptual architecture.

Service collections begin their migration to actors in logical architecture.

Physical architecture is under discussion and possibly out of scope.

Only actors exist in implementation level of architecture and are discussed only to provide definitional clarity.

❑ *Services* represent a particular pattern of behaviour.

See also Architecture Working Party e.g., "haircut."

A given service may also correspond to a message type.

- A *Service* is not an instance.

  e.g., not "the haircut that I had yesterday."

- Different patterns of behaviour can be different services or the same service, at the discretion of whomever is populating the ontology.

  e.g., "haircut" could include both "normal" and "bald barber" behaviour patterns, or "normal haircut" and "barber special" could be separate instances of *Service* – perhaps of a "Haircut" subclass of Service

❑ *Task* is defined as disjoint with the *service*, and is considered an atomic action within each level of architecture.

An atomic *task* is an action which accomplishes a defined result. Tasks are done by people or organizations, specifically by instances of *Actor (at the Implementation level).*

At the Implementation Level *Tasks* are done by actors, furthermore tasks can use services that are performed by technology components.

Task is defined as disjoint with the *Actor/Role.*

❑ *Actors* are people organizations or systems that perform a task at the bequest of a service.

Only actors exist at the implementation layer of architecture

The SOA ontology document is silent regarding the ontology of a role. The ADWP team elected to create a definition leveraging several use case intent, and the definition of a building block from the SOA ontology and the Open Group's Architecture Framework documents. The team is also working with the EU SG-CG team on merging definitions and possible ontology to include important relevant parts of the ENTSO-E role model[192]. Figure C.3.2 shows the ADWP mapping of the relationship between actors and roles to a service.

For the work at hand, the ADWP elected to use "provides" and "consumes" because at all times a service contract is required for interaction. However, below is the reasoning of the SOA ontology document:

Terminology used in an SOA environment often includes the notion of service providers and service consumers. There are two challenges with this terminology:

- It does not distinguish between the contractual obligation aspect of consume/provide and the interaction aspect of consume/provide. A contractual obligation does not necessarily translate to an interaction dependency, if for no other reason than because the realization of the contractual obligation may have been sourced to a third party.

- Consuming or providing a service is a statement that only makes sense in context – either a contractual context or an interaction context. These terms are consequently not well suited for making statements about elements and services in isolation.

The above are the reasons why the ontology has chosen not to adopt "consume" and "provide" as core concepts, rather instead allows "consume" or "provide" terms to be used with contractual obligations and/or interaction rules described by service contracts (see the definition of the Service Contract class). In its simplest form, outside the context of a formal service contract, the interaction aspect of consuming and providing services may even be expressed simply by saying that some element uses (consumes) a service or that some element performs (provides) a service; see the implementation level examples below.

Figure C.3.2. Actor to Service Map

---

[192] European Network of Transmission System Operators for Electricity, "The Harmonized Electricity Market Role Model," version 2014-01, May 2014, https://www.entsoe.eu/fileadmin/user_upload/edi/library/role/harmonised-role-model-2014-01_approved.pdf

- *Provider/Consumer* are intersection of *actor and service.* *

- *As in all service-oriented approaches, a provider/consumer may use multiple services to support its role.*

- *Provider* is domain of *provides.*

- *Consumer* is domain of *consumes.*

- *Provides* and *Consumes* are not transient relations.

  Provides includes *Provides at this instant, has Provided,* and *may in future Provide. Consumes* is similar.

* Note, the team discovered these rules, which helped classify the actors:

- An actor fulfills a business service by invoking an automated service in the context of a role.

- Only roles exist in conceptual architecture.

- Roles begin their migration to actors in logical architecture.

- Only actors exist in implementation architecture.

A set of services may be a collection of services organized in a building block. Thus far, the ADWP team has not identified any building blocks other than there may be a relationship between building blocks and super-set service definitions.

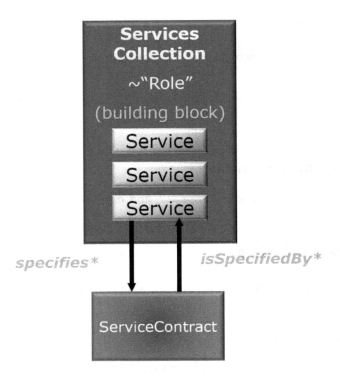

*Deviation from open group isContractFor & hasContract

Figure C.3.3. Role to Service Map

C.4 Architecture Matrix

The Open Group Architecture Methodology (TOGAF) Architecture Development Methodology (TOGAF ADM) development cycle[193] defined the entire lifecycle of the architecture process from vision to maintenance. The intent of defining a reference architecture for smart grid is that only the development phases of the cycle are relevant. Each organization that deploys an architecture must travel a unique path migrating legacy organizational structures, manual and automated processes, applications, networks and various automations to participate in new fashions while ensuring they continue to provide the legacy service for which they were originally intended.

TOGAF and other architecture frameworks have a concept of iterations where requirements are clarified with increasing detail for each level of architecture. The diagram below (see Fig. C.4.1) represents the combination of TOGAF and Zachman architecture principles[194] that is applied to each level of architecture.

---

[193] See http://pubs.opengroup.org/architecture/togaf9-doc/arch/chap05.html

[194] Note the use of TOGAF and Zachman does not infer endorsement or preference, as described previously.

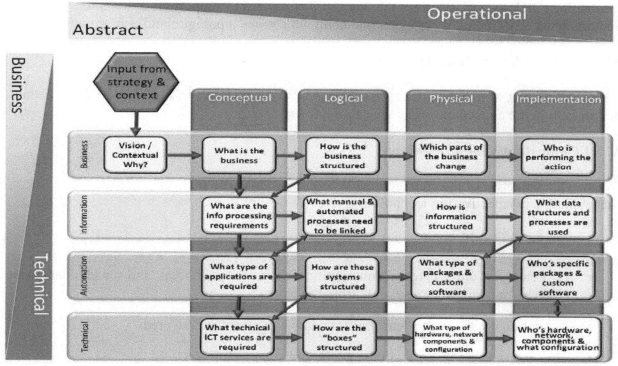

Figure C.4.1. Architecture Layer & Levels

Each cell within this matrix is defined by the intersection of business-to-technical orientation levels and abstract-to- discrete layers. The following sections define these layers and levels.

C.4.1 Business Architecture

Business architecture describes the product and/or service strategy, and the organizational, functional, process, information, and geographic aspects of the business environment. It also identifies what personnel actually perform a task.

C.4.2 Information Architecture

Information architecture defines the structure, organization, flow of information, and protocols. It is a superset of the ICT concept of data architecture.

C.4.3 Automation Architecture

Automation architecture defines what types of automation (applications, sensors, etc.) are required to support the information management requirements of the enterprise.

C.4.4 Technology Architecture

Technology architecture describes the types of ICT needed to support the automation requirements. This includes computer and communications topologies and configurations.

C.5 Layers of Abstraction Definitions

These definitions were developed to assist the ADWP team in identifying a level of architecture for an item in the conceptual architecture's actor list.

C.5.1 Contextual/Vision Definition

What is the objective of the architecture? Which questions need to be answered for the stakeholder's perspective (no technology)?

Context includes identifying:

- Core business units, external communities, governmental bodies, and stakeholders most affected and deriving most value from the work

- Aspirational vision of the capabilities and business value delivered

- The business principles, business goals, and strategic drivers

❑ Example: Why this study? Which objectives, what scope, and which constraints?

C.5.2 Conceptual Definition

Conceptual architecture models the actual business as the owner conceptually thinks the business is, or maybe, wants the business to be. What are the services that are required to satisfy the future needs?

- Conceptual services represent the goals of the stakeholder.
  - o What I want to do, which is driven by my mission?
  - o What I need to do, which is often driven by my mission?
- Conceptual services have a lot of attributes.
  - o Service levels and other quality attributes (historically called non-functional requirements in engineering).
  - o Specifications of functionality.
- Simplest questions to find them:
  - o What are the essential elements within the scope?

o   Which services do I need to provide to the outside world to fulfill my mission?

o   Which services from the outside do I need to do that?

C.5.3 Logical Definition

Logical architecture models of the "systems" of the business, logical representations of the business that define the logical implementation of the business. How is the architecture (ideally) structured?

How are basic elements related, according to the specific objectives and constraints of the architecture? (logical structure)

Are descriptions of the ideal building blocks needed to run the business as defined in the conceptual architecture?

Building blocks are technology-independent services.

For the construction, criteria are needed to cluster the services into these building blocks.

C.5.4 Physical Definition

Physical architecture is the technology-constrained, physical-implementation design of the systems of the business. How is the architecture (ideally) structured?

What software and processes are necessary?

Which elements of structure will be realized, according to strategies and implications? And with what can this be achieved?

Describes components necessary to implement.

Is a representation of components of real building blocks an architect will use, such as:

- A person

- A process

- A piece of software and/or

- A piece of infrastructure

Provides implementation technical specifications, i.e., the details needed for white box development process (e.g., Rational Unified Process), vendor solution, and manual processes (Phase E).

C.5.5 Implementation Definition

This is where the systems specialize.
What software and processes are used to execute?

For ICT, these are the vendor offerings or custom-built applications.

For organizations, these are the personnel and workflow execution.

C.6 Actor List Evolution

The collected actors represent the largest collection of actors available. The sources of this list include use cases, standards organizations, and other reference architecture activities. Currently, the contributing organizations include:

- NIST Framework Document (this document)

- NISTIR 7628 Guidelines for Smart Grid Cybersecurity

- Smart Grid Cybersecurity Committee

- IEC 61968/ 61970 Common Information Model

- IEEE 2030 Draft Guide for Smart Grid Interoperability of Energy Technology and Information Technology Operation with the Electric Power System (EPS), and End-Use Applications and Loads

- Energy Information Standards Alliance (from PAP10 & 17)

- EU Commission Task Force for Smart Grids, Expert Group 3: Roles and Responsibilities of Actors involved in the Smart Grids Deployment (EU EG3) (2011/Aug/08)

- EU Smart Grid Mandate Reference Architecture Working Group (EU M.490 RAWG)

- EU M.490 SP (Sustainable Process WG) and initial IEC TC8 AHG4 Smart Grid Requirements

- EU SG-CG SG Information Security Working Party 1: Second set of SGIS standards (EU SG-CG SGIS WP1)

- European Network of Transmission System Operators for Electricity (ENTSO-E) Market model

- North American Energy Standards Board (NAESB)

- National use case repository extracts

- E-Mobility Coordination Group Ad hoc group for Smart Charging under CEN/CENELEC M468 and M490 (EM-AhG-SmartCharge)

- IEC System Committee Smart Energy (formerly SG3)

- EU SG-CG Generic Use Cases

- DKE Use Case Management Repository (UCMR)

- EU M.441 Smart Meter Coordination Group (SMCG)

- Various national use case repository extracts

This list covers a wide range of applications, and the actor lists are found to have varying degrees of consistency. As a result, an increasing number of actors are created to suit the need at a given time rather than discovering whether a suitable entity is already defined or one exists that may be a better choice than one constructed for a silo-oriented need.

After the ontology was defined to a sufficient degree to identify the terms crisply, the team began working through this list. As mentioned in the ongoing efforts of the SGAC, this effort is still ongoing, with teams in North America and the EU contributing to the effort. The results are not yet ready for peer review. However, the process of identification is described below:

- Semantics should be explicitly documented to reduce ambiguity – this is the foundation of the ontology effort.

- An actor is considered to be a person, organization, or system that has at least one role that initiates or interacts with activities. Actors may be internal or external to an organization.

- A role is the usual or expected function or context in which an actor consumes/provides a service. An actor may play a number of roles.

- At the highest level, a conceptual role represents the goals of the stakeholder (e.g., energy provider). A conceptual role will have many characteristics.

- A logical role or service decomposes/partitions a conceptual role into supporting services or actors. At the logical level, mapping from roles to actors begins; there may not be an actor for every role or service at the logical level.

- There are no physical level roles or conceptual actors.

- A logical actor decomposes/partitions conceptual roles into structural entities.

- A physical actor is an instantiation of a logical actor. A physical actor performs a set of actions which is a physical instantiation of a logical role.

C.7 Relationships Between Layers of Architecture

Here is a conceptual role, "Clearing and Settling Agent," that shows an automation example:

Entity	Type	Entity's Architectural Level
Clearing and Settling Agent	Role	Conceptual Level
Market Clearing	Service	Logical Level
Energy Market Clearinghouse	Service	Logical Level
SG Clearing App	Actor	Physical Level
SG Clearing App – V1.31	Actor	Implementation Level

Here is a conceptual role, "Clearing and Settling Agent," that shows a personnel example:

Entity	Type	Entity's Architectural Level
Clearing and Settling Agent	Role	Conceptual Level
Market Clearing	Service	Logical Level
Energy Market Clearinghouse	Service	Logical Level
Accounting Department	Actor	Physical Level
Joe from Accounting	Actor	Implementation Level

Appendix D: SGIP Committees, DEWGs, and PAPs

This appendix provides descriptions of various entities within the SGIP.

D.1 Committees

SGIP committees include:

- Smart Grid Architecture Committee (SGAC) -- The SGAC is responsible for creating and refining a conceptual reference model and developing a conceptual architectural framework supporting the standards and profiles necessary to implement the vision of the smart grid. Further details on the activities and plans are found in Chapter 5.

- Smart Grid Cybersecurity Committee (SGCC) – The primary objective of the SGCC is to assess standards for applicability and interoperability across the domains of the smart grid, rather than to develop a single set of cybersecurity requirements that are applicable to all elements of the smart grid. These standards will be assessed within an overall risk management framework that focuses on cybersecurity within the smart grid. Further details on the SGCC activities and plans can be found in Chapter 6.

- Smart Grid Testing and Certification Committee (SGTCC) -- The SGTCC creates and maintains the necessary documentation and organizational framework for compliance, interoperability, and cybersecurity testing and certification for smart grid standards recommended by SGIP. Further details on the activities and plans are found in Chapter 7.

- Implementation Methods Committee (IMC) -- The IMC identifies, develops, and supports mechanisms and tools for objective standards impact assessment, transition management, and technology transfer in order to assist in deployment of standards-based smart grid devices, systems, and infrastructure. The committee writes reports and guidelines that address these implementation issues.

D.2 Domain Expert Working Groups (DEWGs)

DEWGs provide expertise in specific application areas, as well as a rich understanding of the current and future requirements for smart grid applications. Due to their broad membership and collaborative process, DEWGs integrate a wide array of stakeholder expertise and interests. Through their understanding of smart grid applications, DEWGs expose and model the applications in use cases, cataloged in the IKB. The applications are analyzed against functional and nonfunctional requirements, and against the potential standards that fulfill them. Through their analyses, DEWGs can allocate functionality to actors, standards, and technologies, and thus support the fulfillment of smart grid applications. By this means, the DEWGs can discover the gaps and overlaps of standards for the smart grid, as well as identify which technologies best fit the requirements necessary for carrying out the applications.

The results of these analyses are the identification of the following:

- Smart grid standards and the nature of their fit to the applications

- Additional PAPs that are needed to address the gaps and overlaps

- High-priority use cases that merit detailed analysis and development

The DEWGs as of October 2013 include:

- Transmission and Distribution (T&D) – This DEWG works to enhance reliability and improve resilience to grid instabilities and disturbances. It also works to improve power quality to meet customer needs and efficiency, and to enable ready access for distributed generators to the grid. Activities in the past several years include creating a list of phasor data concentrator requirements; conducting the initial discussions to determine if efforts related to electromagnetic interference should be a PAP or a Working Group, and recommending to the Governing Board that an Electromagnetic Interoperability Issues (EMII) Working Group be established; creating a white paper on weather-related standards; and providing technical comments to NIST on the Guiding Principles for Identifying Standards for Implementation from Release 1.0.

- Home-to-Grid (H2G) – This DEWG is investigating communications between utilities and home devices to facilitate demand response programs that implement energy management. The DEWG has agreed on a set of goals and has written white papers for the four target segments: government, electric industry, consumers, and residential product manufacturers. The DEWG has produced six white papers: "Requirements"; "The Key Starting Point for a Business-Level Roadmap to Achieve Interoperable Networks, Systems, Devices in the Smart Grid"; "Privacy of Consumer Information in the Electric Power Industry"; "Free Market Choice for Appliance Physical Layer Communications"; "Appliance Socket Interface"; and "Electromagnetic Compatibility Issues for Home-to-Grid Devices101."

- Building-to-Grid (B2G) – This DEWG represents the interests and needs of building consumers. It envisions conditions that enable commercial buildings to participate in energy markets and perform effective energy conservation and management. The DEWG is responsible for identifying interoperability issues relevant to the building customer and providing direction on how to address those issues. The B2G DEWG has examined use cases for weather data exchange and proposed an approach for standard weather data exchange, and it has participated in the formation and further development of the concept of the Energy Services Interface (ESI) and definition of the customer interface. The DEWG has also explored energy management beyond electricity (e.g., combined heat and power [CHP], district energy, thermal storage, etc.).

- Distributed Renewables, Generators, and Storage (DRGS) – This DEWG provides a forum to identify standards and interoperability issues and gaps related to smart grid integration of distributed renewable/clean energy generators and electric storage, and to initiate PAPs and task groups to address identified issues and gaps. Significant technical challenges exist in this area, and resolution of these issues and gaps is essential to enable high penetrations of distributed renewable/clean generator and storage devices while also enhancing rather than degrading grid stability, resiliency, power quality, and safety.

- Industry-to-Grid (I2G) – This DEWG identifies business and policy objectives and requisite interactions for industrial customers of the electric grid, and it also identifies standard services and interfaces needed for interoperability (e.g., syntax and semantics of information transfer, service interface protocols) for these customers. This DEWG is preparing a transition strategy for future energy transfers between industrial facilities and the electric grid, in various manifestations, to meet fluctuating demand at predictable quality and price. This should be accomplished while acknowledging variable supplier delivery capability and regulatory requirements, and while optimizing energy conservation. This DEWG developed a presentation on the Organization for the Advancement of Structured Information Systems (OASIS) Energy Interoperation Technical Committee (EITC), which defines the interaction between the smart grid and smart facilities.

- Vehicle-to-Grid (V2G) – This DEWG identifies the service interfaces and standards needed (e.g., syntax and semantics of information transfer, service interface protocols, cross-cutting issues, business- and policy-level issues) to create the infrastructure to make plug-in electric vehicles (PEV) a reality. This DEWG defines business objectives and prioritizes corresponding PEV-grid interactions (discharging as well as charging) that can occur at different locations under one billing account. The goal for this DEWG is to ensure that the basic infrastructure will be implemented in time to support one million PEVs by 2015.

- Business and Policy (BnP) – This DEWG assists business decision makers and legislative/regulatory policymakers in implementing smart grid policies relevant to interoperability by providing a structured approach that may be used by state and federal policymakers and by trade organizations to implement smart grid policies, and helps to clearly define the interoperability implications and benefits of smart grid policy. This DEWG serves as an educational resource and develops tools and supporting materials. BnP DEWG meetings include discussions with federal and state regulators, including members of the National Association of Regulatory Utility Commissioners (NARUC).

D.3 Additional SGIP Working Groups

In addition to the DEWGs, there are other working groups established to examine issues in particular areas and, if appropriate, recommend the creation of new PAPs. These working groups are described below.

Electromagnetic Interoperability Issues (EMII) – This working group investigates strategies for enhancing the immunity of smart grid devices and systems to the detrimental effects of natural and man-made electromagnetic interference, both radiated and conducted. It addresses these electromagnetic compatibility (EMC) issues and develops recommendations for the application of standards and testing criteria to ensure EMC for the smart grid. In particular, the group focuses on issues directly related to interoperability of smart grid devices and systems, including impacts, avoidance, and generation of electromagnetic interference, as well as mitigation of and immunity to electromagnetic interference. With its focus on interoperability, this effort is not a general review of electromagnetic- and electric power-related issues, such as power quality. These issues are addressed by different groups outside the SGIP.

Gas Technologies Working Group – The Gas Workgroup investigates the interaction between the gas delivery and electric power delivery grids with respect to interoperability standards, common technological paradigms, and associated system implementations. A major emphasis is the investigation of the advantages available to both industries with the development of interoperability standards that will foster the integration of gas systems into the electric-centric smart grid, e.g., distributed gas pressure metering within AMI, and multiple meter integration with Home Area Network (HAN) devices. The recommendations of the Gas Technologies Working Group can be considered by the SGIP for follow-on activity, viz., Priority Action Plan (PAP) creation, and Smart Grid Testing & Certification Committee (SGTCC) action. Because of its focus on interoperability issues pertinent to both the gas and electric power industries, the scope does not include a review of either gas- or electric- power-specific technology systems or issues.

D.4 Priority Action Plans (PAPs)

PAPs are a key activity of the SGIP. They arise from the analysis of the applicability of standards to smart grid use cases and are targeted to resolve specific critical issues. PAPs are created only when the SGIP determines there is a need for interoperability coordination on some urgent issue.

Specifically, a PAP addresses one of the following situations:

- A gap exists, where a standard or standard extension is needed. An example of such a needed standard is the need for meter image-download requirements.

- An overlap exists, where two complementary standards address some information that is in common but different for the same scope of an application. An example of this is metering information, where the Common

Information Model (CIM), 61850, the American National Standards Institute (ANSI) C12.19, Smart Energy Profile (SEP) 1.0, and SEP 2.0 all have non-equivalent methods of representing revenue meter readings.

PAP activities include coordinating with the relevant SDOs and SSOs to get standards developed, revised, or harmonized. Once the standards are completed and reviewed through the SGIP Catalog of Standards (CoS) process, the output of the PAP is a recommendation to the SGIP for consideration for the CoS along with the associated CoS review documentation.

PAPs are created when the SGIP BOD receives proposals (through the SGIP Technical Committee) from SGIP members, working groups, committees, or other interested parties who have identified issues with interoperability standards, such as a gap or overlap among standards. The SGIP BOD approves the PAP proposal, and experts in relevant SDOs and SSOs are brought together to create the PAP working group management team. The PAPs themselves are executed within the scopes of participating SDOs, SSOs, and users groups that sign up for tasks that implement the plans.
The SGIP also offers guidance to the PAP team to move difficult discussions toward resolution. Although PAPs and SDOs work together closely, there may be times when the SDOs and PAPs disagree based on their constituent viewpoints. Specific PAP tasks may diverge from the original intent of the PAP due to the SDOs' natural, and correct, orientation towards their own specific goals and needs. The PAPs, on the other hand, arise from the broader stakeholder involvement in the smart grid problem space, and the goals identified for a PAP reflect this broader scope. In these cases, the parties are brought together for further discussion and mutual understanding.

To date, there have been 25 PAPs[195] established. Of the 25 PAPs that have been established, 14 PAPs are active, and 11 PAPs have completed their work:

Active Priority Action Plans:

- PAP 02 Wireless Communications for the Smart Grid

- PAP 07 Electric Storage Interconnection Guidelines

- PAP 08 CIM for Distribution Grid Management

- PAP 09 Standard DR and DER Signals

- PAP 12 Mapping IEEE 1815 (DNP3) to IEC 61850 Objects

- PAP 15 Harmonize Power Line Carrier Standards for Appliance Communications in the Home

- PAP 16 Wind Plant Communications

---

[195] Because one of the PAPs was designated as PAP 0, the most recently established PAP is the 25th PAP, but its designation is PAP 24.

- PAP 17 Facility Smart Grid Information Standard
- PAP 19 Wholesale Demand Response (DR) Communication Protocol
- PAP 20 Green Button ESPI Evolution
- PAP 21 Weather Information
- PAP 22 Electric Vehicle Sub-Metering
- PAP 23 Testing Profile for IEC 61850, Communication Networks and Systems in Substations
- PAP 24 Microgrid Operational Interfaces

Completed Priority Action Plans (see Table D-1):

- PAP 00 Meter Upgradeability Standard
- PAP 01 Role of IP in the Smart Grid
- PAP 03 Common Price Communication Model
- PAP 04 Common Schedule Communication Mechanism
- PAP 05 Standard Meter Data Profiles
- PAP 06 Common Semantic Model for Meter Data Tables
- PAP 10 Standard Energy Usage Information
- PAP 11 Common Object Models for Electric Transportation
- PAP 13 Harmonization of IEEE C37.118 with IEC 61850 and Precision Time Synchronization
- PAP 14 Transmission and Distribution Power Systems Model Mapping
- PAP 18 SEP 1.x to SEP 2 Transition and Coexistence

Table D-1 Completed Priority Action Plans (PAPs) as of August 2014.

PAP Project	Standards Products
Meter Upgradeability Standard	•NEMA SG-AMI 1-2009: Requirements for Smart Meter Upgradeability
Role of IP in Smart Grid	•IETF RFC6272: Internet Protocols for the Smart Grid
Common Specification for Price and Product Definition	•OASIS EMIX: Energy Market Information eXchange
Common Schedule Communication Mechanism for Energy Transactions	•OASIS WS-Calendar: Web Services Calendar
Standard Meter Data Profiles	•AEIC Metering Guidelines V2.1

PAP Project	Standards Products
Translate ANSI C12.19 to and from a Common Semantic Model	•White Paper: Mapping of ANSI C12.19 End Device Tables to UML model
Standard DR and DER Signals	•OpenADR 2.0 Profile A •SEP 2.0
Standard Energy Usage Information	•NAESB REQ 18/WEQ 19: PAP10 Energy Usage Information
Common Object Models for Electric Transportation	•SAE J1772: Electrical Connector between PEV and EVSE •SAE J2836/1-3: Use Cases for PEV Interactions •SAE J2847/1-3: Communications for PEV Interactions
Harmonization of IEEE C37.118 with IEC 61850 and Precision Time Synchronization	•IEEE C37.238-2011: IEEE Standard Profile for Use of IEEE 1588 Precision Time Protocol •IEC 61850-90-5: Use of IEC 61850 to Transmit Synchrophasor Information per IEEE C37.118
Transmission & Distribution Power Systems Model Mapping	•IEEE C37.239 COMFEDE •Relay Settings Guideline
Harmonize Power Line Carrier Standards for Appliance Communications in the Home	•NISTIR 7862 •IEEE 1901-2010 •ITU-T G.9960 •ITU-T G.9972 •ITU-T G.9961 •ITU-T G.9955 •ITU-T G.9956
SEP 1.x to SEP 2 Transition and Coexistence	•SGIP 2011-0008_1: SEP 1.x to SEP 2.0 Transition and Coexistence White Paper
Wholesale Demand Response Communication Protocol	•OpenADR 2.0 Profile B •Proposed Wholesale Demand Response Communication Protocol (WDRCP) extensions for the IEC Common Information Model

The scope, output, and status of each of the 25 PAPs—as of August 2014—are summarized below in Table D-2.

Table D-2. There are 25 PAPs as of August 2014[196] (including PAP 0).

#	Priority Action Plan	Comments
0	Meter Upgradeability Standard http://collaborate.nist.gov/twiki-sggrid/bin/view/SmartGrid/PAP00MeterUpgradability	Scope: PAP00 defined requirements including secure local and remote upgrades of smart meters. Output: National Electrical Manufacturers Association (NEMA) Meter Upgradeability Standard SG-Advanced Metering Infrastructure (AMI) 1-2009. Date: Completed 2009.
1	Role of IP in the Smart Grid http://collaborate.nist.gov/twiki-sggrid/bin/view/SmartGrid/PAP01InternetProfile	Scope: For interoperable networks it is important to study the suitability of Internet networking technologies for Smart Grid applications. PAP01's work area investigates the capabilities of protocols and technologies in the Internet Protocol Suite by working with key SSO committees to determine the characteristics of each protocol for Smart Grid application areas and types. Output: This PAP's work culminated in publication of a Request for Comment (RFC) cataloguing a core Internet Protocol Suite for IP-based Smart Grid and its acceptance by the SGIPGB in December 2010 as a Smart Grid standard. Date: Completed 2010.
2	Wireless Communications for the Smart Grid http://collaborate.nist.gov/twiki-sggrid/bin/view/SmartGrid/PAP02Wireless	Scope: This PAP's work area investigates and evaluates existing and emerging standards-based physical media for wireless communications. The approach is to work with the appropriate SDOs to determine the communication requirements of Smart Grid applications and how well they can be supported by wireless technologies. Results are used to assess the appropriateness of wireless

---

[196] Due to the dynamic nature of the PAP process, a snapshot in time (such as that provided here as of August 2014) will quickly be out of date. The most up-to-date information about the status of each PAP can be found on the NIST Smart Grid Collaboration Site (http://collaborate.nist.gov/twiki-sggrid/bin/view/SmartGrid/PriorityActionPlans) and the SGIP site (http://sgip.org)

#	Priority Action Plan	Comments
		communications technologies for meeting Smart Grid applications. Output: PAP02 compiled Smart Grid communication requirements and a catalog for wireless standards and their characterizations. The PAP developed an evaluation methodology published in "Guidelines for Assessing Wireless Communications for Smart Grid Applications, Version 1.0" in July 2011. A second version of the document has been approved by the PAP and was published in June 2014.[197] The document is out for a membership vote for inclusion in the CoS. Date: Active.
3	Common Price Communication Model http://collaborate.nist.gov/twiki-sggrid/bin/view/SmartGrid/PAP03PriceProduct	Scope: Coordination of energy supply and demand requires a common understanding of supply and demand. A simple quotation of price, quantity, and characteristics in a consistent way across markets enables new markets and integration of distributed energy resources. Price and product definition are key to transparent market accounting. Better communication of actionable energy prices facilitates effective dynamic pricing and is necessary for net-zero-energy buildings, supply-demand integration, and other efficiency and sustainability initiatives. Common, up-to-the-moment pricing information is also an enabler of local generation and storage of energy, such as electric-charging and thermal-storage technologies for homes and buildings. PAP03 builds on existing work in financial energy markets and existing demand response programs to integrate with schedule and interval specifications under development. This PAP overlaps with others that include price and product information (4, 6, 8, 9, 10, and 11). Outputs: OASIS Energy Market Information Exchange (EMIX) standard

---

[197] See http://www.nist.gov/customcf/get_pdf.cfm?pub_id=914731

#	Priority Action Plan	Comments
		was added to the SGIP Catalog of Standards in 2011 (See http://collaborate.nist.gov/twiki-sggrid/bin/view/SmartGrid/SGIPCosSIFO ASISEMIX). ZigBee Smart Energy 2.0 was completed in April 2013. Date: Completed 2012.
4	Common Schedule Communication Mechanism http://collaborate.nist.gov/twiki-sggrid/bin/view/SmartGrid/PAP04Schedules .	Scope: Under this plan, NIST and collaborators will develop a standard for how schedule and event information is passed between and within services. The output will be a specification that can then be incorporated into price, demand-response, and other specifications. This Project Plan was developed in conjunction with PAP03 (Develop Common Specification for Price and Product Definition). Participants include, but are not limited to, International Electrotechnical Commission (IEC), North American Energy Standards Board (NAESB), other OASIS Technical Committees, and ZigBee Smart Energy Profile. Outputs: A common standard for transmitting calendaring information will enable the coordination necessary to improve energy efficiency and overall performance. The Calendar Consortium completed its current work in 2011 on eXtensible Markup Language (XML) serialization of iCalendar into a Web-service component (OASIS Web Services-(WS)-Calendar). WS-Calendar added to the SGIP Catalog of Standards (see http://collaborate.nist.gov/twiki-sggrid/bin/view/SmartGrid/SGIPCosSIFO ASISWSCalendar) Date: Completed 2011.
5	Standard Meter Data Profiles http://collaborate.nist.gov/twiki-sggrid/bin/view/SmartGrid/PAP05MeterProf iles	Scope: The Smart Grid recognizes that several clients may require local access to meter data, and these data may be on the same order of complexity as the meter itself. Such potential clients might range from thermostats to building automation

#	Priority Action Plan	Comments
		systems. Other potential clients will exist inside and outside of the customers' premises. Meter interface will reach across various domains including Operations (e.g., Metering System), Customer (e.g., Customer Energy Management System (EMS) and Submeter), and Distribution (e.g., Workforce Tool and Field Devices). The ANSI C12.19 standard contains an extensive set of end device (e.g., meter) data tables. This large set of tables makes it time-consuming for utilities (and other service providers) to understand the standard and specify the proper tables for specific applications. The objective of this Priority Action Plan is to develop a smaller set of data tables that will meet the needs of most utilities and simplify the meter procurement process. Outputs: Minimize variation and maximize interoperability of application services and behaviors within ANSI C12.18-2006, ANSI C12.19-2008, ANSI C12.21-2006, and ANSI C12.22-2008. Date: Completed 2012.
6	Common Semantic Model for Meter Data Tables http://collaborate.nist.gov/twiki-sggrid/bin/view/SmartGrid/PAP06Meter	Scope: There are currently several "meter models" in standard existence. These include ANSI C12.19, Device Language Message Specification (DLMS)/ Companion Specification for Energy Metering (COSEM)/IEC 62056, IEC 61968 CIM, and IEC 61850. As the smart grid requires interoperation between meters and many other applications and services, the existence of unique forms of data representation pertinent to a single actor is problematic, requiring complex gateways to translate this representation into alternate formats for information sharing. PAP06 works with industry stakeholders to translate the ANSI C12.19 End Device (meter) data model to and from a common form that will allow the semantics of this and End Device models in other standards to be more readily harmonized. The

#	Priority Action Plan	Comments
		objective is to allow the lossless translation from the common form to the various syntactic representations prevalent in each domain. Details will include the representation of the Decade/Table/Element model. PAP06 develops an exact and reusable representation of the ANSI C12.19 data model in the presentation form of Unified Markup Language (UML). Outputs: A side-by-side comparison of the ANSI C12.19 UML model and the IEC 61968-9 UML model to illustrate gaps and overlaps. White paper published, "PAP06 UML Meta Model and EDL White Paper." Date: Completed 2012.
7	Energy Storage Interconnection Guidelines http://collaborate.nist.gov/twiki-sggrid/bin/view/SmartGrid/PAP07Storage	Scope: Energy storage is expected to play an increasingly important role in the evolution of the power grid, particularly to accommodate increasing penetration of intermittent renewable energy resources and to improve electrical power system (EPS) performance. Coordinated, consistent, electrical interconnection standards; communication standards; and implementation guidelines are required for energy storage devices (ES), power-electronics-connected distributed energy resources (DER), hybrid generation-storage systems (ES-DER), and the ES-DER aspects of plug-in electric vehicles (PEV). A broad set of stakeholders and SDOs are needed to address this coordination and evolution in order to update or augment the IEEE 1547 electrical interconnection standards series as appropriate to accommodate Smart Grid requirements and to extend the ES-DER object models in IEC 61850-7-420 as needed. Coordination with Underwriters Laboratories (UL), Society for Automotive Engineers (SAE), National Electrical Code-(NEC-) National Fire Protection Association (NFPA) 70, and Canadian Standards Association

#	Priority Action Plan	Comments
		(CSA) will be required to ensure safe and reliable implementation. This effort will need to address residential, commercial, and industrial applications at the grid distribution level and utility/Regional Transmission Operator (RTO) applications at the grid transmission level. Expected Outputs: updated IEEE 1547.8, IEC 61850-7-420. Date: Active.
8	CIM for Distribution Grid Management http://collaborate.nist.gov/twiki-sggrid/bin/view/SmartGrid/PAP08DistrObj Multispeak	Scope: Standards are urgently needed to enable the rapid integration of wind, solar, and other renewable resources, and to achieve greater reliability and immunity to grid instabilities resulting from their wide-scale deployment, which is radically changing how the power system must operate. The use of standardized object models, such as the CIM and 61850, will support the interoperability of information exchanges that is critically needed to ensure a more reliable and efficient grid. PAP08 will coordinate with: PAPs 3, 4, 9, or 10 on any use cases involving Demand Response (DR), pricing signals, and other customer interactions; PAP07 on any use cases involving energy storage and Distributed Energy Resources (DER); PAP11 on any use cases involving PEVs; PAP14 on any use cases involving "CIM wires models" or transmission-related interactions; and CSWG on security efforts. Expected Outputs: updated IEC 61968, IEC 61970, and IEC 61850, and Multispeak implementation profile. Date: Active.
9	Standard DR and DER Signals http://collaborate.nist.gov/twiki-sggrid/bin/view/SmartGrid/PAP09DRDER	Scope: Demand Response communications cover interactions between wholesale markets and retail utilities and aggregators, as well as between these entities and the end-load customers who reduce demand in response to grid reliability or price signals. While the value of DR is generally well understood, the interaction patterns,

#	Priority Action Plan	Comments
		semantics, and information conveyed vary. Defining consistent signal semantics for DR will make the information conveyed more consistent across Smart Grid domains. Outputs: OASIS Energy Interoperation standard version 1.0, ZigBee Smart Energy 2.0. Date: Completed 2013.
10	Standard Energy Usage Information http://collaborate.nist.gov/twiki-sggrid/bin/view/SmartGrid/PAP10EnergyUsagetoEMS	Scope: This action plan led to data standards to exchange detailed information about energy usage in a timely manner. The first goal was agreement on the core information set to enable integration of usage information throughout facility decision processes. Customers and customer-authorized third-party service providers will use these standards to access energy usage information from the Smart Grid and meter, enabling them to make better decisions about energy use and conservation. Consumers and premises-based systems will use these standards to provide real-time feedback on present and projected performance. Using the Smart Grid infrastructure, this information will be shared with the facility: a home, building, or industrial installation. Two-way flows of usage information will improve collaboration and energy efficiency. Outputs: Implementation of a plan to expedite harmonized standards development and adoption: OASIS, IEC61970/61968, IEC61850, ANSI C12.19/22, PAP17/ American Society of Heating, Refrigerating and Air Conditioning Engineers (ASHRAE) SPC201, and ZigBee Smart Energy Profile (SEP) 2.0. NAESB REQ18/WEQ19: Energy Usage Information was added to the Catalog of Standards, http://collaborate.nist.gov/twiki-sggrid/bin/view/SmartGrid/SGIPCosSIFNAESBREQ18WEQ19. Date: Completed 2012.

#	Priority Action Plan	Comments
11	Common Object Models for Electric Transportation http://collaborate.nist.gov/twiki-sggrid/bin/view/SmartGrid/PAP11PEV	Scope: PAP11 ensures that the grid can support the massive charging of cars and help to popularize the adoption of PEVs. Standards will optimize charging capabilities and vendor innovation, allowing for more creative engineering and automobile amenities. This PAP also supports energy storage integration with the distribution grid as addressed by PAP07. Outputs: SAE J1772, SAE J2836/1, and SAE J2847/1. All have now been completed and approved (See http://collaborate.nist.gov/twiki-sggrid/bin/view/SmartGrid/SGIPCosSIFSAEJ1772 (SAE J1772), http://collaborate.nist.gov/twiki-sggrid/bin/view/SmartGrid/SGIPCosSIFSAEJ283613 (SAE J2836/1), and http://collaborate.nist.gov/twiki-sggrid/bin/view/SmartGrid/SGIPCosSIFSAEJ284713 (SAE 2847-1). Date: Completed 2011.
12	Mapping IEEE 1815 (DNP3) to IEC 61850 Objects http://collaborate.nist.gov/twiki-sggrid/bin/view/SmartGrid/PAP12DNP361850	Scope: This action plan focuses on developing the means to enable transport of select Smart Grid data and related services over legacy Distributed Network Protocol (DNP) 3 networks. This will be accomplished, in part, by defining a method to map the exchange of certain data types and services between DNP3 and the newer IEC 61850 Standard for Communication Networks and Systems in Substations. This is to be published as IEC 61850-80-2, Standard for Exchanging Information between Networks Implementing IEC 61850 and IEEE Standard 1815 (DNP3). DNP3 was adopted by IEEE as Standard 1815 in 2010. IEEE is now developing Standard 1815.1 which includes upgraded security. Expected Outputs: IEEE 1815 was approved and placed on the Catalog of Standards in 2011 (See

#	Priority Action Plan	Comments
		http://collaborate.nist.gov/twiki-sggrid/bin/view/SmartGrid/SGIPCosSIFIEEE18152010). IEC 61850-80-2, IEEE 1815.1 will follow. Date: Active.
13	Harmonization of IEEE C37.118 with IEC 61850 and Precision Time Synchronization http://collaborate.nist.gov/twiki-sggrid/bin/view/SmartGrid/PAP1361850C27118HarmSynch	Scope: The current primary standard for the communication of phasor measurement unit (PMU) and phasor data concentrator (PDC) data and information is the IEEE Standard C37.118, which was published in 2005. This standard also includes requirements for the measurement and determination of phasor values. IEC 61850 is seen as a key standard for all substation and field equipment operating under both real-time and non-real time applications. The use of IEC 61850 for wide-area communication is already discussed in IEC 61850-90-1 (Draft Technical Report) in the context of communication between substations. It appears possible to use a similar approach for the transmission of PMU and PDC data, but the capability needs to be formally defined in IEC 61850. This action plan seeks to assist and accelerate the integration of standards that can impact phasor measurement and applications depending on PMU- and PDC-based data and information. Outputs: IEEE C37.118.1, IEEE C37.118.2 (updated version), IEC 61850-90-5, and IEEE C37.238. IEEE C37.238 approved and placed on the Catalog of Standards in 2011 (see http://collaborate.nist.gov/twiki-sggrid/bin/view/SmartGrid/SGIPCosSIFIEEC372382011). IEC 61850-90-5 approved and placed on the Catalog of Standards in 2012 (see http://collaborate.nist.gov/twiki-sggrid/bin/view/SmartGrid/SGIPCosSIFIECTR61850905) IEEE C37118.1 and IEEE C27.118.2 will follow. Date: Completed 2012.
14	Transmission and Distribution Power Systems Model Mapping	Scope: PAP14's work defines strategies for integrating standards across different

#	Priority Action Plan	Comments
	http://collaborate.nist.gov/twiki-sggrid/bin/view/SmartGrid/PAP14TDModels	environments to support different real-time and back-office applications. Strategies call for defining key applications and evaluating the available standards for meeting the requirements of such applications. Modeling of the electric power system, multifunctional Intelligent Electronic Devices (IEDs), and definition of standard methods for reporting events and exchanging relay settings will meet the requirements for improvements of the efficiency of many protection, control, engineering, commissioning, and analysis tasks. Field equipment can supply the raw data for objects and measured parameters used across the enterprise based on the standard models and file formats defined. Outputs: updates to IEC 61850, IEC 61970, IEC 61968, IEEE C37.239, IEEE C37.237, and MultiSpeak v1-v4. The IEEE C37.239 (COMFEDE) Standard has been approved for the SGIP Catalog of Standards (see http://collaborate.nist.gov/twiki-sggrid/bin/view/SmartGrid/SGIPCosSIFIEEEC372392010). Date: Completed 2013.
15	Harmonize Power Line Carrier Standards for Appliance Communications in the Home http://collaborate.nist.gov/twiki-sggrid/bin/view/SmartGrid/PAP15PLCForLowBitRates	Scope: The goal of this PAP is to enable the development of an interoperable profile containing common features for home appliance applications where the resulting implementation of this profile leads to interoperable products. Expected Outputs: Updates to relevant standards including ITU G.Hn (G.9960, G.9961, G.9972), IEEE P1901 (HomePlug ™, High Definition Power Line Communication (HD-PLC™), and Inter-System Protocol (ISP)), and ANSI/ Consumer Electronics Association (CEA) 709.2 (Lonworks™). Date: Active.
16	Wind Plant Communications	Scope: The goal of PAP16 is development of a wind power plant communications standard.

#	Priority Action Plan	Comments
	http://collaborate.nist.gov/twiki-sggrid/bin/view/SmartGrid/PAP16WindPlantCommunications	Expected Output: IEC 61400-25, Wind Plant Communications, based on IEC 61850. Date: Active.
17	Facility Smart Grid Information Standard http://collaborate.nist.gov/twiki-sggrid/bin/view/SmartGrid/PAP17FacilitySmartGridInformationStandard	Scope: This priority action plan will lead to development of a data model standard to enable energy-consuming devices and control systems in the customer premises to manage electrical loads and generation sources in response to communication with the Smart Grid. It will be possible to communicate information about those electrical loads to utilities, other electrical service providers, and market operators. This PAP will leverage the parallel PAP10 effort and other related activities and models, such as IEC CIM, SEP 2.0, IEC 61850.7-420, and PAPs 3, 4, and 9. Expected Output: Development of an ANSI-approved Facility Smart Grid Information Standard that is independent of the communication protocol used to implement it. Date: Active.
18	SEP 1.x to SEP 2 Transition and Coexistence http://collaborate.nist.gov/twiki-sggrid/bin/view/SmartGrid/PAP18SEP1To2TransitionAndCoexistence	Scope: This action plan focuses on developing specific requirements to allow the coexistence of SEP 1.x and 2.0 and to support the migration of 1.x implementations to 2.0. Because it is a deployment-specific issue, the PAP will not address whether new deployments should be 1.x or 2.0. The effort assumes 1.x in the field as the starting point and assumes that the meters themselves are capable of running SEP 1.x or 2.0 via remote firmware upgrade. Output: The PAP produced a white paper summarizing the key issues with migration and making specific recommendations, and a requirements document thatthat was submitted to the ZigBee Alliance for consideration in developing the technology-specific recommendations, solutions, and any required changes to the

#	Priority Action Plan	Comments
		SEP 2.0 specifications themselves. (See http://collaborate.nist.gov/twiki-sggrid/bin/view/SmartGrid/PAP18SEP1To2TransitionAndCoexistence). Date: Completed 2011.
19	Wholesale Demand Response (DR) Communication Protocol http://collaborate.nist.gov/twiki-sggrid/bin/view/SmartGrid/PAP19WholesaleDR	Scope: The purpose of this work is to build an information model for wholesale demand response communications based on the International Electrotechnical Commission (IEC) Common Information Model (CIM), profiles from which may be mapped to other relevant profiles such as OpenADR 2.0b and MultiSpeak. Output: This PAP will establish a common wholesale market (ISO/RTO) to market participant Demand Response interface profile(s) (based on standards such as CIM) to support pricing or grid condition communications with minimal translation of semantics as information flows from market participants to consumers in cascade. Date: Active.
20	Green Button ESPI Evolution http://collaborate.nist.gov/twiki-sggrid/bin/view/SmartGrid/GreenButtonESPIEvolution	Scope: Green Button Challenge is one step towards realizing the common-sense idea that consumers should have access to their own energy usage information in a downloadable, easy-to-use electronic format, offered by their utility or retail energy service provider. Green Button is based on the SGIP shepherded standards for Energy Usage Information (EUI) that was part of PAP10 including NAESB REQ18/WEQ19 and later NAESB REQ21 (Energy Service Provider Interface (ESPI). This Priority Action Plan follows the evolution of the Green Button and ESPI fostering the requirements for and establishment of standards evolution, testing and certification specifications, and sample or reference implementations and test harnesses. Collectively, these actions will support a robust and rapid penetration of

#	Priority Action Plan	Comments
		interoperable goods and services in support of exchange of EUI. Expected output: The PAP will produce a set of deliverables to support the growing support for a critical standard of the smart grid - the ubiquitous availability of Energy Usage Information, and, a marketplace of sources and uses of that data. Date: Active.
21	Weather Information	Scope: This PAP will coordinate development of Use Cases with inputs from a wide range of industries including Renewable/DER, distribution utilities, ISO/RTO markets, and forecasters. It will produce a set of information requirements designed to facilitate the harmonization of information models and exchange models to be used in smart grid applications. Expected output: Harmonized standards for bi-directional exchange of weather information that are produced in WMO, IEC, & ASHRAE and other identified SSOs. This will enable a robust ecosystem for weather exchange between government, energy industry, and building management industry. Date: Active.
22	EV Fueling Submetering Requirements http://www.sgip.org/pap-22-ev-fueling-submetering-requirements/#sthash.NVaqy1jW.dpbs	Scope: This PAP will compile the core requirements for sub metering as they apply to form factor, accuracy, performance, security, data format, and certification for embedded, portable and stationary applications. These requirements will be coordinated with the SDOs to develop appropriate standards and specifications for the development of next-generation sub meters. Any new standards developed based on these requirements will be vetted for suitability by the PAP Working Group through a comprehensive requirements compliance analysis. The PAP will establish and administer a coordinated collaborative teaming of the cognizant SDOs, and industry stakeholder representatives and organizations. The

#	Priority Action Plan	Comments
		primary focus of this effort is to define the requirements, identify gaps and coordinate with the SDOs to develop standards for sub metering of EV electricity fuel consumption. Though submetering requirements are common to many end-uses, there is an immediate need to address EV specific requirements. Date: Active.
23	Testing Profile for IEC 61850, Communication Networks and Systems in Substations http://www.sgip.org/PAP-23-Testing-Profile-for-IEC-61850-Communication-Networks-and-Systems-in-Substations	Scope: This PAP will select one Business Application Profile (BAP) and develop technical requirements to support it. The PAP team will focus on IEC 61850 devices connected to the grid that measure basic electrical characteristics (voltage, current, real power, apparent power, etc.). Focusing on a simple application profile related to the minimum expected measurement elements for the MMXU (Measurement Unit) and MMTR (Metering) logical nodes would be useful because a significant percentage of IEC 61850 devices are capable of measuring a set of basic electrical quantities. This input will then be fed back to the UCAIug for use in their test program and collaboration with other partners. Date: Active.
24	Microgrid Operational Interfaces http://www.sgip.org/PAP-24---Microgrid-Operational-Interfaces	Scope: Coordinated and consistent electrical interconnection standards, communication standards, and implementation guidelines are required for microgrids and their interaction with the macrogrid. Although there are standards that define the basic microgrid connection and disconnection process, there are no standards that define the grid interactive functions and operations of microgrids with the macrogrid. Because standards already exist for managing loads and DER devices themselves within the various physical domains of the microgrid, the priority action plan (PAP) will focus on the grid facing functionalities and communications (e.g., microgrid to/from

#	Priority Action Plan	Comments
		macrogrid). The PAP will address consistency and interoperability of the information models and signals used by microgrid controllers. Date: Active

www.ingramcontent.com/pod-product-compliance
Lightning Source LLC
Chambersburg PA
CBHW060542060326
40690CB00017B/3574